# A POLITICS OF SORROW

# A POLITICS OF SORROW

## The Disintegration of Yugoslavia

### Davorka Ljubisic

Montréal/New York/London

Black Rose Books No. GG324

National Library of Canada Cataloguing in Publication Data

Ljubisic, Davorka

A politics of sorrow : the disintegration of Yugoslavia / Davorka Ljubisic

Includes bibliographical references and index.
Hardcover ISBN: 1-55164-233-6 (bound)  Paperback ISBN: 1-55164-232-8 (pbk.)

1. Yugoslav War, 1991-1995—Causes. 2. Nationalism—Yugoslavia.
3. Yugoslavia—Ethnic relations. I. Title.

DR1316.L59 2003      949.703      C2003-904158-1

Every effort has been made to secure permission for materials reproduced herein.
Montage on page vii from paintings by
Desa Lozo entitled *L'espoir éclaté* and *Je me souviens*.

*Cover design: Associés libres*

**BLACK ROSE BOOKS**

| | | |
|---|---|---|
| C.P. 1258 | 2250 Military Road | 99 Wallis Road |
| Succ. Place du Parc | Tonawanda, NY | London, E9 5LN |
| Montréal, H2X 4A7 | 14150 | England |
| Canada | USA | UK |

To order books:

In Canada: (phone) 1-800-565-9523 (fax) 1-800-221-9985
email: utpbooks@utpress.utoronto.ca

In United States: (phone) 1-800-283-3572  (fax)  1-651-917-6406

In the UK & Europe: (phone) London 44 (0)20 8986-4854 (fax) 44 (0)20 8533-5821
email: order@centralbooks.com

Our Web Site address: http://www.web.net/blackrosebooks

A publication of the Institute of Policy Alternatives of Montréal (IPAM)

Printed in Canada

The Canada Council | Le Conseil des Arts
for the Arts | du Canada

# Table of Contents

# List of Illustrations

# List of Tables

Crimes committed with extraordinary boldness are more likely to succeed than any others.

—Fyodor Dostoyevsky, *The Brothers Karamazov*

Hitler circulated millions of copies of his book in which he stated that to be successful, a lie must be enormous.

—Hannah Arendt, *The Origins of Totalitarianism*

From *L'espoir éclaté* and *Je me souviens*. Artist: Desa Lozo

To the memory of my parents

and

Yugoslavia (SFRY)


For my sister and brother

# Preface

This book is based on my belief that love, and its companion, creation, is the driving force of humanity and not hatred which is accompanied by destruction. As Erich Fromm asserted not so long ago: "Love is the only satisfactory answer to the problem of human existence" (*The Art of Loving*). I do nevertheless acknowledge the simultaneous existence of both forces, Eros and Thanatos, as inseparable parts of human nature. Life is, in this sense, a permanent struggle between the two. The unanswered question however remains: At what time and in which conditions does one prevail over the other, or more precisely, when does the innate and unconscious tendency towards self-destruction overcome the desire to live and love? Since Victor Frankl's amazing psychological study of Auschwitz in his book *Man's Search for Meaning*, we have known that the instinct for survival, inherent to Eros, is a primary human inclination, embedded in the hope that the end of 'evil' will come soon. This is why people more often than not, choose life and love instead of self-destructiveness. Even in such extremely inhuman conditions, as were the concentration camps, suicide was the exception rather than the rule. To find meaning in life in these factories of death was the 'art of living.'

This dialectics of life and death, the struggle for survival and overcoming fear of death or extinction, is central to my understanding of the disintegration of the former Yugoslavia. The question that I am exploring in the following pages is: How does one explain why the Yugoslav peoples, whose history is marked by their love of freedom and who built their common homeland upon the belief that creation is stronger than destruction, become in the 1990s so hateful and violent towards each other? Why did yesterday's good neighbors and friends become sworn enemies and foes? More importantly, did all citizens of Yugoslavia suddenly begin to hate each other? Nationalism does have the strength to evoke both life and death, to force people to 'choose' between the two, if they are in position to choose. But nationalism is not necessarily centered on destruction and death, it is also about love and creation. Tom Nairn eloquently depicts the faces of nationalism as the modern Janus who simultaneously gazes in the past and in the future. Moreover, nationalism has many faces, or forms, developed across history.

My approach to the topic of nationalism includes a critique of the two main theoretical frameworks—primordialism and constructivism—particularly in regard to their strong and extreme variants, which have explained the 1990s Yugoslavia crisis as a result of either 'ancient ethnic hatreds' or 'artificiality' of the state. It may well be that my critique does not distinguish enough of the double sense involved in the term 'imagined community,' as both a lived and a fictional way of thinking about the nation. In the hope of getting at a more balanced approach, I have chosen to emphasize the need for a critique of its one-sided usage as fictional or 'artificial' in the constructivist literature on the Yugoslavia case. Also, since I have focused on the destruction of the Yugoslav Nation and entailed statelessness, I have not looked at the question of nation-building and state development, nor at the distinction between these processes and nationalism.

To write about Yugoslavia is like writing about Pandora's box. It is a never-ending story with an open and unpredictable future that makes it hard to find the beginning or the end of the story. Even before its creation as a state, and particularly with regard to its destruction, every single issue or event, as soon as it was mentioned, begged some new question and every answer provided needed more detailed explanation, which, in turn, raised new questions. To prevent getting lost in this labyrinthine, I wrote *A Politics of Sorrow* in a spiral way without a clear beginning or a certain end, where the beginning is actually the end and the end becomes the beginning. I present the historical and contemporary events as they happened, without embellishment, without making them uglier, selecting those that were most important, and relevant, and avoiding, for the most part, the overwhelming details in order not to further complicate an already very complex setting.

*Davorka Ljubisic*
*Montreal, November 2003*

# ACKNOWLEDGMENTS

Without the kind and generous support of my professors, colleagues and friends, from at least three continents, this book would have had a much harder time to see the light of a day. Perhaps, it would have never been written.

There are no words to describe the depths of my gratitude to Greg Nielsen for his much-needed help with the abyss and labyrinth of nationalism, for our never-ending dialogues and the 'aesthetical consummation' of different and similar points of view. It is my pleasure to acknowledge my debt to Neil Gerlach whose insightful remarks were more than welcomed and whose comments helped me to clarify my thoughts and arguments. I also thank Vered Amit for her constructive criticism, which motivates my further questioning and thinking. My appreciation goes to Paul and Anouk Bélanger who offered indispensable advice and input. I am grateful to Michel Chossudovsky who has kept me well informed for years with his objective analysis of 'what is wrong' in Yugoslavia.

My eternal gratitude goes to Diane Bélanger, whose emotional support and intellectual stimulus have been crucial to the manuscript, a constant source of inspiration and encouragement. I extend a warm thank you to my very special friends and colleagues, in particular Tamara Vukov and Tammy Saxton who helped in editing the final version, but also to Donavan Rocher, John Brooks, Laura Shea, Randal Rogers, Rodrigo Molina, Sylvia de Sousa, and Marc Lajoie for their generous, priceless help.

My special gratitude goes to my respondents for their kind participation in my survey, for their patience and stimulation, as well for sharing their pleasant and unpleasant memories, historical knowledge and life experiences.

Finally, I acknowledge that a shorter version of chapter five was originally a part of the Culture of Cities Project financed by the SSHRC Major Collaboration Research Initiatives. I also thank Karl Polanyi Institute of Political Economy at Concordia University for being a valuable resource not only of inspiration but has also offered a warm ambience.

# Introduction

The Socialist Federal Republic of Yugoslavia (SFRY: 1945-1991) was created as a multinational federation based on the equality of its nations and national minorities living in any of its six constitutive republics: Bosnia and Herzegovina, Croatia, Macedonia, Montenegro, Serbia, and Slovenia. The disintegration of this, in many respects, unique country is a story about crimes committed with extraordinary boldness and with great deception propagated by politicians and media inside and outside Yugoslavia. In order to understand this tragedy of the Balkans, or to grasp what really went wrong in Yugoslavia, it is crucial to distinguish between the external and internal aspects of so-called "Balkanization," or political fragmentation of the Balkans.[1] To do so provides a more accurate account of the complexity of the collapse of the former Yugoslavia. In contrast to the widespread media representation of exclusively internal Balkanization, or the division of the territories among internal-Balkan forces resulting in civil or ethnic wars, it is necessary to bring into play a broader spectrum of geopolitics, of foreign involvement and of the phenomenon of statelessness. My intention is to present some of the essential elements of the dissolution of Yugoslavia and the refugee crisis that followed. As no simple theory can examine comprehensively such an intricate situation, I will use concepts already developed by other scholars from various disciplines. To explain the complexity of "the Yugoslav Drama," to use Mihailo Crnobrnja's[2] term, I will describe a number of key points of the multitude of external and internal factors that contributed to the disintegration of Yugoslavia.

The book embraces and links both *macro* and *micro* analyses, seeking thus to overcome the dualism between theory and praxis. I approach the labyrinth of the creation and destruction of Yugoslavia primarily by a method of deduction, originating from the general to particular, first demonstrating the broader theoretical, historical, economic and political background, and then applying it to particular issues pertaining to the life experiences of refugees now living in Canada and their consummation of Montreal's urban culture. While the macro analysis deals with theories of nation and nationalism as well with the global historical-political context of the Balkans, the micro analysis examines the history of uprootedness and the lifeworld of Bosnian refugees in Montreal. Indeed, Bosnia is the focus of my analysis since it was the most culturally and religiously mixed republic, called 'Yugoslavia in miniature.'

Thus, included here are both historical and political analyses combined with elements of the socio-economic context of Yugoslavia's crisis.[3] I argue that a foreign-external dimension, particularly the role of the United States (U.S.) and Germany, was decisive in the emergence of internal Balkanization or violent ethnic nationalism. External Balkanization came prior, historically and in the contemporary period, to the internal divisions of the country and the bloody civil wars that followed. I will demonstrate that external Balkanization predates the settlement of the South Slavs[4] in the Balkan peninsula in the sixth and seventh centuries and that the divisions of the Balkans were primarily a product of the well-known ancient Romans' conquering formula: 'Divide and Rule.' For this reason, ethnic nationalism in this region is primarily a product of external (foreign) conquest or colonization of the Balkans. 'A Politics of Sorrow' then demonstrates that a complete picture of the recent crisis and war must take into account *both* external and internal Balkanization since both forces were at work as main protagonists in this tragedy. Both are responsible for the civil war and its victims, which includes the casualties and the survivors, particularly for the massive displacement of people, or the refugee crisis. In this regard, I concur with Michael Parenti's analysis in his article "The Rational Destruction of Yugoslavia," particularly with his argument about the correlation between ethnic enmity and U.S. 'diplomacy':

> When different national groups are living together with some measure of social and material security, they tend to get along. There is intermingling and even intermarriage. But when the economy goes into a tailspin, thanks to sanctions and IMF [International Monetary Fund] destabalization, then it becomes easier to induce internecine conflicts and social discombobulation. In order to hasten that process in Yugoslavia, the Western powers provided the most retrograde separatist elements with every advantage in money, organization, propaganda, arms, hired thugs, and the full might of the U.S. national security state at their backs. *Once more the Balkans are to be balkanized.*[5]

While ethnic nationalism was an indispensable ingredient of the conflict, it was certainly not the sole reason for the breakdown of the former Yugoslavia. In the first two chapters I will focus upon definitions and arguments of two main theories of nation and nationalism, namely primordialism and constructivism. While the advocates of primordialism claim that nations are prehistoric, premodern or 'primordial' formations, constructivists argue that nations are socially 'constructed' categories or 'imagined communities,' a product of modernity emerging in the so-called age of nationalism and led by nationalist elites. I argue that both schools of thought in sociology and anthropology have failed to satisfactorily explain the Yugoslav crisis. This is because each version is fixated on ethnic nationalism as the only reason for the destruction of Yugoslavia. While for primordialists Yugoslavia disintegrated because of historically rooted religious and ethnic hatreds, for constructivists it was simply an 'artificial imagined community' and, thus, not actually real. Extreme primordialism is often presented, as Alexander Motyl notes, as the "ancient hatreds thesis," or "Dark Gods theory," that has also been embraced by journalists and policy makers as well as advocated by some scholars of whom the most prominent is Samuel Huntington.[6] This ancient hatreds thesis is central in the representation of the crisis and war in the Balkans by the world's media and by Western politicians. It lies at the core of the image of the barbarian Balkan tribes who have historically fought against each other. This distorted media image denies both the national status of various ethnic groups living in Yugoslavia and their membership in European civilization.[7] It has also been the basis of the division between 'good' and 'bad' guys in the Yugoslav conflict.

In this regard, Huntington's hypothesis about "the clash of civilizations"[8] influenced U.S. foreign policy in the Balkans and provided a theoretical framework for the Hollywood-like scenario invoked to understand Yugoslavia. For Huntington, Yugoslavia, in particular Bosnia, are illustrative examples confirming his claim that future conflicts will occur as clashes between civilizations, because all of the three major civilizations he describes meet there: Western Catholic, Eastern Orthodox and Islam—anchored mostly among Bosnian Muslims and Kosovo's ethnic Albanians. According to Huntington, from Yugoslavia to the Middle East and Central Asia, the fault lines of civilizations are the next battlefields. For him, the future conflicts will not be primarily ideological or economic, but cultural:

Nation states will remain the most powerful actors in world affairs, but the principal conflicts of global politics will occur between nations and groups of different civilizations. The clash of civilizations will dominate global politics. The fault lines between civilizations will be the battle lines of the future. Conflict between civilizations will be the latest phase in the evolution of conflict in the modern world.[9]

While Motyl discredits extreme primordialist claims on the theoretical level, I argue that Huntington's hypothesis is also unsustainable on the empirical level with regards to Yugoslavia and more specifically Bosnia. Indeed, the history of Yugoslavia supports neither Huntington's claim about 'ancient hatreds' among Yugoslav nations nor his vision of the clash of civilizations in Bosnia. On the contrary, the conflict between the Serbs, Croats and Muslims is a recent phenomenon, occurring within the twentieth century. As well, it is not a 'clash of civilizations' since the Yugoslav peoples are of the same ethnic stock and have similar rather than different cultures. Even though religious differences played an important role in recent conflicts, there is also a history of their mutual tolerance and coexistence.[10] I further challenge Huntington's hypothesis with my own concept of external Balkanization, or foreign involvement in the drama of Yugoslavia. There is a long history of foreign occupation of the Balkans, as well as of popular and political resistance to it. This contradicts Huntington's argument regarding the 'clash of civilizations.' He inaccurately explains foreign involvement in the conflicts, like the recent one in the Balkans, as the "kin-country syndrome," that is, a natural phenomenon of "civilization rallying" between nations and civilizations.[11] In Huntington's words, "Groups or states belonging to one civilization that become involved in war with people from a different civilization naturally try to rally support from other members of their own civilization."[12] On the contrary, both ancient and recent agendas of external Balkanization have been tied to very specific geopolitical, strategic and economic interests in the Balkans, such as those of the U.S. led Western powers this time.

I concur with Michel Chossudovsky's argument that Western media and politicians have misled public opinion. The representation of Yugoslavia's crisis as the outcome of aggressive nationalism resulting from deep-seated ethnic and religious tensions historically rooted is, as Chossudovsky writes, simply wrong and deceptive.[13] He points out that a deep-seated economic crisis was induced with the first round of IMF macro structural adjustment reforms enforced in 1980, on the eve of Tito's death.[14] In his words:

> ...the economic and social causes of the civil war have been carefully concealed. The *strategic* interests of Germany and the U.S. are not mentioned, the deep-seated *economic crisis* which *preceded* the civil war has long been for-

gotten. In the eyes of the global media, Western powers bear no responsibility for the impoverishment and destruction of a nation of 24 million people. Yet the break up of the Yugoslav federation bears *a direct relationship* to the programme of macro-economic restructuring imposed on the Belgrade government by its external creditors. This programme, adopted in several stages since 1980, contributed to triggering the collapse of the national economy, leading to the disintegration of the industrial sector and the piecemeal dismantling of the welfare state. Secessionist tendencies feeding on social and ethnic divisions, gained impetus precisely during a period of brutal impoverishment of the Yugoslav population.[15]

Furthermore, while Robert Hayden's analysis of ethnic cleansing and constitutional nationalism in the successor states of the former Yugoslavia is accurate and powerful, I take issue with his constructivist approach that claims the artificiality of Yugoslavia as an 'imagined community.' Although I disagree with as it is found entrenched among intellectuals and especially postmodern scholars, my critique is primarily directed against extreme primordialism because of its strong influence on both Western journalists and politicians. Arguments against both theories are presented in the first three chapters of this book; as well I outline the main points of Hayden's valuable and very relevant analysis of the impact and 'hidden agenda' of ethnic cleansing in the fourth chapter. For now, I recapitulate Hayden's basic arguments and, in general, those of the constructivist school of thought. While I agree with Hayden's explanation of the viability of the Yugoslav community, I disagree with his contradictory constructivist approach:

> To reverse Benedict Anderson's evocative phrase (1983), the disintegration of Yugoslavia into its warring components in 1991-92 marked *the failure of the imagination of a Yugoslav community.* This failure of the imagination, however, had real and tragic consequences: the Yugoslav community that could not be maintained, and thus has become unimaginable, had actually existed in many parts of the country. Indeed, it is my argument that the spatial patterning of the war and its terrible ferocity are due to the fact that *in some regions the various Yugoslav people were not only coexisting but also becoming increasingly intermingled.*[16]

Indeed, this argument is unclear and essentially not much different from the primordialist claim about 'ancient hatreds.' Both theories end in a 'deadlock' or circularity with the same conclusion: Yugoslavia was either 'an artificial community' or was built up on 'ancient hatreds,' and therefore, it had to disintegrate sooner or later. Hayden at the same time supplements and contrasts the primordialist argument because he is drawing on Anderson's . He states that "extreme nationalism in the former Yugoslavia has not been only a matter of imagining allegedly 'primordial' communities, but rather of making existing heterogeneous ones unimaginable."[17] For Hayden, in these mixed heterogeneous regions "the idea that the Yugoslav peoples could not live peacefully together was empirical nonsense."[18] He then argues that "the power of an imagined ethnic community" to dismantle Yugoslavia's actually existing communities is "clear and apparent."[19] Therefore, for Hayden, the former Yugoslavia was an artificial 'imagined community' but the new successor states are also, in the same sense, 'artificially imagined communities' as they are building their homogenous nation-states in heterogeneous territories. In this sense, there is no difference between the 'old' Yugoslavia and the new successor states: both are unnaturally 'imagined' communities, making, thus, unviable national formations. This constructivist argument suffers from circularity, explaining neither the complex environment that brought about the collapse of Yugoslavia nor the conditions that enabled the emergence of the new successor states.

Hayden rightly points out that Yugoslav peoples were living peacefully together and that the new successor states are 'cleansing' their heterogeneous regions in order to build ethnically homogenous nation-states. But, he falls into a circular argument of never ending emergence and collapse of the artificially imagined communities. Thus, from the constructivist point of view, all national communities are imagined, and in this sense, all nations are artificial. For both theories of nations and nationalism, the Balkans is an inherently unstable region. This is either due to the ancient hatreds of belligerent ethnic groups in the primordialist sense, or it is due to the artificiality of the imagined communities in the constructivist point of view. According to both theories, peaceful and stable nation-state(s) are thus impossible in the Balkans even though different reasons are provided for this instability.

Up to now, there has been no satisfactory explanation for the victorious 'ethnic vote' in the first free multi-party elections in the 1990, especially in Bosnia, which is a key point in the constructivist claim about the artificiality of Yugoslavia. In regard to this controversial event, one of the unsolved political enigmas of the Balkans, I agree with Catherine Samary who emphasizes that the 'ethnic vote' in Bosnia was not so much ethnic, but rather an anti-Communist vote.[20] In fact, if the peoples of Yugoslavia wanted socio-economic and political changes, this did not in any way mean that they were in favor of national divisions or civil wars. One might also argue that there was at that time no real political choice: on the one side were Communists and on the other were nationalists![21] I also assert that in every country, especially in Yugoslavia, the popular memories of Nazi terror and especially of mutual atrocities committed by domestic Fascist forces are still very vivid. It was not, therefore, difficult to induce ethnic mistrust and collective paranoia through a politics of fear.[22] One should not ignore the fact that the recent civil wars in the 1990s were fought under the same flags and symbols used during World War II.

Contradicting both arguments regarding ancient hatreds and the artificiality of the former Yugoslavia, and particularly in opposition to Huntington's hypothesis of the clash of civilizations, is the following opinion of Lord Owen, who was one of the peace negotiators in Bosnia. In an interview for *Foreign Affairs* magazine in 1993, he provides a more realistic point of view and a more accurate prediction for the future of ethnic relations in the Balkans. When asked: "Given the hatred and the bloodshed of the past two years and the historic ethnic enmities, is it realistic to hope these groups will lie down together and live in peace?" Lord Owen stated,

> I think it's realistic because these people are of the same ethnic stock. I believe some political leaders in the Balkans are not authentically speaking for all their people. There are still very strong elements of modernization within Bosnia-Herzegovina. Many people there still see themselves as European and even now don't think of themselves as Muslim, Croat or Serb; some deliberately and proudly call themselves just Bosnians. That sentiment is reflected in the degree of intermarriage. It's reflected in the fact that, even now, you can go to Sarajevo under bombardment and see Muslims, Serbs and Croats living together in the same streets and apartments. Throughout Yugoslavia people are still all mixed in together and, in many cases, living peaceably.[23]

Certainly, the complexity of the disintegration of the Yugoslav federation far exceeds both primordialist and constructivist arguments. The answer to the question "Why did Yugoslavia collapse?" cannot be reduced to internal factors, or to internal Balkanization in my terms, as both schools have done. Neither can it be reduced strictly to external factors. An accurate picture must include both factors. As argued in more detail later, I am not suggesting that both theories of the nation and nationalism are simply wrong. Rather, my critique is directed towards their strong and extreme variants, while acknowledging that weaker versions are more reasonable and moderate. The third chapter demonstrates the importance and the crucial role of external Balkanization. Indeed, historical and recent divisions of the Balkans by outside powers are my basic counter argument to the extremism of both schools of thought. Following Crnobrnja's account of the drama of Yugoslavia, I also hope that my book can help the reader reach the conclusion as to whether "the creation of Yugoslavia was a noble experiment...or an impossible task from the start."[24] A good starting point for better understanding a number of key historical and political facts about the Yugoslav nations, specifically about the origins of the Yugoslav idea for the creation of a common state of all South Slavs, is to acknowledge both the centrality of Croats and Serbs for Yugoslav unity as well as the interchangeability of the synonymous concepts of 'ethnic group' and 'nation' in Yugoslavia's context. Aleksa Djilas best explains both:

> Since the creation of Yugoslavia in 1918, the conflict between Croats and Serbs has posed the greatest threat to the Yugoslav union. Its causes can be traced to their development of separate cultural and political identities as they took crucial steps toward becoming modern nations in the nineteenth century. Non-Slav observers did not distinguish between Croats and Serbs until the ninth century. These two names became established when the first forms of political organization appeared. The Croatian and Serbian tribes, though identical in ethnic and linguistic origin, developed distinct political organisms. The formation of two separate polities was, from the beginning, an important differentiating force between Croats and Serbs...From the time of their settlement in southeastern Europe during the sixth and early seventh centuries, Croatian tribes were influenced by Latin and Germanic political orders and cultures. The Croats were at the periphery of this western civilization. To the east lived the Serbian tribes, adjacent to the Byzantine world. In the following centuries these eastern and western influences, especially Eastern Orthodox and Roman Catholic, frequently transgressed the borders—which were never firmly established anyway—between Croatian and Serbian tribes and Croatian and Serbian states, creating a pluralistic mosaic rather than a simple division between 'western Croats' and 'eastern Serbs.'[25]

Worldwide public opinion has largely been misled by Western media sources and politicians about the 'real and true' story of the Yugoslav crisis. In line with the authors presented in this book,[26] I argue that ethnic nationalism and religious conflicts were not the primary cause or reason for the war. The common image of 'good guys' (Croats, Muslims, and more recently Albanians) and 'bad guys' (Serbs) is misleading. The ethnic or national identities of refugees and internally displaced people as civilian survivors of the war and 'ethnic cleansing' are misinterpreted in these simplistic and one-sided official explanations and media representations.

One illustrative example of such misinterpretation can be found in the fact that even though refugees from Bosnia are commonly called 'Bosnians,'[27] there is no clear understanding or official explanation of the national composition of these 'Bosnians.' This confusion is further enhanced by the recent emergence and usage of the neologism 'Bosniaks.'[28] Much of the Western media and politicians promote both terms without any explanation of the difference between them, or why they are used interchangeably in such a confusing and contradictory manner. While Huntington, for instance, wrongly refers *only* to Bosnian Muslims as 'the Bosnians,' Lord Owen more accurately uses the same word to describe all three major Bosnian nations, or ethnic groups: the Bosnian Muslims, the Bosnian Croats and the Bosnian Serbs. Furthermore, most official and media reports largely failed to include the 'Yugoslav' national identity as a viable category, even though many Yugoslavs, particularly Bosnians, chose to declared it in the final census conducted in socialist Yugoslavia in 1991. Some people went so far as to jokingly declare themselves 'Eskimos'[29] as a way of rejecting any local national identity inherent to the region. Besides an explanation of these terms, I will show in the fourth chapter how these 'Yugoslavs, Bosnians and Eskimos' are being forced to disappear without a trace, as if these national and personal identities never existed.

I will further illustrate in the latter chapters how and to what extent the concise life histories and experiences of a small sample of Bosnian refugees living in Montreal support my argument that the reasons for the civil war and the ethnic identities of victims of ethnic cleansing are different and far more complex than what is usually assumed in the West. There is rather a multitude of key factors that led to the war, of which the foremost is a crisis in the socio-economic and political system brought about by the post Cold War new world order and its free-market agenda. As I will demonstrate, there is strong evidence showing that the victims and perpetrators of the war crimes include all of the nations involved in the conflict, for example, the Serbs, the Croats and the Muslims in multinational, or multi-ethnic Bosnia. Above all, the civilian victims, the casualties and the survivors, of the civil war in the former Yugoslavia are in essence nationally 'mixed' people, or 'mixed' families, and the 'newly created' national minorities, such as Serbs, Croats and Muslims in Bosnia. Both groups, the 'mixed' and the 'new' minorities, became by definition 'undesirable' populations. Similarly to many authors,[30] I suggest that all of the parties involved in the conflict, particularly in Bosnia, had the same goal: to avoid the national minority status that ultimately meant their expulsion or treatment as second-class citizens.

With regard to the expulsion of 'undesirables' and the subsequent emergence of apatrides or refugees from Yugoslavia due to both external and the consequent internal Balkanization, the last chapter describes the historical and political background of this hundred year old story dating from the very creation of the first Yugoslavia in 1918. I deduce my arguments from the previous chapters and link them with the life histories of Bosnian refugees now living in Montreal. My historical and comparative analysis of present day Bosnian refugees and the first modern European, and Yugoslav, apatrides examines the phenomena of statelessness, homelessness and rightlessness as the common ground of both groups. Drawing on Hannah Arendt's remarkable analysis of these phenomena, based on her account of the very emergence of the first modern apatrides or refugees, I will show that present day refugees from Yugoslavia, more specifically from Bosnia, like those analyzed by Arendt, consider themselves to be stateless, homeless and rightless because of the dismemberment of Yugoslavia. This historical-comparative approach seeks to link the macro and micro levels of this book, as I examine the refugee problematic within a global and historical context.

The main purpose of my empirical research, or my *micro* analysis, presented mostly in the fourth and fifth chapters, is to explore and describe the complexity of issues pertaining to the past and present life experiences of refugees from Bosnia. I look at the main reasons and circumstances under which they resettled in Canada, as well at the main barriers in rebuilding a 'lost home,' or making a new life in Montreal. At the heart of my analysis of this 'Yugoslav Saga,' is the foregrounding of these refugees' own opinions about their displacement and consequent resettlement, including examination of the obstacles or difficulties in their new life. I do not seek to offer an indepth analysis of their complex life

histories, as I concur with David Albahari's mother's expressed scepticism regarding the writing of her own life history: "there is no book that could embrace
the whole life, or even a part of it."[31] This is, rather, a preliminary study that explores such fundamental questions as: Who are the refugees from the former Yugoslavia? Who are these Bosnians, Yugoslavs and 'Eskimos'? For what specific
reasons and under what circumstances did they come to Canada? What are their
main problems or obstacles in creating a new home in Montreal, or rebuilding a
lost one? How are they supported by the various urban community organizations, particularly by ethnic one(s)? What kind of help do they have and to what
extent are their needs being fulfilled?

By linking the relevant parts of these refugees' extraordinarily rich life experiences and points of view with a broader historical and socio-political context, I
intend to provide different insights into both the 'Yugoslav Drama' and the consequent 'Yugoslav Saga,' or respectively the war and the refugee crisis. This combination of theoretical and empirical research offers a more profound
understanding of the complexity of historical, socio-economical and political
context of this 'Odyssey,' the intimate relationship between life experiences of
Yugoslav refugees with the history and the politics within and outside of the Balkans. I reveal different aspects of the history and the geography of ethnic cleansing in Bosnia by linking various theoretical arguments with the findings of my
survey research on refugees, conducted in Montreal, January 2001.

Central to my main argument is the claim that Western politicians and
much of the media misled public opinion at home and at large with regards to
both the civil war in the former Yugoslavia and the ethnic or national identities
of refugees. As a consequence, people who were certainly against national piety
and the ethnic division of their homeland—composed especially of those from
'mixed' marriages and their children in combination with those who perceived
themselves as 'Yugoslavs' and more recently as 'Eskimos'—are *invisible* victims of
the civil war and its ethnic cleansing, since they are completely excluded from all
mainstream accounts. These anti-nationalistically oriented Yugoslavs, Eskimos
and Bosnians[32] are also excluded from Canada's multicultural agenda for three
basic reasons: their practical 'non-existence' due to media exclusion; being a
small group incapable of leadership; and the existence of Serbian, Croatian and
other ethnic or cultural community organizations.

The fact that Yugoslavia's various nations and national minorities were increasingly intermingling, and, that its people, for the most part, considered

themselves officially or personally to be Yugoslavs, combined with a history of peaceful coexistence in spite of the mutual atrocities committed in World War II, is living proof of the reality contrary to the 'truth' maintained and propagated by most of the media. The fact that there are people who are anti-nationalists and of mixed national origins or families demonstrates the inaccuracy of both arguments, regarding the 'artificiality' of the Yugoslav or Bosnian imagined community and historically rooted ethnic hatreds and aggressive-chauvinist nationalism. According to the vast majority of Western media reports, ancient hatreds and ethnic nationalism were at the heart of the Yugoslav crisis. On the contrary, the majority of people did not perceive Yugoslavia as an artificial country or as an unstable region due to ancient hatreds. Particularly not mixed families, who, combined with the old and new 'undesirable' national minorities, composed the vast majority of civilian causalities and refugees in the series of civil wars of the 1990s. Consequently, this invisibility in the media and the exclusion of the very people who believed in peaceful multinational coexistence from the framework of multiculturalism in Canada has resulted in a lack of appropriate multinational community organization in their 'new homeland.'

The very existence of supranational Yugoslavs, Bosnians or 'Eskimos,' reflected especially in the large numbers of 'mixed' marriages, illustrates both the nonsense and the criminality of ethnic division or 'purification' of the heterogeneous territories of the former Yugoslavia. These postnational peoples certainly believed in the Yugoslav idea promoted by civic nationalism, based on socialist internationalism and respect for each nation and, as such, transcended ethnic nationalism. They were definitely the first among those people who were against the partition of Bosnia and Yugoslavia along ethnic and religious lines. Popular slogans often promoted Yugoslavia's foreign policy of socialist internationalism and peaceful coexistence, of which the most prominent was "Svoje nedamo, Tudje necemo" that stands for "we protect and defend what is ours and we do not want what belongs to others" (my translation). The national identity of 'Yugoslavs,' as the seventh nation of Yugoslavia, was based on the very principle of 'supranationality.' Even though 'Yugoslavs' were composed of ethnic or national Serbs, Croats, Muslims, etc., Yugoslavs were a political nation that transcended ethnic nationalism. I want to mention for now that these declared and undeclared 'Yugoslavs,' or simply people who loved Yugoslavia, represent in my view, a majority of the former Yugoslavia's population, definitively did not support the break up of Yugoslavia. As Crnobrnja points out in his analysis of the role of the "Intelligentsia and Nationalism in the Yugoslav Drama," the idea of holding a referendum throughout Yugoslavia based on the principle of "one person-one vote" was refused by both the republican nationalist governments and the intelligentsia.[33]

It seems to me that citizens of the former Yugoslavia were ignored as individuals and reduced to ethnic 'nationals' or Serbs, Croats, Muslims, etc. This transition or, in my opinion, regression from civic to ethnic nationalism, is best expressed by the well-known intellectual Slavenka Drakulic, whose descriptions of the new Croatian state is an apt and passionate analysis that applies to all of the successor states of the former Yugoslavia at that time:

> Being Croat has become my destiny...*I am defined by my nationality, and by it alone...*Along with millions of other Croats, I was pinned to the wall of nationhood—not only by outside pressure from Serbia and the Federal Army but by national homogenization within Croatia itself. That is what the war is doing to us, reducing us to one dimension: the Nation. The trouble with this nationhood, however, is that whereas before, I was defined by my education, my job, my ideas, my character—and, yes, my nationality too—now I feel stripped of all that. *I am nobody because I am not a person any more.* I am one of 4.5 million Croats...I am not in a position to choose any longer. Nor, I think, is anyone else...there is no escape...One doesn't have to succumb voluntarily to this ideology of the nation—one is sucked into it. So right now, in the new state of Croatia, no one is allowed not to be a Croat.[34]

It comes as no surprise then that some people resisted this whole process of national homogenization by declaring themselves, in a sarcastic manner, to be 'Eskimos' in the last census of 1991. Some of these Yugoslav 'Eskimos,' now already Canadian citizens, ironically and symbolically predicted their resettlement in Canada, which is in fact the homeland of the real 'Eskimos': the Inuit people. It is interesting to note that, similar to the term 'Yugoslav,' which refers to the peoples of Yugoslavia, the national identity or the term 'Inuit' also means 'people.' While 'Inuk' means 'a person,' similarly, the peoples of Yugoslavia were defined by personality, as persons, and not by nationality. Likewise, the term 'Bosnians' also referred to all nations and nationalities living in Bosnia. Both supranational identities, Yugoslav and Bosnian, were based on civil projects in contrast to the more recent ethnic claims.

The non-recognition of Yugoslavs, Bosnians, Eskimos and others who were against ethnic divisions and the war, means that those who immigrated to Canada lack multi-ethnic Yugoslav community organization in their new homeland that would be inclusive of all nations and national minorities of Yugoslavia. If we do not understand or know who the refugees from the former Yugoslavia are and what happened to them, then we cannot understand the impact of resettlement in Canada nor the nature of their main problems and obstacles in rebuilding a lost home. It is impossible however to separate past, present and future, if one wants to truly understand what happened to the peoples of Bosnia and what these refugees' lifeworld in Montreal looks like.

In order to elaborate these claims and provide the necessary theoretical support and empirical evidence, this book is divided into five interrelated chapters. While the first chapter provides an overview of the key theories of the nation and nationalism already outlined, the second one examines their application in the Yugoslav context. This theoretical background is crucial for understanding the complexity of the national question in Yugoslavia and the role of ethnic nationalism in the disintegration of Yugoslavia. The third chapter is a brief summary of the historical and political context of Balkanization, particularly the external form that is equivalent to the old and new world orders, and their 'Divide and Rule' politics, embracing the constant division of the territories of Yugoslavia and the Balkans at large. This legacy of continual conflict due to external Balkanization and its impact on the crisis and war in the 1990s will then be linked to the geography of ethnic cleansing in the next chapter. The fourth chapter thus describes the heterogeneous ethnic composition of the republics of the former Yugoslavia that consequently reflects the various national identities of refugees from Bosnia who immigrated to Canada. The final chapter reveals the correlation between the destiny of these refugees and the first European apatrides, both groups being labelled 'undesirables.' This historical and political analysis of the phenomena of statelessness and homelessness provides a necessary conceptual introduction to the refugee problematic and, additionally, links the macro and micro analyses of this book. This last chapter also explores some of the positive and negative implications of multiculturalism and its impact on the life and urban experience of Bosnian refugees in Montreal. Finally, the main difficulties and obstacles to successful integration into Quebec society will be identified. Along with these thematics and arguments, each chapter also includes a number of sub-discussions on related issues in order to avoid the over-simplification of complex social settings and phenomena; something that is all too common in Western accounts of the breakup of the former Yugoslavia (SFRY).

## NOTES

1. The verb "balkanize" means to break up a region or group into smaller, often hostile, units.

2. Mihailo Crnobrnja was the last ambassador of the former Yugoslavia to the European Union and a participant in the Peace Conference on Yugoslavia in The Hague in 1991. He is also the author of *The Yugoslav Drama*. Montreal: McGill-Queen's University Press, 1994.

3. My approach points out key components of the conflict, which excludes in-depth analyses of the socio-economic and political crisis prior to the eruption of ethnic nationalism as well as the role of media, within and outside Yugoslavia.

4. In this book the term *South Slavs* (meaning Yugoslavs, 'south' is 'yug' in Serbo-Croatian language), refers to all seven South Slavic nations of the former Yugoslavia: in alphabetical order, Croats, Macedonians, Montenegrins, Muslims, Slovenes, Serbs, and controversial Yugoslavs. Concerning the exclusion of the Bulgarians, see "Introduction" and notes to it in Aleksa Djilas. *The Contested Country: Yugoslav Unity and Communist Revolution*. Cambridge Massachusetts: Harvard University Press, 1996.

5. Michael Parenti. "The Rational Destruction of Yugoslavia," in Michael Parenti Political Archive at http://www.michaelparenti.org/yugoslavia.html, 2000, accessed 24 May 2001, my emphasis.

6. Alexander Motyl. *Revolutions, Nations, Empires: Conceptual Limits and Theoretical Possibilities*. New York: Columbia University Press, 1999, pp. 85, 86.

7. I use the terms "ethnic group" and "nation" interchangeably in this book because they are conceptually synonymous and for the sake of clarity and simplicity. In the former Yugoslavia, and now in the new successor states, the word 'nation' or 'narod' signifies what Americans view as 'ethnic.' Also, in the Constitutions and in public usage there is the well-established word 'people' or '*narod*' that refers to the nation that again in the North America means 'ethnic'. In Yugoslav official and popular vocabulary we find words '*narod and narodnosti*' where the former refers to people or nation and the latter to nationalities or national minorities. See also Djilas, 1996; Hayden, 1996; Samary, 1995, et al.

8. Samuel P. Huntington. "The Clash of Civilizations." *Foreign Affairs*. New York: Council on Foreign Relations. Volume 72, Number 3. Summer 1993. This article he further elaborated in his book *The Clash of Civilizations and the Remaking of World Order*. New York: Simon&Schuster, 1996.

9. Huntington, 1993, *ibid.*, p. 22.

10. Not to mention that after all socialist Yugoslavia officially separated the State from the Church. As well, by the personal choice of peoples it was mainly an atheist country.

11. Huntington, 1993, *op. cit.*, pp. 35-39.

12. *Ibid.*, p. 35.

13. Chossudovsky is referring to the account of Warren Zimmerman, the former U.S. Ambassador to Yugoslavia, in Michel Chossudovsky. *The Globalization of Poverty: Impacts of IMF and World Bank Reforms*. London and New Jersey: Zed Books, 1997, pp. 243, 260, note 1.

14. *Ibid.*, pp. 243, 244.

15. *Ibid.*, p. 244, my emphasis.

16. Robert Hayden "Imagined Communities and Real Victims: Self-determination and Ethnic Cleansing in Yugoslavia." *American Ethnologist.* Vol. 23 (4), 1996, p. 788, my emphasis.

17. *Ibid.*, p. 783.

18. *Ibid.*, p. 790.

19. *Ibid.*, pp. 793, 794.

20. See Catharine Samary. *Yugoslavia Dismembered.* Translated from French by Peter Drucker. New York: Monthly Review Press, 1995. Samary rightly explains, that first of all, "the votes of rural municipalities help explain nationalists' electoral success. But it is neither a sufficient explanation nor even a wholly convincing one (since voting for a 'national' party does not necessarily imply support for all its policies)" (p. 90). Moreover, she accurately states that "on the eve of Bosnia-Herzegovina's elections, all the poles forecast a majority for the non-nationalist parties...the principle of 'national' parties had been rejected in polls shortly before the elections, because people were so conscious of the deathly danger that such parties represented in Bosnia-Herzegovina. This sentiment was so widespread that on election day several nationalist parties, unable to believe that they were actually winning, declared that the elections were being rigged" (p. 91). Finally, she claims that "reasoning in the context of the prior regime's economic and moral crisis, voters logically pronounced their verdict on the clear failure of the late 1980s by casting a non-Communist vote...the 'ethnic vote' in the first elections can thus be interpreted as a vote to punish those responsible for the crisis and as an (illusory) safeguard against Bosnia's break-up [since the three nationalist parties promised to govern jointly]. The 'ethnic vote' only embraced 55 percent of the electorate anyway; 25 percent voted for non-nationalist parties and 20 percent abstained. So it cannot be said that these elections expressed a popular will for separation" (p. 92). The greatest 'mystery' however, was the fact that Fikret Abdic, a Muslim non-nationalist, who was a pillar of the secular wing of the Muslim Party for Democratic Action (SDA) and who was very popular as a trustworthy person, won more votes than Alija Izerbegovic, but Abdic 'mysteriously' decided to leave the presidency of Bosnia to Izerbegovic.

21. To attract voters, the main opposition parties across Yugoslavia promoted their programs as democratic or liberal, thus 'hiding' their pure nationalist agendas and goals. This was apparent in their names, of which all included buzzwords democratic or liberal, omitting completely the word 'national' or leaving it to the ultra-nationalist parties. Consider for example these names of Bosnia's opposition: HDZ stands for "Croatian Democratic Community," SDA is a Muslim party called "Party of Democratic Action" and SDS stands for "Serbian Democratic Action."

22. See Crnobrnja, 1994, *op. cit.*, as well as his article "Intelligentsia and Nationalism in the Yugoslav Drama" in *Europe: Central and East (Critical Perspective on Historic Issues, Volume 6)* Edited by Marguerite Mendell and Klaus Nielsen. New York: Black Rose Books. 1995.

23. The Editors. "The Future of the Balkans: An Interview with David Owen." *Foreign Affairs.* New York: Council on Foreign Relations. Spring 1993, pp. 6, 7.

24. Crnobrnja, 1994, *op. cit.*, p. 34.

25. Djilas, *op. cit.*, p. 4.

26. Baudson, 1996; Chossudovsky, 1996, 1997; Crnobrnja, 1994, 1995; Parenti, 2000; Samary, 1995, et al.

27. *Bosanci*, singular *Bosanac* in Serbo-Croatian.

28. *Bosnjaci*, singular *Bosnjak* in Serbo-Croatian.

29. The word '*Eskimo*' is used in this book in an entirely positive sense. Catherine Samary similarly emphasizes this positive connotation of the term "Eskimo" in her aforementioned book *Yugoslavia Dismembered*, dedicated to all her friends of all nations and nationalities from the former Yugoslavia, including those that have resisted the ethnic or national division of Yugoslavia, and have chosen rather to declare themselves as 'Eskimos,' instead of Serbs, Croats or Muslims, in the last Census in 1991.

30. Gerard Baudson, 1996; Hayden, 1996; Samary, 1995, et al.

31. David Albahari. *Mamac* (*A Bait*, my translation), Belgrade: Narodne Novine, 1997, p. 133. Albahari is a well-known Yugoslav writer of mixed Jewish and Serbian origins, who in the 1990s immigrated to Canada. In this book, he depicts interweaving similarities of his mother's life with his own destiny.

32. In this book and in reality the term 'Bosnians' includes Bosnian Croats, Bosnian Muslims, Bosnian Serbs and other various Bosnian national minorities.

33. See Crnobrnja, 1995, *op. cit*, p. 135.

34. Slavenka Drakulic. *The Balkan Express: Fragments from the other Side of War*, New York: W.W. Norton, 1993, pp. 50-52, cited in Rogers Brubaker. *Nationalism Reframed*, 1999 (1996), p. 20, note 17, my emphasis.

# Chapter One
# Theories of Nation and Nationalism

In the next two chapters, I review a modest amount of literature written about the nation and nationalism in order to provide a theoretical framework for further comprehension of the complexity surrounding the national question in Yugoslavia (1918-2003), as well as an explanation of terms and concepts used throughout this book.[1] While in this first chapter I introduce a debate on issues related equally to nationalism and multiculturalism, in the following chapter I will examine the origins of the Yugoslav idea of the unification of all South Slavs, or Yugoslavs, in a common state, through this explanatory prism. The following overview of concepts and definitions of the nation, ethnicity, national and ethnic minority together with theories of nationalism will ultimately enrich my historical and sociological analyses of the emergence and dissolution of Yugoslavia. It will also provide an insight into the differences between the federal models of both Canada and the former Yugoslavia, which I compare at the end of the second chapter. In particular, it will facilitate an understanding of the central question regarding whether Yugoslavia disintegrated because of ancient ethnic hatreds as advocated by the primordialists, or due to its artificially as an imagined community, as constructivists argue. Both arguments, in fact, impose a false dilemma upon Yugoslavia by ignoring the importance of the international dimension and external geopolitical and economic factors. The focus in both approaches is on ethnic nationalism as the primary cause of the collapse of Yugoslavia and subsequent civil war, while external Balkanization is pushed aside as a distant secondary cause.

However, I agree with Kai Nielsen and Alexander Motyl who claim that for any nation to be born, its people have to see themselves as a nation, distinguishing themselves from 'others' while sharing a belief system about a common historicity or a common future, as well as expressing the desire and political will to form the state on the territory that the nation has, in most cases, historically in-habited. In line with these claims, my analysis of the disintegration of the former Yugoslavia goes one step further. My account of the 'Politics of Sorrow,' which ultimately refers to a loss of one's native homeland, shows that for the emer-gence or the disappearance of a country or a nation, it is not sufficient that its people see or cease to see themselves as a nation. What ultimately counts is that the nation becomes internationally recognized as such, as a full-fledged partner in the family of nations, or in the international political, economic and cultural community.

My strategy for approaching and analyzing the key elements of modern na-tionalist conflicts is to conceptualize diverse forms of nationalism and multicul-turalism by providing much needed definitions and distinctions between nations, national minorities, ethnic or immigrant groups and tribes. In order to explain these distinctions, I will examine the different meanings and goals of these social groups by drawing upon the analyses of various scholars, of whom I will present a few of the most relevant for my analysis of national issues in Yugo-slavia. I first introduce a discussion on nationalism and multiculturalism from the vantage point of two internationally renowned political philosophers, Kai Nielsen and Will Kymlicka. In particular, I present Nielsen's notion of liberal na-tionalism and Kymlicka's analysis of multiculturalism in Canada, especially with regard to difference between a national minority and an ethnic or immigrant group. After this introduction into the complexity of modern society and em-bedded nationalist conflicts, I will proceed with a more detailed presentation of theories of nation and nationalism, including the arguments of Craig Calhoun and Alexander Motyl's eloquent critique of both primordial and constructivist schools of thought.

## Nationalism and Multiculturalism

Kai Nielsen advocates the concept of a multi-nation state based on equal part-nership of its composing nations, which would simultaneously enable the inte-gration of cultural minorities without assimilation.[2] He promotes the idea of what he calls a "liberal nationalism" and a "pluralistic multiculturalism," arguing that these concepts do not exclude each other but rather are "compatible" mod-ern movements.[3] For Nielsen, multiculturalism cannot be ignored in our con-temporary reality because it is an obvious social fact. In his definition of a nation, national membership implies,

*...a people* who constitute a political community. A nation is a group of people with a) a distinctive history, distinctive traditions, customs, typically, but not always (e.g., the Scots), with a distinctive language...with a distinctive encompassing (societal) culture and b) as well, with *a sense that they are a people* sustaining or seeking some form of self-governance. To be a nation a people will almost invariably inhabit a territory which they regard as their homeland or, if in Diaspora, they will have an aspiration to inhabit a place that will become their homeland.[4]

For Nielsen, there is a multitude of different forms of nationalism, of which he distinguishes two main categories: "good," or liberal nationalism, and "bad," or ethnic nationalism. He justifies this division by claiming that while "some forms are barbaric and vicious, others are liberal and tolerant."[5] Ethnic nationalism is non-liberal because of its obvious demand for a membership in the nation based exclusively on descent or blood, which is therefore contrary to Nielsen's notion of universalism or cosmopolitanism, evidently also clashing with multiculturalism. Ethnic nationalism, in his words, is "barbaric...xenophobic, exclusionist, typically racist," with a tendency of engagement "in genocide and ethnic cleansing," if there is an "opportunity."[6] In contrast to ethnic nationalism, Nielsen asserts that in modernity there also exists a tradition of liberal nationalism, which is at the same time particular, or local, and universal or cosmopolitan. This liberal form of nationalism is, in his view, committed simultaneously to the "near and dear," or particularism, and to "pluralism and tolerance," or universalism.[7] Unlike ethnic nationalism, liberal nationalism is open and tolerant, as national membership or nationality is not attained through descent or blood but rather through "cultural attunement, a willingness to accept membership in the nation and to recognize others similarly attuned and similarly inclined as members."[8]

Nielsen acknowledges that even though both forms of nationalism are an inherent part of our modern reality, liberal nationalism occurs less often worldwide than ethnic nationalism. He bases his argument for the suitability of liberal nationalism in democratic society on examples of the struggles for the independence of Norway from Sweden in 1905 and Iceland from Denmark in 1944, emphasizing that both countries fought for their independence in a purely democratic way. Drawing upon these two historic events, he makes a parallel with the case of Quebec's independence from Canada. For Nielsen there is no doubt that the inhabitants of Quebec, or Quebecois, have a right to become a sovereign nation because they see themselves as a 'people.' As well, their nationalism is a liberal one as they are seeking to achieve their sovereignty peacefully and democratically. Thus, they struggle to become a nation by liberal rather than violent means. Nielsen views this struggle for a sovereign Quebec as "intense and bitter, as was the struggle for Norwegian and Icelandic sovereignty, but it will be fought out within the limits of liberal democracy alone. However it gets settled, if it ever gets settled, it will be settled with words and votes and not guns and tanks."[9] He stretches his argument so far as to claim that both Quebec and African-American nationalist struggles are in essence reasonable and justified overall. Even though the level of national awareness and consciousness differ between Quebecois and African-Americans, both groups perceive themselves as a people, having thus a legitimate reason to become a nation. In Nielsen's own words,

> African-Americans are by now, and have been for a long time, *a people* and as a people they could aspire to some form of political community with some form of self-governance...There is a subjective factor that is also crucial to nationhood, namely that to *be a nation, people must see themselves as a people, as a nation*...Moreover, to recognize that you are a people is to recognize that you can become a nation (a political community).[10]

He further argues that nations are distinct from ethnic or immigrant groups who primarily seek to integrate into existing society without assimilation, having no desire to form their own national or political community. Nations are also very different from national minorities, which Nielsen defines as a people who are "historically located in a nation and as a distinct part of that nation, but who have as well another encompassing (societal) culture which is that of an adjacent nation (e.g., Anglophones in Quebec and Francophones in Ontario)."[11] While a more detailed description of the concept of the nation and of the ethnic group will be provided later, I want to now proceed with the distinction between national and ethnocultural minorities in the Canadian context. Kymlicka explains this difference succinctly in his analysis of the ethnocultural relations and limits of multiculturalism in Canada.

For Kymlicka, Canada is "a world leader in three of the most important areas of ethnocultural relations: immigration, indigenous peoples, and the accommodation of minority nationalisms."[12] He distinguishes two main sources of Canada's increasing ethnic and cultural diversity, one of the existence of the First Nations, or Aboriginal peoples, and French Canadians prior to the arrival of the British who both remained as national minorities; the other of mass immigration of both ethnocultural groups: immigrant and ethnic ones. In this sense, Kymlicka defines a national minority as a "historical society, with its own language and institutions, whose territory has been incorporated (often involuntary, as is case with Quebec) into a larger country."[13] He explains that, for example, the Quebecois, Aboriginal peoples and Puerto Ricans in North America[14] are all national minorities because these groups see themselves as 'nations' and they create nationalist movements in order to protect their linguistic rights and obtain some degree of autonomy. As well, all of them have a history of struggling for different forms of self-governance and for the preservation of their culturally different societies that have been incorporated into a larger state. With regard to the second source of Canadian ethnocultural diversity, Kymlicka maintains that mass immigration is a common ground for both immigrant and ethnic groups. He explains that even though some 'older' immigrant groups such as Irish, German or Ukrainian Canadians are perceived by many people, including themselves, as 'ethnic groups,' their origins in Canada nevertheless "lie in the act of immigration...[and] these groups have very different histories from the 'nations within.' They are the result not of the involuntary incorporation of complete societies settled in their historic lands, but of the decisions of individuals and families to leave their original homelands for a new life."[15]

For this reason, Kymlicka uses concepts of an immigrant and an ethnic group interchangeably as both groups have origins in immigration, which, in the case of refugees or African-Americans, is not a voluntary but rather a forced act. He draws a demarcation line between ethnocultural groups, who all immigrated, and national minorities, including both founding peoples of Canada, the Aboriginals and French-Canadians, who were already living here when the British arrived. Like Nielsen, Kymlicka asserts that Canadian immigrant or ethnic groups historically and contemporarily have primarily demanded social and political integration and not self-government or an independent state. Kymlicka thus defines the 'Canadian model' of multiculturalism as a policy that comforts and nourishes the existence of its various ethnocultural groups. In his examination of the limits of multiculturalism, he claims that "multiculturalism is working well, and fears of ethnocultural separatism are misplaced."[16]

He points out however that Canada is more successful in dealing with its immigrant and ethnic groups than in resolving disputed issues with its national minorities and their nationalism. He states that, at the moment, there are no hopeful prospects for the settlement of national differences in Canada, because of pronounced opposition to the existing model of 'symmetrical federalism' by both the Quebecois and Aboriginal peoples who oppose this national strategy for preserving state unity. Although not very optimistic about the model of multi-national federation advocated by both groups, he admits that this proposed model might be the only way to preserve Canada as a state. According to Kymlicka:

> In recent years, both the Quebecois and Aboriginal peoples have strongly asserted their distinctive national identities. For them, Canada is a single country that contains more than one 'nation': their citizenship is Canadian, but their national identity is Quebecois, Cree, etc. As a result Canada is, sociologically speaking, a 'multination' state, and like all multination states it must find a way to accommodate minority nationalisms...The sort of 'multination' federalism desired by most Quebecois and Aboriginal people rests on a model of federalism fundamentally opposed to the model of symmetrical federalism that is endorsed by the (non-Aboriginal, non-Quebecois) majority in Canada.[17]

Kymlicka further elaborates on the differences between national minorities and immigrant or ethnic groups, while also introducing a distinction between ethnic and civic nations. He explains the latter difference by arguing that ethnic nations "take the reproduction of a particular ethnonational culture and identity as one of their most important goals," while in contrast, civic nations are " 'neutral' with respect to the ethnocultural identities of their citizens, and define national membership purely in terms of adherence to certain principles of democracy and justice."[18] Kymlicka also claims that national minorities are peoples who have always resisted integration and especially the adoption of a majority language, while at the same time immigrants have always integrated and learnt the language of the dominant group. Therefore, he states that in Canada and in other Western countries, only national minorities have historically resisted integration or assimilation, and have fought for self-government or sovereignty.

Kymlicka argues that the very demanding project of nation building is traceable exclusively to non-immigrant national minorities, regardless of whether they live inside or outside Canada. In contrast, immigrant groups have typically integrated into dominant culture for two main reasons; one is that immigrants have voluntarily left their own native land with a will to integrate in their new chosen homeland, the other is that they have arrived individually or with families and not as whole communities. Therefore, they usually have neither a territory nor essential institutions for developing their culturally and linguistically distinct societies within an existing state. Kymlicka thus argues that multiculturalism, in all its forms, does not constitute a separatist movement, as none of its programs are related to the project of nation building or the logic of self-governing territories. In his words, "immigrants are very different from national minorities, for whom nation-building threatens a culturally distinct society that already exists and has functioned for generations. Historically, the nationalist option has been neither desirable nor feasible for immigrants."[19] Kymlicka also states that his differentiation of national minorities from immigrants with regard to the process of integration in Canada has one exception, that of the case of colonialism where "colonial settlers did not see themselves as 'immigrants,' since they had no expectation of integrating into another culture: rather they aimed to reproduce their original society in a new land."[20]

Thus, both scholars Nielsen and Kymlicka agree that ethnic or immigrants groups are completely benign in terms of claims to self-government or to independent state formation. In contrast to national minorities, these ethnocultural groups usually integrate into the existing state without assimilation, as well as without any desire to become a distinct political community. However, in discussing the accommodation of national minorities, Nielsen goes further than Kymlicka and more radically argues for the formation of multi-nation states, such that would, for example, include African-Americans in the U.S. and Quebecois in Canada. Nielsen also contributes to the debate on nationalism by making a clear distinction between violent-bad and peaceful-good forms of nationalism, respectively ethnic and liberal nationalism, such as, for example, the Quebecois or the Scottish form of civic or liberal nationalism in contrast to the violent Irish, Basques or Corsican ethnic nationalism. Kymlicka is much more reserved in commenting on the Quebec question and the formation of a multi-nation Canadian state. For Kymlicka, the idea of a multi-national federation is the last resort since, in his view, the Quebecois are better served within the existing, thus unchanged, Canada.

## The Origins of the Nation and Nationalism

Returning now to theories of the nation and nationalism, Craig Calhoun, who belongs to the so-called constructivist school of sociology and anthropology, points out that none of the offered definitions of the nation, or nationalism and nationality, "has ever gained general acceptance."[21] Even though Calhoun acknowledges different forms of nationalism that range from horrifying to more gentle variations, in contrast to Nielsen's fundamental division between good and bad nationalism, he argues that too many scholars devote themselves to finding the key to differentiate between good and bad nationalism, or between patriotism and chauvinism. For Calhoun, thus, these two disputed forms of nationalism are not as drastically different social phenomena as some scholars claim them to be. By doing so, social scientists tend to ignore their similarities, provoking unnecessary confusion between positive and negative sides of national identity. However, in an extremely constructivist manner, Calhoun argues that nationalism is "a discursive formation," and therefore, "national identity and loyalty are shaped by the common discourse of nationalism."[22]

For Calhoun and the constructivist school, nationalism is a distinctly modern phenomenon. It is the very product of modern social development in which new collective identities were shaped by the process of industrialization that brought about new communication and transportation facilities and many other technological innovations that completely changed traditional ways of living. In spite of the modernity of nationalism, Calhoun argues that it is "important analytically to distinguish nationalism from ethnicity...and both from kinship...since ethnicity is often presented as an extension of kinship and nationalists commonly present nations as large families sharing bonds of culture and descent."[23] In this regard, he points out that there are two very different, almost antagonistic, theories for analyzing nationalism; one emphasizes the role of ethnicity, while the other stipulates the political project for building a state led by nationalist elites. For this reason, the literature on nation and nationalism is respectively divided between the primordialist approach and the constructivist or instrumentalist approach. According to Calhoun, the basic difference is that while primordialists emphasize trans-historical "continuities between modern national cultures and their antecedents...like family and ethnic bonds," in contrast, constructivists "underestimate the power of culture," by emphasizing rather "the historical and sociological processes by which nations are created," in particular the role of nationalist elites whose "leaders often manipulate...their followers...on the basis of nationalist ideology."[24]

In his analysis of the differences between a tribe, an ethnic group and a nation, Calhoun argues that even though almost all modern nations have originated from previously existing ethnic groups, nevertheless, nationalism implies a completely different conception of collective identity and the organization of a society as a whole. In terms of how people had organized their society in the past, Calhoun maintains that ethnicity is only one of the historical expressions of collective identities; the other one of kinship and descent, or tribal identity, was much more crucial and omnipresent. He argues that historically speaking, all known communities primarily organized their social life and contacts with other groups through kinship and descent. Thus, the first collective identities in the past were formed through marriage and blood. However, Calhoun emphasizes that in the contemporary period, the role of these relations is different in modern Western countries than in technologically less developed societies. He provides the example of Northern Ghana in Africa, where almost the whole social order is based on kinship and descent. For Calhoun then, it is wrong to use concepts of kinship and descent when referring to nations, as modern nationalist movements often do incorporate in their rhetoric. He illustrates this difference through the case of contemporary Serbia, Croatia and Bosnia, arguing that although kinship and family are valued and more important "in organizing social life than, say, in England, the United States or Australia...they are not the template of the whole social order" as in traditional societies.[25]

Calhoun explains that the Tallensi of Northern Ghana have organized their society on the basis of both kinship and descent, as well as "clans," which are exogamous organization of "kin relations between individuals...[who] share common identities as equal members of a unitary whole."[26] While Tallensi identify themselves through their family ties and clans, or only through kinship and descent, Bosnians or Americans could identify with their family, school, city, state or country. In contrast to the Tallensi whose prayers are devoted to their ancestors, Orthodox Christians or Serbs, Catholics or Croats and Bosnian Muslims pray to their different Gods. As well, they do not inherit the presidential office, as is the case with the Tallensi. Another significant difference is that economic system and employment policy in Croatia, Bosnia or Serbia are not based on kinship and descent, but rather on international trade, money exchange and professional competition. Moreover, while Tallensi are members of a fragmented lineage society that is identical to clan structure, Serbs, Croats and Muslims live in nuclear families composed of parents and their children. Thus, Calhoun asserts that even though the nationalist rhetoric of Serbian or Croatian leaders implies that "we are one family," the notion of 'we' is not fragmented by any loyalty to smaller groups, or in his words "there is no single, fixed unit so primary that a Tallensi would always think of it."[27] For Calhoun then, nationalist rhetoric is distinctive in the sense that it refers to the country as a whole, which implies that the concept of the nation is above any kind of fractional claims. In his terms:

Nationality, thus, becomes one large categorical identity that encompasses many smaller categories ('tribes,' ethnic groups) each of which may be organized internally on the basis of further categories and complex networks of interpersonal relationships. Nationalist rhetoric posits whole categories of people without reference to their internal differentiation, or claims priority over all such internal differences; ideal-typically, one is a member of a nation directly as an individual.[28]

Furthermore, the basic difference between a tribe and an ethnic group is that the former is centred on kin relations that, in turn, are completely irrelevant for the latter. Calhoun maintains that kin embraces people who are related either by having a common ancestor and blood or by marriage. In his words, kinship "can be used inclusively to refer to the whole set of relationships and identities formed by affinal and consanguinal ties—'in-laws' and 'blood'."[29] Ethnicity, on the other hand, is situated between kinship and nationality having, thus, an intermediary position between the two. For Calhoun, it is an oversimplification to assume that ethnicity is merely a historical continuation of kinship, because ethnicity is based on much broader and inclusive criterion than kinship. In other words, ethnic identities are historically developed when very different social groups who live in the same region have had to interact with each other.

Calhoun explains that ethnic identities have emerged due to "the concentration of population in a city, the development of economic links beyond the local level, and/or the creation of a state, particularly an empire," where distinct peoples had to deal "with each other or with the state itself."[30] Even though internally any given ethnic group can be arranged through kinship and descent, on the external level, such group always acts as an egalitarian partner among other ethnic groups. For Calhoun, the intermediate position of an ethnic group is very apparent in both Roman and Ottoman Empires, where central authorities in Rome and Istanbul showed no interest for interference in the internal organization of ethnic groups living on the periphery of their empires. In this sense, Calhoun points out that Romans distinguished themselves from non-Romans, or from Jews, Greeks, Gauls and others, as did the Ottomans with Jews, Armenian Christians, Greek Christians and other ethnic communities. With respect to the difference between a nation and an ethnic group, Calhoun notes that the root of the word 'nation' comes from the Roman term 'natio,'[31] which, in its original usage, was equivalent to ethnicity as "it meant simply people of common ancestry and thereby common character."[32]

Calhoun argues that on the one hand, ethnic identity resembles national identity in the sense that both formations have to demonstrate their likeness within the group emphasizing at the same time their distinctiveness from other groups. On the other hand, ethnic identity differs essentially from nationality, which, as a modern product, is intimately related with the notion of individualism. For Calhoun, the modernization of Europe demanded the transformation of ethnic groups, because it brought forth both migration and integration of different territories into common or larger states. As Calhoun notes, "while nations may have ideologies of common descent and shared kinship, they are organized primarily as categories of individual members, identified on the basis of various cultural attributes—common language, religion, customs, names, etc."[33] He maintains that modern Western thought understands nations in the same manner as individuals, who likewise co-exist and interact with each other. Thus, each nation, like each individual, has its unique and distinctive identity.

Ethnicity, according to Calhoun, does not provide sociocultural groups with the ingredient to become nations; rather, it is only one factor that helps to transform an ethnic group into a nation. He claims that even though ethnic groups promote social solidarity and have a distinct common culture, their collective identity is neither exclusively rooted nor defined by their common culture since it could also be based on common political goals. In this regard, Calhoun provides the examples of Switzerland, Canada and the United States that all have developed "political cultures—and consumer and media cultures—that are not reducible to the culture of any of the many ethnic groups within them."[34] These countries obviously have distinct political cultures despite their internal ethnic differences. They show that although nationalism draws on and reflects previous ethnic identities and traditions, it also changes or enriches their traditional cultures. For Calhoun, ethnic origins and cultural differences are very important but they are not the only determining factor for the emergence of modern nations or states. He asserts that the example of the United States demonstrates his claim of national unification for political purposes since American independence from Britain was won by its many diverse ethnic groups, such as the English, Scottish, Irish, Welsh, Dutch, French, descendants of African slaves and Native Americans. Calhoun states that the United States also illustrates one of the distinct meanings between civic and ethnic nationalism as it "has retained a national identity even while absorbing a wide range of immigrants and allowing them to retain considerable ethnic distinctiveness. Part of the key is that the

United States was conceptualized—at least in part—as a willed community...not just ethnic or other categorization."[35]

Therefore, Calhoun argues that nationalism has many different faces and manifestations that draw upon a plethora of moral and political foundations. Nationalism can mean modernization and unification, but can also reflect chauvinistic tribalism. Calhoun rejects the division of positive-good and negative-bad nationalism and the whole discourse around such a radical separation. He maintains that "the modern idea of nation grew up alongside the idea of democracy as part of an effort to base politics in the will of 'the people.' The nation could be identified with the people of a country against their rulers—whether these were foreigners or simply monarchs who lacked popular support."[36] Calhoun asserts that the distinction between ethnic versus liberal nationalism is historically unfounded. For example, between the 1780s to the 1870s, ethnic territorial claims emerged alongside the liberal project of promoting freedom for all peoples and not just for the dominant ethnic group. According to Calhoun:

> In short, the discourse of nationalism is too basic and too widespread to pigeonhole as either positive or negative...there is a strong inclination among some groups of scholars to distinguish patriotism as 'good' love of country from nationalism as a 'bad' distortion. This is not only rooted in a general desire to maintain sharp distinctions between good and bad, but it reflects some of the history of nationalist discourse itself.[37]

He further explains that liberal nationalism in its early stage promoted loyalty to the nation and not to the king or emperor, aiming to achieve both a democratic state and independence from foreign rule. Calhoun notes that the so-called liberal theory labelled Western European nationalist movements as desirable expressions of patriotism, thus distinguishing them from the Eastern European experience that was seen as 'bad' nationalism. While Western nations in this schema have stable national identities, the Eastern peoples have problematic or unstable national identities. Calhoun states that although, for example, the Poles, Magyars and Germans might think of their nationalist projects as similar or identical to the patriotism of French and English, their Eastern nationalism, with its emotional destructiveness and instability, was in direct opposition to the Western vision of both stable states and the concept of patriotism. The difference then between civic and ethnic nationalism which formed respectively Western and Eastern nationality, implies, in Calhoun's view, that:

This West/East contrast is cognate with the opposition between 'political' or 'civic' nationalisms and 'cultural' or 'ethnic' nationalisms. In the former case, national identity is understood to be something established by legitimate membership in a constituted political state; members of the nation are understood first and foremost through their political identities as citizens. In the latter case, national identity is defined on the basis of some cultural or ethnic criteria distinct from, and arguably prior to, political citizenship.[38]

Central to Calhoun's argument against the division or classification of 'good' and 'bad' nationalisms is his claim that although Germans are considered to be the example of an ethnic or cultural nation and the French of political or civic nation, these two types of nationalism are not fundamentally dissimilar social phenomena. This is due to the fact that there is always a civic component inherent to ethnic nationalism, and more generally, that every type of nationalism contains both ethno-cultural and political elements. In his own words: "France and Germany, and all of Western and Eastern Europe, have been shaped by the international discourse of nationalism—including both ethnic claims and civil projects of popular political participation."[39]

## Primordial Versus Imagined Community

Alexander Motyl, a political scientist, goes further than Calhoun and completely discredits any distinction between civic and ethnic nationalism. He enriches the debate about nation, nationalism and ethnicity by providing both a more comprehensive account of the meaning behind nation and nationalism and an outstanding critique of both the primordialist and constructivist approaches. Although Motyl disagrees with the arguments of both schools of thought, he argues that the recent division between good-constructivist and bad-primordialist theoretical frameworks is inappropriate. Motyl criticizes primordialist and constructivist theories of nations by explaining that while the former claims that nations are prehistoric categories standing outside history or existing forever, in contrast, the latter claims that nations and nationalism are just like any other social construction that had been imagined or invented by nationalist elites in the age of nationalism and, therefore, their place is not in history but in modernity. Motyl maintains that, on the contrary, nations come into being when requirements regarding historicity and otherness meet and fuse within the belief system of a particular group of people. He rightly points out that it is impossible to know what kind of logic and dynamic makes these propositions compatible in the sense that they become sufficient conditions for the emergence of a nation.

Motyl asserts that nationalism is usually defined in relation to an ideology, common social action or shared cultural heritage. In a more general sense, nationalism is primarily placed in the sphere of ideology and ideas, or in Motyl's own terms within belief systems. On the one hand, collective actions are very similar to social movements, since both are carefully planned and organized group activities. Motyl thereby argues, with regard to collective social actions, that there are no significant differences between, for example, Fascist, Communist or nationalist movements. On the other hand, he states that the relationship between nationalism and cultural identity along with ethnic solidarity is even more problematic, because nationalism cannot be reduced either to culture or to nationality. Motyl argues that the awareness of one's ethnic characteristics such as, for example, language, religion or customs, and especially one's loyalty or love for one's own nation, are not nationalist expressions but rather universally desirable inclinations towards one's national group. He states that the reduction of nationalism to any of these forms would mean to assume that all human beings are nationalists. Therefore, Motyl claims that:

> If nationalism is neither action nor culture, all we are left with is belief system. That is, nationalism must be a specific type of belief, idea, doctrine, or ideology...Nationalism is not just any ideal, however, but a distinctly political ideal: that is, it posits certain political ends and highlights certain optimal political relationships. Nationalism, obviously, is about nations, but it is about much more than that as well. Nationalism connects nations with the 'essence' of the political—states—and claims that all nations should have their own political organizations in control of administration and coercion in some geographic space...*Nationalism is a political ideal that views statehood as the optimal form of political existence for each nation.*[40]

Having outlined Calhoun's analysis of the origins of the modern nations, I want to juxtapose Motyl's notable critique of the key constructivist claim that national identities like nations are invented or imagined categories of practice, as both nationality and loyalty are shaped by the discourse of nationalism and by nationalist elites. Motyl eloquently argues that the constructivist proposition that national identity is constructed by nationalist elites is problematic, because, in his view, they are irrelevant for both the emergence of national identity and for the transmission of national myths and cultural traditions. Motyl claims that instead of nationalist elites, the determining factor for defining any national identity is rather a shared belief system. In contrast to constructivist claims that national identity is an outcome of the rational and conscious action of nationalist elites, Motyl states that human agency plays a much more spontaneous role in this process. For Motyl, nationality can be also a product of the unconscious acts of both elites and ordinary people. He maintains that "many established elites, the office holders, construct identity simply by 'doing their job,' by 'mindlessly' following the rules, patterns, habits, and procedures prescribed by institutions."[41] The same logic holds for ordinary people who can in a similar, thus, unintended, way contribute to the formation of national identity.

Besides the irrelevance of nationalist elites in nation-building project, Motyl further explains that even though national identity is based on both common history and distinctiveness from other national or ethnic groups, nationality is not, however, defined exclusively with regard to a common past. While historicity is an indispensable element of the nation that gives the nation a temporal dimension, national historicity can also be claimed in regard to a common future. Motyl provides the example of the Ukrainian socialists who, in the nineteenth century, became nationalists, and whose agenda and rhetoric emphasized a common future for the Ukrainian nation rather than common history. For Motyl then, the nation can find its historical place in the past, in the present or in the future. Therefore, Motyl argues that nations are:

> ...groups of people who believe in two things: that their group, as a group, has a place in history, and that their group differs from other existing groups in ways other than historicity. If a national identity must consist of both sets of propositions, it can do so if and only if they fit together in a single propositional package...A nation, then, exists, or comes into being, when people sharing a lifeworld believe in a set of logically complementary propositions regarding historicity and otherness.[42]

Using the example of contemporary Ukraine, Motyl strongly supports his claim that the distinction between civic and ethnic national identity is both confusing and misleading. He notes that the origins of the Ukrainian nation can be traced back to the Kievan Rus' state that existed approximately a thousand years ago, in which the Ukrainians strictly distinguished themselves from the Russians—'the others.' For Motyl, Ukrainians fulfill both sets of national propositions: historicity and otherness. He argues in this regard that "inasmuch as these two complementary propositional sets exist in contemporary Ukraine and are believed by some of its inhabitants, they make of their believers a nation even if, as is indeed the case, many 'Ukrainians' might dispute their nationhood or prefer the term *narod* (people) to *natsiia* (nation)."[43] For this reason, Motyl argues that there is no clear-cut line between civic and ethnic nationalism, as all nations are basically ethnic nations in the sense that the concepts of ethnicity and nationality are synonyms, though not exactly the same. Also, he maintains that since all nations claim a unique historical place and to have certain boundaries *vis-à-vis* others, they are all to some extent closed communities with a rather exclusionary agenda. Even the idea of the so-called 'constitutional patriotism'[44] promoted by German intellectuals like Jürgen Habermas includes only speakers of the German language. Motyl stresses, therefore, that:

> The quality of being more or less exclusionary or inclusionary has nothing to do with whether a putative ethnicity underlies the putative nation, because there is...no meaningful difference between an ethnic group (or ethnie) and a nation. Both entities accept propositions about their place in history and both draw boundaries. Even if we conclude that nations are merely ethnic groups writ large or modern-day ethnic groups, we still posit a fundamental continuity that overrides whatever differences may emerge in the course of time.[45]

In contrast then to constructivists who argue that nationalism is a modern phenomenon, Motyl emphasizes that there is nothing modern about a given belief system. For him, nationalism is not necessarily modern, because history shows that both nations and nationalism existed long before the modern invention of nationalism. He states that even though the origins of the ideal type of nationalism are rooted in the modern age, there is nothing particularly modern about a belief system and even less modern is to form resembling political organizations. Motyl argues that while the "self-styled ideal called nationalism" is undeniably modern, it is also possible to find "instances of unself-styled nationalism in prenationalist times as it is possible to find nationalism among modern-day movements that sincerely reject the nationalist label (such as the non-Russian popular fronts in 'support of perestroika')."[46] Thus, for Motyl, it is unsustainable to claim that nationalism must be modern, since nationalism and the nation existed prior to modernity, both being products of spontaneous thus unpredictable collective action and group consciousness.

Central to Motyl's argument is his claim that the formation of national identity occurred prior to the age of nationalism, with or without elites that need not necessarily be nationalists. For Motyl, the ancient Israelites, the Romans and the Byzantine Greeks were nations in the same sense that contemporary nations are; they all had developed particular belief systems that located them in time and space, and that distinguished them from 'others,' usually perceived as 'barbarians.' In Motyl's view, nations flourished in recent centuries and not in the distant past due to six 'modern' conditions that enabled the emergence of national identity, namely secularism, modernization, the market, the state, democracy, and nationalism. He states that:

> These six conditions may explain why nations have multiplied with modernity; if so, they also suggest that nations are likely to be with us for a long time to come...We can, in sum, expect nationalism to grow in intensity as modern states become even more modern and unmodern states embark on the road to modernity... *modernity can only continue to breed nationalism.*[47]

Motyl remarkably argues that the two theories of the nation are not in any sense opposing analytical approaches but, rather, they are related to each other, having similarities and differences. He maintains that primordialism and constructivism only appear to be two independent theoretical approaches for analyzing nations and, as such, they seem to demonstrate bipolar opposition. In this regard, Motyl explains that while the former claims "undifferentiated notions of immutability, objectiveness, timelessness, and naturalness," the latter must advocate "similarly undifferentiated notions of mutability, subjectiveness, temporal boundedness, and artificiality."[48] Motyl asserts that their similarities tend to disguise their important differences. Nevertheless, he states that there are three key points that separate primordialist from constructivist approach to the nation:

> First, with respect to how nations are caused, all primordialisms contend that they are not purposefully constructed—or not necessarily constructed—by self-conscious nation builders. Second, with respect to where nations are located in time, all primordialisms countenance the possibility that nations could have emerged before what Ernest Gellner calls the 'age of nationalism'—a period that began sometime between the English Revolution of 1688 and the French Revolution of 1789 and that continues to this day—and may exist, or even emerge, in the future. Third, with respect to the properties of nations, all primordialisms argue that, because they are not easily susceptible to elite manipulation, they are more or less stable. In contrast,

all constructivisms argue that nations are constructed, invented, or imagined in the age of nationalism by constructors, inventors, or imaginers.[49] Motyl analyzes both theoretical approaches in their weak, strong and extreme variations, arguing that extreme variants of both schools make very radical and exaggerated claims while weak forms are more modest and acceptable. The strong variants are in the middle of the two. Turning now to Motyl's critique of primordialism, I begin with its extreme variation that politicians and journalists often present as the ancient hatreds thesis or Dark Gods theory. Motyl maintains that for extreme primordialism "nations are temporally transcendent human communities with immutable properties immanent in life itself. Extending from the distant past, through the present, and into the distant future, nations effectively are outside history."[50] He points out that according to this thesis, the recent war in Bosnia-Herzegovina is the conflict between bellicose nations historically fighting against each other. Samuel Huntington is one of the most popular scholars who, in Motyl's words, "takes extreme primordialism to new heights by effectively attributing its characteristics to human communities that are even larger and more complex than mere nations. For all practical purposes Huntington's civilizations…stand outside history, appear to have no identifiable cause, and do not change."[51]

For Motyl, strong primordialism is a weaker variant of the ancient hatreds thesis, making less radical and uncompromising claim that nations have permanent and stable characteristics because they are a historical product of the convergence of various social forces and factors. The advocates of this variation emphasize "the importance of a political culture…[that] involves a deeply… rooted set of beliefs, attitudes, norms and significations."[52] Thus, central to a strong primordialist definition of the nation is that each nation has its distinct national political culture, or national character.

According to Motyl, weak primordialism is a more modest version, because in contrast to all other variants of primordialism and all variants of constructivism, it simply claims that there are no barriers to the emergence of nations: it can happen at any time, anywhere in the world in, for example, Serbia, Rome, or Sparta. In other words, nations may exist in the present, past and future, as well as for brief or long periods of time. For this reason, Motyl argues that "the combination of theoretical self-restraint and open-endedness enables weak primordialism to propose an irenic alternative to primordialism's claim that nations are virtually timeless and to constructivism's claim that they are fleetingly contemporary."[53] On the other hand, Motyl maintains that weak primordialism cannot provide a comprehensive theory of the nation because of "so much variation" in its claim that "the properties of nations are determined conceptually and are always possible historically."[54]

Similar to weak primordialism, weak constructivism is also the least radical constructivist approach. According to Motyl, weak constructivism modestly claims that nations are human products dating no longer than modernity, thus emerging only in the so-called age of nationalism. Although Motyl agrees that nations are human constructs, he argues that there is no reason to think that nations are constructed only by nationalist elites in nationalist times.

In a more uncompromising stance, strong constructivism claims that "the nation is a malleable human community with properties that were created, invented, or imagined by self-styled nationalist elites pursuing conscious, goal-oriented action in nationalist—that is to say, modern—times."[55] As it claims the necessity of nationalist elites, strong constructivism is extremely attractive to nationalist leaders and, therefore, it is often anchored in a majority of modern nationalist ideologies. However, Motyl argues that strong constructivism is not able to explain the origins of nationalist elites without putting them into historical perspective, which is not problematic for strong primordialism which can always argue that, at one point in history, various forces caused social elites suffering from resentment to simply turn from non-nationalists into nationalist elites. As Motyl rightly points out, historical explanation can not be confined to the age of nationalism, and "the further back in history strong constructivism goes—as it must in order to account for nationalist elites and thereby salvage itself—the more it comes to resemble strong primordialism."[56]

Finally, extreme constructivism like that of Calhoun and Rogers Brubaker, claims, even more radically, that although "nationalism as a discourse is ontologically real, nations, being contemporary discursive constructs, are only words. As such, the word *nation* is an empty signifier, lacking an empirical referent and having no real place in history."[57] Brubaker's extreme argument comes to the logical dead end of claiming that "nationalist conflicts are in principle, by their very nature, irresolvable."[58] This is not only an illogical conclusion, conceivable perhaps only as a subjectless category of discourse at the abstract theoretical level, but empirically, it is an unsustainable and ahistorical argument. In contrast to the attractiveness of strong constructivism, this extreme variation is not as interesting an idea for nationalists. As Motyl notes, while nationalists apparently would never accept the reduction of both nation and nationalism to empty words, the advocates of postmodernism definitely would embrace such an appealing argument. However, Motyl concludes his analysis of the strengths and weaknesses of both schools by arguing that "extreme primordialism is no less preposterous than extreme constructivism, and strong primordialism is no less flawed than strong constructivism, whereas weak primordialism is only slightly less modest than weak constructivism."[59]

I now want to conclude my expose of the debate on nation and nationalism by bringing together key points that link these theories with the context of Yugoslavia. Like Motyl and Calhoun, Greg Nielsen, a Quebecois sociologist and internationally renowned Bakhtinian scholar, eloquently argues against a radical conceptual and empirical division between the primordial or ethnic nation and the modern civic nation. In line with these authors, I maintain that historically and in current conditions we can find both premises embedded in the nation and nationalism, that of emphasizing the component of 'ethnos' and the other involving political-civic nation based on the idea of 'demos.' In the Bahktinian legacy, Greg Nielsen goes further and refines this distinction by insisting on the uniqueness of every nation and the creativity of nationalism, in the sense of advocating for a convergence and a dialogue between 'ethnos' and 'demos.' For Nielsen, a nation should be understood as an open creation of both forces, that is, of the political participation of demos, or citizens, and of the simultaneous accommodation of cultural ethnos, or respect for the ethno-national principle. Nielsen defines a nation as "a form of two-sided answerability wherein *ethnos* and *demos* are unconsummated in the sense that their relation is never finalized but is rather in a process of historical becoming."[60] This is the main theme of the next chapter, in which I examine the historical becoming of the multinational and socialist state of Yugoslavia founded upon both civic and ethnic principles, whereby 'demos' and 'ethnos' together created this, in many respects, unique country. We will see that Tito's Yugoslavia was conceived from the very beginning as an advanced multinational federation, which further evolved into a distinct multinational and multicultural political community based on the equal rights of its numerous nations and national minorities.

## Summary

The above overview of theories of nation and nationalism, including definitions of the key terms and concepts used in this book, provides a necessary theoretical framework for the next chapter, which deals with the national question in Yugoslavia. Not only is there no widely accepted definition of the nation and nationalism, but we have also seen through Motyl's critique of both primordialist and constructivist schools that their claims—especially extreme and strong variants—are theoretically and empirically unsustainable. This critique is particularly relevant for analyzing Yugoslavia's context. Motyl's argument that primordialism and constructivism are not monolithic theories that are binary opposites, but, rather, related theoretical approaches, is appealing. Although primordialism is theoretically discredited, Motyl disagrees with the recent distinction between a 'bad' primordialism versus 'good' constructivism, because the divergence from constructivism makes primordialism a valuable competitive or alternative approach. In contrast to constructivism, Motyl demonstrates that nationalism is not necessarily modern and that nationalist elites are irrelevant for the emergence of nations and nationalism. He also discredits primordialist claim that nations are life itself, involving timelessness, and placed exclusively in the past. As Motyl remarks, weak primordialism offers a more reasonable claim by simply arguing that nations are human communities with stable and permanent properties, thereby implying that nations are always and everywhere possible. Although this is a persuasive claim, I accept Motyl's contention that national characteristics are not predetermined and known in an abstract or conceptual manner, as assumed by weak primordialism. For this reason, weak primordialism cannot provide 'a grand theory' of the nation. Drawing upon Motyl's valuable critique of both schools and, in particular, using his argument that it is impossible to know what kind of logic and dynamic ultimately makes existing conditions become the 'sufficient conditions' for the emergence or disappearance of a nation, I will apply both theoretical frameworks in Yugoslavia's context. Let me now conclude this chapter with the suggestion that the convergence of both weak variants of primordialism and of constructivism provides a reasonable ground for understanding the phenomena of nations and nationalism.

A POLITICS OF SORROW

## NOTES

1. Kai Nielsen, 1999; Will Kymlicka, 1998; Craig Calhoun, 1997; Alexander Motyl, 1999; Rogers Brubaker, 1998, 1999; Benedict Anderson, 1983; Anthony Smith, 1983; Greg Nielsen, 2002; Samuel Huntington, 1993, 1996; Robert Hayden, 1996; Aleksa Djilas, 1996; Mihailo Crnobrnja, 1994, 1995; Catherine Samary, 1995; Gerard Baudson, 1996.

2. In fact, the former Yugoslavia was such a state, as I will illustrate later on.

3. Kai Nielsen. "Cosmopolitanism, Universalism and Particularism in an Age of Nationalism and Multiculturalism" in *Philosophical Exchange*. Vol. 29. 1999, pp. 27, 10.

4. *Ibid.*, p. 9.

5. *Ibid.*, pp. 8-10.

6. *Ibid.*, p. 9.

7. *Ibid.*, pp. 8, 10.

8. *Ibid.*, p. 10.

9. *Ibid.*, p. 11.

10. *Ibid.*, p. 12.

11. *Ibid.*, p. 9.

12. Will Kymlicka. *Finding Our Way: Rethinking Ethnocultural Relations in Canada.* Toronto: Oxford University Press, 1998, p. 2.

13. *Ibid.*

14. Or Catalans, Basques and Flemish in Europe.

15. Kymlicka, *op. cit*, p. 7.

16. *Ibid.*, p. 10.

17. *Ibid.*

18. *Ibid.*, p. 26.

19. *Ibid.*, p. 35.

20. *Ibid.*, p. 37.

21. Craig Calhoun. *Nationalism*. Buckingham: Open University Press, 1997, p. 127, note 1.

22. *Ibid.*, p. 3.

23. *Ibid.*, p. 29.

24. *Ibid.*, pp. 30, 32.

25. *Ibid.*, p. 38.

26. *Ibid.*, p. 39.

27. *Ibid.*, p. 38.

28. *Ibid.*, p. 39.

29. *Ibid.*, p. 131, note 10.

30. *Ibid.*, p. 40.

31. Tomas Spira best explains both the origins and the historical usage of word *nation*: "In ancient Roman times, *natio* meant a backward, exotic tribe, today's natives. During that period, civilized people were called gens. The Roman people, as the bearers of sovereignty, called themselves *populus*, or populace. In later ancient times, the Latin Vulgate desig-

nated *natio* and *gens* to refer to the Gentiles, or non-Romans, while the Romans continued to be called *populus*. In the ecclesiastical society of the Roman Catholic Church in the Middle Ages nation meant a specific territory and its people. The most important attributes of the medieval nation were common dialect, traditions and customs." Tomas Spira. *Nationalism and Ethnicity Terminologies: An Encyclopedic Dictionary and Research Guide. Volume 1*, 1999, pp. 419-420.

32. Calhoun, *op. cit.*, p. 132, note 13.

33. *Ibid.*, p. 44.

34. *Ibid.*, p. 48.

35. *Ibid.*, p. 49.

36. *Ibid.*, p. 87.

37. *Ibid.*, p. 86.

38. *Ibid.*, pp. 88, 89.

39. *Ibid.*, p. 89.

40. Alexander J. Motyl. *Revolutions, Nations, Empires: Conceptual Limits and Theoretical Possibilities*. New York: Columbia University Press, 1999, p. 80, my emphasis.

41. *Ibid.*, p. 76.

42. *Ibid.*, pp. 77, 78.

43. *Ibid.*, p. 78.

44. See more details also in Calhoun, 1997, and Brubaker, 1999 (1996).

45. Motyl, *op. cit.*, p. 78.

46. *Ibid.*, pp. 81, 82.

47. *Ibid.*, pp. 102, 113, my emphasis.

48. *Ibid.*, p. 83.

49. *Ibid.*, pp. 83, 84.

50. *Ibid.*, p. 85.

51. *Ibid.*, p. 86.

52. *Ibid.*, p. 87.

53. *Ibid.*, p. 96.

54. *Ibid.*, p. 95.

55. *Ibid.*, p. 89.

56. *Ibid.*, p. 90.

57. *Ibid.*, p. 91.

58. Rogers Brubaker. "Myths and Misconceptions in the Study of Nationalism" in *The State of the Nation: Ernest Gellner and The Theory of Nationalism*. Edited by John Hall. London: Cambridge University Press, 1998, p. 273.

59. Motyl, *op. cit.*, p. 96.

60. Greg M. Nielsen. *The Norms of Answerability: Social Theory Between Bakhtin and Habermas*. Albany: State University of New York Press, 2002, p. 163.

# Chapter Two
## The National Question in Yugoslavia

While it is very important that a particular group of people see and identify themselves as a nation or a political community in Kai Nielsen's sense, it is even more important how the outside world or 'the others' see this particular group. Indeed, international recognition has the ultimate word in determining which peoples can become or cease to exist as a nation. The membership in the international community of nations depends then not only on how people identify themselves but also on how others perceive that group of people. For this reason, I claim that the explanations provided by advocates of both primordialist and constructivist theories have simplified the intricacy of the national question in Yugoslavia and its dismemberment as a state. In fact, both theses—the ancient hatreds and the artificiality of the country—have imposed a false dilemma on Yugoslavia's case by ignoring the broader international, particularly geopolitical, context. Such a complex question regarding the disintegration of an internationally respected country needs and deserves at least a complex answer, which neither theory provides.

Like the last chapter, this chapter discusses the issues related to nationalism and its discourse, including common explanations and definitions of terms and concepts used in my analysis of the disintegration of Yugoslavia. Since the historic development of the national question in Yugoslavia is a broad issue, I open a debate about some basic questions regarding the collapse of Yugoslavia in the following pages, such as: Was Yugoslavia a federation of nations or republics? Are the new successor states of Yugoslavia one-national or multi-national? How does the notion of ethnic and civic nationalism fit into Yugoslavia's context? What are the differences between the idea of Yugoslavism and the recent ethnic nationalism? What are similarities and differences between the federal models of the former Yugoslavia and of Canada?

## The Yugoslav Idea Between Primordialism and Constructivism

Returning now to the question of the creation and destruction of Yugoslavia, I first acknowledge the existence of three states bearing the name of Yugoslavia. The first was created in 1918 and dissolved under the Nazi occupation in 1941; the second formed after World War II, and the third, or last one, had the shortest lifetime, from 1992 to 2003. Although I will briefly examine all three, my focus in this chapter, and the whole book, is the second, socialist or former Yugoslavia. Its disintegration surpasses the theoretical frameworks of both primordialism and constructivism that are, as mentioned, insufficient and inadequate for grasping the complexity of its particular context. I agree with Mihailo Crnobrnja who maintains that "it is not easy to hold together all the elements necessary to a comprehensive study of *what went wrong*. But then nothing about Yugoslavia is really easy. Answers to some very important, fundamental questions can be reached only by complex analysis."[1] If such a comprehensive analysis is beyond the scope of this book, my goal is nevertheless to examine historical, economic and political elements that are important key parts of the external and internal environment surrounding the collapse of Yugoslavia. Even though weak variations of both primordialism and constructivism are not necessarily wrong in their analyses of the dissolution of Yugoslavia, I argue that they fail to take hold of the complexity of the case as they avoid looking at the external factors, which they consider to have a sporadic—if any—role, thus, being of a distant secondary importance compared to the key role of ethnic nationalism.

For the purpose of my analysis, it is not so important whether primordialism and constructivism are, in Motyl's terms, related theoretical approaches or a binary opposition of two monolithic theories. The Yugoslav crisis can simultaneously 'fit' into the explanations of both and neither of the two theories, because ethnic nationalism was not the only reason for its disintegration. Although we can find some historical evidence to support both theses (for example, a history of genocide, the controversial 'ethnic vote' in the 1990 and a low percentage of declared 'Yugoslavs'), I argue that their arguments are too limited to explain why Yugoslavia dismembered since neither theory takes into account historical and current postcolonial 'Divide and Rule' politics of the external Balkanization.

Indeed, Yugoslavia was not dismantled due to 'the ancient ethnic hatreds' between its hostile nations as primordialists argue, nor because it was an artificial 'imagined community' that, as such, had to dismember as constructivists claim. If both, or any of these, claims would be such an imperative, Yugoslavia(s) would not have existed for the past 85 years. In particular, it would never have been able to enjoy such international respect as a socialist country that it did; it was notably one of the founders of both the United Nations (UN) and the Non-Alignment Movement, the latter established as the 'third way' in the antagonistic and hostile Cold War bipolarity of the world commonly known as the anti-bloc international policy of 'peaceful and active coexistence.' In this regard, I agree with Crnobrnja who maintains that the destruction of Yugoslavia goes hand in hand with the fall of communism in Europe. The domino effect of this historic event meant that Yugoslavia, a country which, in Crnobrnja's words, "only a few years ago not only seemed to be but *was* stable, reasonably prosperous and certainly very interesting as a maverick in the socialist camp, became engulfed in a destructive, ultra-nationalistic and national-chauvinistic turmoil which has left deep scars and wounds and untold inflicted suffering on the population."[2]

I draw upon Crnobrnja's historical and political analysis, being very similar to other authors, which demonstrates that "nationalism was a necessary but not sufficient condition for the destruction of Yugoslavia."[3] If ethnic nationalism was not a sufficient condition, then both schools of thought fail to explain the real causes and circumstances under which Yugoslavia was dismembered. I argue that there is neither sufficient historical evidence for the 'ancient hatreds' thesis nor for the constructivist view that the Yugoslav idea was defeated because of being an artificially imagined political community. I claim instead that Yugoslavia was dismembered due to a multitude of external and internal factors elaborated later in the next chapters which deal with both external and internal Balkanization. I also agree with Crnobrnja's remark that we still need, in 1995 as we do now in 2003, more of "the necessary *historical distance* to objectively and dispassionately explain, judge and evaluate the processes and the forces which have brought about this tragic outcome."[4]

Although Crnobrnja underestimates the importance of the foreign dimension in his explanation of the dissolution of Yugoslavia in both economic and geopolitical sense, nonetheless, I find his account pertinent as well as appealing. Not easily categorized in primordialist or constructivist terms since his approach is much broader and goes beyond the boundaries of ethnic nationalism as the only reason for the war, Crnobrnja identifies three key elements at play in the Yugoslav crisis: ethnic nationalism, political structures and the foreign factor. His account of the role of aggressive nationalism and of human agency can be seen, to some extent, as both a weak primordialist argument as well as a weak constructivist argument. Crnobrnja obviously clashes with the extreme primordialism in claiming that hostility and armed conflicts among Yugoslav nations are not so ancient phenomena, but rather stem from the twentieth century. He argues instead that Yugoslavia dismembered in a violent way primarily due to the unsolved question of borders, or the fact that the 'invisible' ethnic borders were not identical with the administrative borders of the republics. Indeed, the borders between republics were created exclusively for administrative purpose and they did not reflect ethnic or national structure of republics. Except Slovenia, which was the most ethnically homogenous republic, all other republics were ethnically mixed, or multinational. I will show later that in addition to the fact that the republics were composed of more than one nation, their various nations and nationalities were increasingly intermingled, particularly in Bosnia that had the highest rate of mixed marriages and children of mixed origins. These 'mixed people' were, and still are, the core of the Yugoslav national identity as they usually declared themselves as Yugoslavs. Of course, Yugoslavs are not exclusively people of mixed national origins. This fact of bi- or multi-national composition of republics, and the consequently unresolved issue of borders, is at the heart of the conflict being the foremost cause of the violent, as opposed to peaceful or democratic, disintegration of Yugoslavia.

Similar to Robert Hayden, Crnobrnja maintains that the aggressive nationalism and the failure of Yugoslavia as an imagined community are the main reasons for its breakdown. Although Crnobrnja does not use the same term of an 'imagined community,' he uses concepts that echo Hayden's constructivist approach. Crnobrnja's valuable analysis of the external and internal forces that played key roles in the destruction of Yugoslavia shows that national revival in the republics led to the triumph of an aggressive-chauvinist nationalism resulting in conflicts that ended in fraternal wars. According to Crnobrnja, this aggressive form of nationalism is "the moving spirit of the drama, if not its principal actor."[5] He defines nationalism in a general sense as the process of national awakening followed by the emergence of a national movement with its specific political agenda. Crnobrnja notes that, for example, the Slovenes, Croats and Macedonians, as well as Bosnian Muslims who became a nation officially in 1963, did not undertake all the steps of national development before joining the Yugoslav federation.[6] He also emphasizes that since the republican leaders of recent nationalist movements from the 1990s were "unable or unwilling" to offer "contemporary national programs," they simply re-appropriated them from "the ideologies and experience of the national movements of the past."[7] Similarly to Kai Nielsen's distinction between good-civic and bad-ethnic nationalism, Crnobrnja maintains that nationalism is not necessarily aggressive or ethnic-violent in Nielsen's terms. Like Nielsen, Crnobrnja argues that there are "benign-romantic" and "malign-aggressive" forms of nationalism:

> *Romantic nationalism* rejects the idea of national aggrandizement through the imperial domination or assimilation of other nations. This benign ideology visualizes universal peace and harmony when national communities each obtain their own national state. Although benign nationalism is best suited to territories that have substantial national and ethnic mixes, the sad truth, one that is also valid for Yugoslavia, is that these are precisely the areas where aggressive nationalism has a much better base for operation. The other, aggressive version of nationalism is the 'integral' kind, insisting on the 'completeness' of the nation in question. Depending on specific circumstances it can be and often is assimilationist and therefore dangerous to the integrity of neighboring nations. *Integral nationalism* emerged in the second half of the nineteenth century as part of the process of liberal decline, adapting itself to the positivist spirit of the age.[8]

For Crnobrnja this violent and irrational form of nationalism is the core problem of the drama of Yugoslavia. In his view, the aggressive nationalism of the 1990s was the outcome of national revival in the republics that unfortunately took a wrong direction leading to war. According to Crnobrnja, this was partially due to the rigidity of the political system, as Yugoslavia was largely ruled by some form of totalitarian regime (or more accurately, authoritarian), since its first state was formed in 1918. Although Communism and Tito's rule are directly responsible for the lack of resolution of the national question and for suppressing any democratic or national opinion, the recent events in Yugoslavia cannot be reduced only to the Communist worsening of the problematic national issues. On the contrary, communists were the main protagonists of the Yugoslav crisis, of which the majority became nationalist leaders in their republics by simply changing sides.[9] Indeed, as Crnobrnja points out, in the aftermath of Tito's death in 1980, political opportunists very soon occupied key positions within social and political elites searching for expanding careers. In Crnobrnja's words, "with the exception of the leader of Bosnian Muslims, all other nationalist leaders in Yugoslavia, and most of the national ideologues, were previously either high Communist officials or at least card-carrying members of the

Communist Party."[10] In this sense, the new nationalist elite was formed by and from the former Communist elite. This fact additionally complicates the constructivist claim about the importance of nationalist elites. For this reason, I agree with Motyl's critique that nations and nationalism can emerge with or without nationalist elites. In the Yugoslav case it was done by both Communists and intellectuals who turned into nationalists.

With further regard to the role of human agency, in particular to the importance of nationalist elites central to the constructivist approach, Crnobrnja notes that despite the fact that the intelligentsia is usually characterized as open, tolerant and liberal, the majority of Yugoslavian intellectuals on all sides did not advocate any of these values. He asserts that only "a minority defended cosmopolitan interests and a universal understanding of people and their human and civil rights," though there were "notable exceptions" of intellectuals from all sides who fought against "nationalistic one-sidedness, close-mindedness and collective paranoia," risking the label of "national traitors."[11] Also, many intellectuals stepped aside, refusing to get pulled into nationalist euphoria and followed passively the disintegration of Yugoslavia either from inside the country or from their new homeland in which they would probably become its citizens. For Crnobrnja, many of the intellectuals should be,

> ...held *directly* responsible for generating and nurturing the national exclusiveness, intolerance, suspicion and hatred toward members of other nationalities through their writings and speeches. Without infusing the social psyche of the Yugoslav nations with this intolerance, no politicians, no matter how crafty they were, could have started the bloody conflict.[12]

In Crnobrnja's view, this early intellectual contribution was an indispensable ingredient for the rapid spread of nationalism. Many intellectuals, regardless of their nationality, did this job passionately as the leaders of nationalist movements or their main ideologists. I agree with Crnobrnja's assertion that intellectuals became nationalists for the same reason that communist bureaucracies in their republics led nationalist movements. The driving force of both the communists and intellectuals towards chauvinist nationalism was apparently, in an Orwellian sense, 'power for power's sake.' Crnobrnja argues that while the communists "played their last card...of nationalism...in a desperate attempt to hold on to power"; the intellectuals saw "an opportunity to rewrite history," to become popular and heard by masses and not simply to be known among their peers.[13] Those intellectuals who turned into nationalists immediately reduced the concept of 'individual' and individualism respectively into the 'national' and nationalism, such that belonging and loyalty to the nation became an imperative. Thus, the nation had completely conquered the state. Crnobrnja notes that the intelligentsia grabbed the opportunity to come into power and rewrite history as the communists did after World War II; in other words, it was not due to their desire for revenge or resentment of communist oppression. He stresses that:

> It could probably be argued that a large segment of the intelligentsia was actually conditioned to accept nationalism following a prolonged period of a totalitarian and essentially nonhumanistic rule by the communist elite. Being a victim of power under communism, a large segment of the intelligentsia became transfixed by the concept of power per se. Living for decades in a prescribed ideological mould, which accommodated rather than actually accepted them, thereby depriving them of any real influence or power, the intelligentsia now saw an opportunity to approach power, to even *be part of it*. It now felt needed, even if it was for a historically questionable role.[14]

For Crnobrnja, the most tragic phase of the Yugoslav crisis is the civil war that partially resulted from the manipulation of the population by communists-turned-nationalists and intellectual elites. This internal manipulation of the mass population was by large possible since Yugoslavia historically lacked a democratic political culture; therefore, it was not hard to turn public opinion towards the desired, though evidently wrong, direction. Although in different terms, Crnobrnja argues, like Hayden and the constructivist school, that Yugoslavia failed as an imagined community.[15] Crnobrnja maintains that a deep-rooted cause of the disintegration of the country is anchored in the paradox of Yugoslav national identity: although Yugoslavs had a nationality, they never became a nation. He draws his argument from Ernest Renan, a French historian, whose definition of the nation emphasizes its spiritual principle originating in a history of common struggle and shared heritage, manifested in a desire to live together in solidarity. In this sense, Crnobrnja maintains both a weak primordialist and weak constructivist approach, emphasizing the spirit of Yugoslavism and its failure:

The spirit of Yugoslavism had to coexist with, or in spite of, the spirits of the various nations forming it. Yugoslavism did not emerge as a kind of melting-pot blend of the various nationalities composing it. That is why the revival of centrifugal nationalist forces within it acted to destroy what did come together in the state of Yugoslavia. There was an insufficient history of common struggle and sacrifice; the identification with Yugoslavia was not strong enough and daily made weaker by the aggressive propaganda of the nationalist champions...the length and type of union that Yugoslavia represented was insufficient to cement firmly and unequivocally the willingness to embrace the present, and especially future, solidarity.[16]

Similarly to Crnobrnja's argument about the failure of Yugoslavism and the victory of aggressive nationalism, Robert Hayden maintains that the triumph of ethnic nationalism in the 1990s reflects the inability of various Yugoslav nations to coexist in a common state, thus preferring division into a number of smaller but nationally homogenous states. For Hayden, "the electoral success of this message meant the defeat of the 'Yugoslav idea' of a common state of the south Slavic peoples, an ideology that had been devised as a counter and rival to the separate national ideologies of each group."[17] To support this claim, Hayden refers to Aleksa Djilas who provides an excellent analysis of the historical and political development of the origins of 'the Yugoslav idea' as well as the unsolved national question in Yugoslavia(s). In order to properly understand Hayden's claim about this defeat of the Yugoslav idea and thus the failure of the 'artificial' Yugoslav community, it is important to look at the main points of Djilas' remarkable analysis of the Communist revolution and Yugoslav unity in order to understand the complexity of the national question in the multinational Socialist Federal Republic of Yugoslavia (SFRY).

Djilas argues that there is an intimate relationship between the origins of Yugoslavism and so-called 'progressive' ideas. This connection traces back its roots to the development of early ties with the eighteenth century "Enlightenment and its heirs, liberal democracy and revolutionary, mostly socialist, radicalism."[18] According to Djilas, these early liberal democrats and socialists, later renamed communists, opted for the idea of Yugoslavism and the unity of all South Slavs under a common state toward the creation of a new national Yugoslav identity. Both social movements and ideologies promoted values inspired by the Enlightenment and by European critical rationalism. Djilas further explains that there was also an early correlation between these progressive ideas and national radicalism. In his words,

> There was an important connection between radicalism on social questions and radicalism on the national question. Most revolutionary South Slav socialists were national revolutionaries struggling both for the destruction of Austria-Hungary and for the unity of all South Slavs and an independent South Slav state. This intertwining of 'progressive' and national radicalism stemmed from the tendency to seek radical solutions in all spheres of political and social life.[19]

The idea of Yugoslavism was attractive to the socialists because it was compatible with the notion of internationalism, which they passionately advocated at the time in a strong belief that it was possible to unite all nations of the world into a common stateless society. Socialists, therefore, suppressed the national question in Yugoslavia as they considered it to be of a secondary importance compared to the paramount priority of the class struggle. In their view, all Southern Slavs had similar or essentially the same language,[20] they shared a common origin and they were ethnically and culturally more similar than different. As Djilas notes, many socialists prior to the unification of the country saw "the South Slav peoples as tribes—usually Croats, Serbs, and Slovenes—that ought to be unified into *one modern Yugoslav nation*."[21] At that time, the radicalism of the Yugoslav idea of creating a common state was ubiquitous and very appealing since it anticipated the dismantling of the Austro-Hungarian Empire. For this reason, as Djilas points out, the Croatian socialists pushed for faster formation of a modern Yugoslav nation and state. Both Croatian and Slovenian socialists, in discussing the settlement of the national question, argued that the emergence of the Yugoslav nation was necessary for the overall victory of socialism in the territories inhabited by South Slavs. Djilas emphasizes that Yugoslav socialists were then strictly against any division between South Slavs along regional, religious or ethnic lines, which were perceived as the main obstacles to modern democratic development. However, they organized a socialist conference[22] for all South Slavs held in Ljubljana in Slovenia in 1909 in order to solve the 'Yugoslav question.' Djilas explains that:

> This term did not refer to relations among Croats, Serbs, and Slovenes. All of these were considered to be *one nation* (or at least suitable material for a future nation), and it was assumed that relations among them would

pose no real problem. Rather, the Yugoslav question concerned the relations of all the South Slavs with the Austro-Hungarian monarchy in general, and with Austro-German and Hungarian nationalism. The socialists at the Ljubljana conference did not call for destruction of the Austro-Hungarian monarchy, but they demanded political as well as linguistic and cultural autonomy. For the first time the idea appeared that socialism could unify the South Slavs...only the workers and the working-class party...could be the creators of the Yugoslav nation.[23]

For Djilas, like for Crnobrnja, the national question was unsolved in both Yugoslavias: in King Alexander's absolutist unitary monarchy (1918-1941) and in Tito's subsequent socialist and multinational federation (1945-1991). Djilas notes that in the interwar period, particularly immediately after the Great War, even communists advocated 'unitarism' and 'centralism' as they failed to recognize the importance of the national question, or the multi-nationality of the first Yugoslavia, called 'The Kingdom of Serbs, Croats and Slovenes' and later renamed 'The Kindom of Yugoslavia'. In this regard, Yugoslav communists at the Congress of Unification held in the April of 1919 firmly believed that Serbs, Croats and Slovenes were the same nation, thus considering Yugoslavia to be a one-national (*jednonacionalna* in Serbo-Croatian) state. Djilas remarks that even though this Congress neither admitted nor recognized the multi-nationality of Yugoslavia, it "strongly opposed any form of national oppression, protesting sharply against the central government's discriminatory policies toward non-South Slav national minorities (especially Albanians and Hungarians, but also Germans)."[24] The turning point however was the Third Party Conference in 1924 in Belgrade when communists finally recognized the urgent need to address and solve the national question in Yugoslavia, particularly regarding growing disputes between Croats and Serbs. According to Djilas, even in 1924, "no one in the Yugoslav [Communist] party or in the Comintern seemed to be aware that there might be more than three nations in Yugoslavia."[25]

However, communists in the 1920s also became more concerned with the national frustration that had emerged due to Serbian hegemony in Macedonia, Montenegro and Bosnia, which were all incorporated into Serbia and their peoples considered Serbs, or a national minority. At that time, Macedonians and Bosnian Muslims were not considered to be distinct nations. For this reason, after the Nazi occupation of Yugoslavia during World War II, which brought about a bloody civil-fraternal war and the parallel socialist revolution, Yugoslav peoples led by communists voluntarily and willingly united in the second, multi-national state named 'The Federal People's Republic of Yugoslavia' (FNRY), which was renamed the 'Socialist Federal Republic of Yugoslavia' (SFRY) by the constitution of 1963 in order to underscore its distinct self-managed socialism. Djilas accurately notes that Article 1 of the first constitution of 1946 stated that all nations of Yugoslavia were equal in their rights and duties; in other words, there was no leading or dominant nation. This second Yugoslavia under Tito was thus defined as a community of peoples with equal rights, recognizing finally its multi-national composition. In contrast to the first Yugoslavia, there were five such peoples or nations: Croats, Macedonians, Montenegrins, Serbs, and Slovenes. The Yugoslav federation was composed of six republics (see Map 1), which were constitutionally guaranteed equal rights and responsibilities.

Besides the rich cultural and ethnic diversity of socialist Yugoslavia (see Map 2), Bosnia was notably the only republic without a majority nation, it was a homeland to three constitutive nations: Croats, Slavic Muslims and Serbs. However, Bosnian Muslims were not officially recognized as a nation until 1963; previously they were treated as a special Slavic group. Although the equality of the republics was based in their sovereignty, they were not in fact sovereign enti-ties, since the constitutional right of self-determination, including the right to secession, referred only to the constitutive nations of Yugoslavia and never to the republics. As Djilas best explains,

> The republics' borders were created on partly national and partly histori-cal principles. Because of the mixed population, it would have been im-possible to create purely national republics even if that had been the primary concern of the CPY [Communist Party of Yugoslavia]. Yet the republics were defined as sovereign homelands of sovereign nations: Croatia of Croats, Serbia of Serbs, [Bosnia of Croats, Serbs and Muslims] and so on. Minorities in the republics, however, had the same rights and duties as the majority. They therefore had the right to take part in all de-cisions affecting the sovereignty of the predominant national group and its republic. At the same time, minorities were defined as part of their own nation; thus, the Serbian minority in Croatia was a part of the sov-ereign Serbian nation. This meant that Serbs were entitled to sovereign rights within three sovereign republics—Serbia, Bosnia and Herzegovina, and Croatia—two of which were the sovereign homelands of other sover-eign nations. The same was valid for Croats, who lived not only in

Croatia but also in Bosnia and Herzegovina and in Serbia. Finally, since all citizens of Yugoslavia had the same rights everywhere in its territory and could move freely from one republic to another, a citizen of any republic had the right to political participation in any other, if he decided to settle in it.[26]

These basic principles outlined in the constitution of 1946 were never modified, even though the constitutional law of 1953 fundamentally changed a number of main directions and points and was, for this reason, perceived as being the constitution itself. After the conflict with the Stalinist Soviet Union and the Comintern in 1948, this constitutional law aimed to radically abandon the preceding Soviet model of 1946, because Yugoslav Communists wanted to emphasize their independence from the USSR as well as the uniqueness of the Yugoslav revolution and its distinct socialist self-management system.[27] This "new and original" constitutional law of 1953, as Djilas explains,

> ...defined Yugoslavia primarily as a union of producers and a community of people whose 'socialist consciousness,' based on the practice of self-management, superseded their national consciousness. The sovereignty of the individual republics was founded on the working people (the producers) and not the people as a whole...the constitutional law omitted the right of secession, mentioned in article 1 of the 1946 constitution. Although even that article implied that the creation of Yugoslavia was irreversible, its absence from the new constitution was a clear sign of further development toward Yugoslav unity.[28]

For all of the above reasons, I argue that, first of all, even though the republics were the homelands of sovereign nations, the republics, from the creation to the destruction of the former Yugoslavia (1945-1991), were themselves never sovereign. It was the Yugoslav nations that were sovereign, not the republics. Secondly, the citizens of Yugoslavia always had equal rights and freedoms within the whole territory of Yugoslavia: they could freely move and live in any of the six republics. Thirdly, the borders between republics were of an administrative nature and, as such, were never congruent with the national composition of republics. Excluding Slovenia, the most homogeneous republic, all republics were, to different degrees, ethnically heterogeneous, or multinational, particularly Bosnia. The four geographically central republics, Croatia, Bosnia, Serbia and Montenegro, the core of Yugoslav unity, were all nationally heterogeneous while their peoples spoke the same language called both Serbo-Croatian (in the

Map 1:   The Former Yugoslavia (SFRY), 1945-1991.

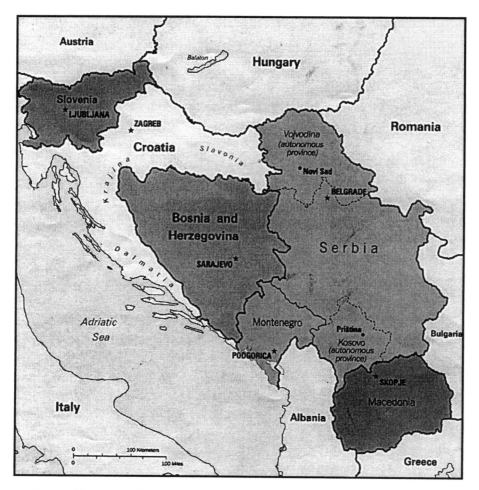

Source: University of Texas Library Online (www.lib.utexas.edu/maps).

Map 2:   Ethnic Composition of the Republics

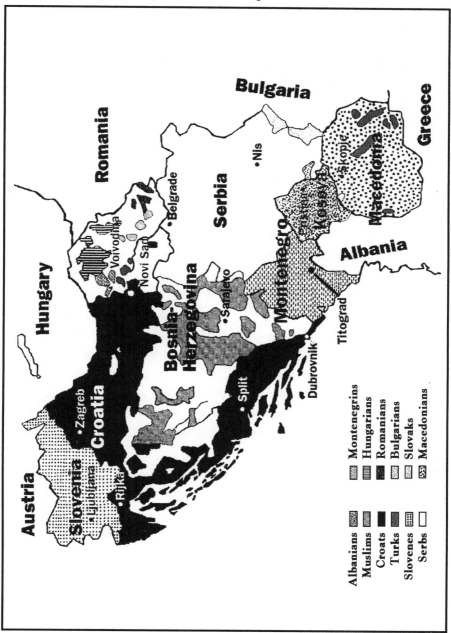

Source: Samary, Catherine. *Yugoslavia Dismembered*, 1995, p. 18.

Eastern part of the country) and the Croatian or Serbian (in the Western part). In contrast, Slovenia and Macedonia were both, to different extents, nationally homogenous and had two officially recognized distinct languages, Slovenian and Macedonian. More precisely, Slovenia was indeed the only homogeneous republic (about 90% Slovenes) while nonetheless having various national minorities, such as Italians and Hungarians, which were not as significant in numbers as was the case in Macedonia or Montenegro. While Macedonia had a significant Albanian national minority (about 20%), Montenegro, similarly to Macedonia, was primarily inhabited by Montenegrins, though there were also many Slavic Muslims, Serbs and ethnic Albanians living there. While all six republics had various, mainly non-Slavic, national minorities, it was the four central republics that were multinational in the sense that they were composed of more than one sovereign nation, or ethnonational majority.

In this regard, both Djilas and Craig Calhoun point out that the republic of Croatia was bi-national, because a significant number of Serbian people (12%), one of the constitutive nations of Yugoslavia, lived there. In this sense, the last constitution of socialist Yugoslavia of 1974, similarly to the first one from 1946, stated in its opening sentence that:

> Based on the right of every *narod* [nation, or people] to self-determination, including the right to secession, *narodi* [nations] of Yugoslavia...together with *narodnosti* [nationalities, or national minorities] with whom they live, are united in a federal republic of free and equal *narodi* and *narodnosti* [nations and nationalities] in the creation of a socialist federal community of the working people—Socialist Federal Republic of Yugoslavia.[29]

For this reason, I agree with Hayden who lucidly notes that the socialist constitutions of the republics, in accordance with the federal constitution, grounded the state in 'the dual sovereignty' of both the working class, or all working people, and the nations and nationalities of Yugoslavia. To supplement Hayden's remark, this dual sovereignty might perhaps be further seen as a triple one since both the federal and republican constitutions of 1974 also included the sovereignty of citizens, *gradani* in Serbo-Croatian *or obcani* in Slovenian.[30] Hayden emphasizes that according to the constitution of 1974 (which in this regard had not changed since 1946) "the right of every nation to self-determination, including the right to secession referred, not to the populations or citizens of republics, but to the nations, *narodi* (singular: *narod*), of Yugoslavia, ethnically defined."[31]

Since the Soviet Union was a federation of republics and not a federation of nations as was Yugoslavia, Hayden correctly claims that the Yugoslav republics did not enjoy the same constitutional right of self-determination and of secession.

Similar to Crnobrnja and many other scholars, Hayden argues that the collapse of socialism in Yugoslavia simply meant shifting from state socialism to state chauvinist nationalism since all of the successor states of Yugoslavia, or its former republics, developed identical or resembling forms of 'constitutional nationalism.' In other words, the end of socialism entailed a loss of sovereignty of the working people and citizens, who were reduced to the single dimension of their national identity. The new constitutions of the successor states thereby legitimized 'bureaucratic ethnic cleansing' or 'constitutional nationalism' in Hayden's terms, as they excluded those that did not belong to the national majority group. It is important to stress here one notable exception to this constitutional nationalist tide, to be found in the constitutions of the third or the last Yugoslavia (1992-2003), the Federal Republic of Yugoslavia (FRY), and its two constitutive republics of Serbia, including both provinces of Kosovo and Vojvodina, and of Montenegro. Both federal and republican constitutions provided a legal framework for a 'civic' and not an 'ethnic' state. According to the federal constitution of 1992, this mutilated state, also known as Milosevic's Yugoslavia, was a civic state (*drzava gradana*) promoting the rights of citizens (*gradani*) and not of national groups. Hayden similarly notes that the constitution of Republic of Serbia was very progressive, even though it was incompatible with the authoritarian rule of Slobodan Milosevic. Given that Milosevic is now in a prison in The Hague, and that 'his' Yugoslavia recently ceased to exist under this name as a federal state, it is noteworthy that this final constitution of the third Yugoslavia was in fact the sixth one since the creation of the first Yugoslavia in 1918. Article 1 of the Federal Republic of Yugoslavia states:

> Yugoslavia is defined by three elements: sovereignty, a federal system, and the constitutive elements typical for federation—citizens [*gradani*] and federal units (republics—members of federation)...the third element ...in contrast to the constitution of Socialist Federal Republic of Yugoslavia from 1974, there is no place for national [*nacionalne*] states, national economies and state nationalism.[32]

Hayden also rightly states that the question of citizenship in the successor states of the former Yugoslavia was not only new but of paramount importance, because people who did not obtain this 'new' citizenship were consequently denied both the rights and the means needed for everyday, normal, life. For many people the cruel reality of this new citizenship policy mirrored what Hayden accurately calls a process of denaturalization. As Hayden explains it,

> The constitution of Yugoslavia had provided for a single, uniform Yugoslav citizenship and guaranteed the equality of Yugoslav citizens throughout the country. Suddenly, however, the citizenship of many residents in the newly independent states became questionable. New citizenship laws, written to privilege the members of the sovereign majority in each case, have worked to discriminate against residents who were not members of the majority groups. In essence, the new citizenship regimes have simultaneously extended citizenship to nonresident members of the majority ethnonation through easy naturalization while denying citizenship to many residents who are not of the right group. This last process turns residents who had been equal citizens of federal Yugoslavia into foreigners of their own republics, a process we might call *denaturalization.*[33]

As we can notice by now, all of the presented authors interchangeably use both terms 'nation' and 'ethnic group,' most frequently in terms of an ethnonation or ethnonational group, when referring to Yugoslav nations. It is notable that that neither federal nor republican constitutions of the former Yugoslavia, nor the new ones of the successor states, use the term 'ethnic' to describe any of the Yugoslav nations. This interchangeability and the usage of the term 'ethnonation' occurred due to several reasons. I agree with Alexander Motyl's claim that 'nation' and 'ethnic group' are conceptually synonymous. In particular, this distinction is non-existent in Yugoslavia's official terminology or documents, where we find no mention of ethnic groups but, instead, only the terms nations and national minorities. For the convenience of reading, I use both terms interchangeably although in principle I prefer the more accurate term nation to ethnic group when addressing the Yugoslav peoples.

To clarify, the Yugoslav nations are ethnonational groups, since they are simultaneously both an ethnic group and a nation. In other words, they are ethnocultural nations. In all of Yugoslavia's Slavic languages, the term 'narod' refers to the people, and it was used both officially and popularly instead of the conceptually synonymous term 'nacija,' which has a more national connotation and was often invoked passionately by nationalists who insisted on their national belonging and distinctiveness. However, the difference between these two synonyms is that while the much broader term 'narod' literarily means 'people' in a civic sense, including a notion of citizens or 'demos,' the term 'nacija' refers primarily to an ethnic or national identity, emphasizing 'ethnos.' In Serbo-Croatian dictionaries, the English term 'nation' is translated as both 'narod' and 'nacija.' Yet the meaning of the former is further described as people, folk, nation, population and crowd, while the latter refers only to a nation.[34] The word 'narod' is a compound of the prefix 'na,' referring to nation or nationality while the root 'rod' comes from the verb 'roditi' meaning literally 'to give birth, to be born.' Fused together in 'na-rod,' this term simply defines all people who are born or live in that particular country, or who are, by the fact of their birth, a part of that particular state or nation. In this sense, the meanings of both terms nation and ethnic group are incorporated in the word 'narod' from which also comes a derivation *narodnost* referring to one's nationality. As nationality in socialist Yugoslavia was defined in terms of civic citizenship based on the place of birth and not one's ethnicity, its various peoples were accordingly described as different *narodi* (peoples/nations) rather than *nacije* (nations), notably, they never called themselves ethnic groups. This is to say that in practical terms, for example, the Serbian 'narod,' people or nation, refers to all ethnic Serbs regardless of where they live: the Serbs from Serbia, Croatian Serbs, Bosnian Serbs, Canadian Serbs, etc. In contrast, the Serbian 'nacija,' or nation, more specifically refers to the Serbian national state, thus, prior to the civil war of the 1990s, it included all Serbs living across the former Yugoslavia and more specifically in the Republic of Serbia. Under the current circumstances, in which Serbs have either been banished or became a national minority in the new successor states of the former Yugoslavia, the Serbian 'nacija' refers only to the Serbs living in the present day Republic of Serbia, a constitutive part of a transitional unity of the Republics of Serbia and Montenegro, the new successor state of the last or third Yugoslavia.

Another important reason for the interchangeability or practical irrelevance of the concepts 'ethnic group' and 'nation' within the specific context of Yugoslavia concerns the complexity of the historical and current national development of each South Slavic nation. Like Crnobrnja, Djilas introduces this contested country by stating that:

> Yugoslavia is a difficult country to understand. Its many nations, languages, and religions generate centrifugal tendencies. At the same time there exist powerful centripetal forces: the common South Slav origin of the majority of the population is the basis for many ethnic, linguistic, and cultural similarities; and there are also many shared historical experiences.[35]

With regard to the history and complexity of the national question in Yugoslavia, I accept Motyl's argument that both schools, primordialism and constructivism, exaggerate or simplify the historical dimension of nations and nationalism. As we have seen, while primordialism situates the nation 'outside' history as a 'prehistoric' category, for constructivism there is no place for the nation in history since it is an 'imagined,' or invented, social construct that has emerged in the age of nationalism, or modernity. Therefore, one of my goals in this chapter is to bring the Yugoslav nations back into history, from which they have been, to some extent, 'uprooted' by both schools, stripping them of their historical struggles and achievements of nationality and nationhood. I agree with Motyl who argues that, contrary to the constructivist claim of the modernity of nations and nationalisms, we can find examples of nations and nationalism which existed long before the modern age of nationalism, such as, the Ukrainians, the Greeks, the Croats and the Serbs. All Yugoslav nations, however, grounded their national identities in their medieval states. Yet, much of the Western media and politicians, in an extremely primordialist manner, refer to all of the Yugoslav nations as hostile ethnic groups fighting forever over territories, emphasizing exclusively their 'tribalism' and recent barbarism as reflected in ethnic cleansing. To be successful and persuasive in establishing and maintaining such a negative or biased image, particularly that of the 'bad side,' it is imperative to ignore the history of Yugoslavia, especially the complexity of the national question and its development. The perpetual maintenance of this a-historical but extremely spectacular media image is, in my view, the foremost reason that the peoples of Yugoslavia have so successfully been stripped of their national identities. However, a closer historical analysis puts into question the credibility of Western media reports and the official statements about the disintegration of Yugoslavia.[36]

A comprehensive analysis of the emergence and development of distinct nations and nationalisms in Yugoslavia requires an examination of each nation, with its specific form of nationalism, from its particular historical context, since in addition to similarities there are important differences between the Yugoslav nations. In particular, special emphasis should be given to the analysis of Croatian and Serbian nationalism as central to both the creation and destruction of both Yugoslavias (the third Yugoslavia is excluded here since it is a different case). The bloodiest fraternal-civil war that occurred from 1941 to 1945 must be a central focus of such analysis for two crucial reasons. Firstly, because it resulted in the genocide of Serbs, Jews and Gypsies, too often misinterpreted, neglected, or exaggerated by politicians and media with respect to the the primordialist claim of the 'ancient ethnic hatreds.' The second reason is that the current nationalist revival was built up on these recent, not ancient, hatreds stemming from World War II. This includes the explicit re-appropriation of both national ideology and symbols from that time. There is also a significant resemblance between the crimes committed in the 1990s and the horrific atrocities of the 1940s, both having been committed with an extraordinary and 'successful' boldness. However, Crnobrnja accurately remarks, that during World War II there was a huge difference between Croatian and Serbian ethnic nationalism even though both ultra-nationalist groups collaborated at different levels with Nazi and Fascist occupying forces. According to Crnobrnja, one of the major distinctions between the Serbian 'Chetniks' and the Croatian 'Ustashi' was that "the former were relatively isolated guerrilla units, especially in territories were they mixed with other ethnic groups, while the latter had a state organization. Thus the scale of murder, plunder, and 'ethnic cleansing' performed by the latter far outstripped the evil deeds of the former."[37] Needless to say, these mixed territories included the so-called 'Krajina' in Croatia and the whole of Bosnia, where most of the crimes were committed in both civil-fraternal wars; that is, during World War II when the Nazi state of Croatia incorporated all of Bosnia, and recently from 1991 to 1995. Furthermore, ethnic nationalism, or more precisely, the irredentism of the Albanian national minority in Kosovo and Macedonia need also be put into historical perspective and analyzed from its particular context. In fact, the only two wars fought in the 1990s in Yugoslavia that would accurately fit into a definition of an 'ethnic war' would be the one fought between the Serbs and Kosovo's Albanians in 1999, as well as the subsequent one between Macedonians and Albanians since the latter are indeed a different ethnic group of non-South Slavic origin.

For these reasons, Djilas' definition of the Yugoslav nations best explains the distinctiveness between a nation and an ethnic group from a historical perspective. In Djilas's words, the "American media use the term *nation* to describe the people in the territory of one state, under one government. In this book the term *nation* means a community of people with territory, culture, and identity based on historical memories. This is also how Serbs, Croats, and so on see themselves—they never describe themselves as 'ethnic groups'."[38]

Therefore, I argue that the Croats and the Serbs, like Motyl's Ukrainians, were nations before the modern invention of nations. Similar to Ukrainians, all Yugoslav nations perceived themselves as *narod* (people) rather than as *nacija* (nation), which means the same as *natsiia* for Ukrainians. In fact, semantically and phonetically speaking there is no difference between the terms *nacija* and *natsia* in Russian, Ukrainian or Serbo-Croatian languages. This is also the case for the word *narod*. As mentioned, all of Yugoslavia's constitutions used the term *narod* rather than *nacija*, even though both referred to a nation. In no case does the term 'ethnic group' appear. Like Ukrainians who define themselves in contrast to their prototypical 'other'—the Russians, the Croats and the Serbs define themselves as distinct from each other as well as from the other Yugoslav nations. Following Motyl, I maintain that there is no radical distinction between an ethnic group (or an ethnie) and a nation, because "all nations are ethnic nations, inasmuch as ethnicity and nationhood are conceptually synonymous."[39] Similar to the Ukrainian case, the national identities of Croats and Serbs and so on, are rooted in the memories and traditions of their medieval kingdoms.

For all of the aforementioned reasons, I agree with both Calhoun and Djilas who argue that the Yugoslav nations have the same ethnic origins. Calhoun challenges the 'ancient ethnic hatreds' thesis, which was also advocated at the time by U.S. Secretary Christopher, by stating that while the Croats and the Serbs are "now presented as an ancient ethnic-national distinction, as late as the early nineteenth century this was mainly a difference of religion between people who *shared the same language and ethnic stock*."[40] Similarly, Djilas' concluding remark best illustrates why Croats and Serbs are simultaneously both ethnic groups and nations, and moreover, why the whole of Yugoslavia should be defined as a mono-ethnic state rather than a poly-ethnic country as Anthony Smith wrongly concludes:[41]

> *The Croats and the Serbs*, as separate nations have a history whose beginnings are lost in the depths of time...Despite the fact that they *are old nations*, neither their national identities nor the states they created were continuous...The instability of the Croatian and Serbian medieval states, followed by the Ottoman conquests, interrupted the development of either two clearly separate identities or a homogeneous proto-Yugoslav one. In the nineteenth century the Croats and the Serbs, found themselves lacking the strong state tradition that allowed the 'old, continuous' nations to emerge as modern nation states...*Ethnically and linguistically*

*they were not separate*, so differentiation rested primarily on historical memory, traditions, and religion. One could even say that Croats and Serbs are *ethnically almost homogeneous*, but are heterogeneous from the standpoint of national consciousness and loyalties. In fact the whole of Yugoslavia could be defined as a *mono-ethnic state* with three closely related languages (Macedonian, Slovenian, and Croato-Serbian or Serbo-Croatian) and many different national political consciousnesses. When Yugoslavia was created in 1918, the South Slavs were not one nation. They had largely different political and state loyalties. Between the two world wars, national ideologies developed further and became widely disseminated.[42]

## The Viability of Yugoslav Unity and the Avoidable War

I agree with Greg Nielsen, Calhoun and Motyl who argue that the distinction between ethnic/cultural and civic/political nationalism is an inappropriate approach for analyzing nationalism. Calhoun correctly claims that national development in Western and Eastern Europe shows that this division between ethnic and civic nationalism does not hold, because historically this development included both ethnic and political projects. I argue that Yugoslavia is a good example in support of this claim, because both forms of nationalism shaped it. As we have seen, since the Enlightenment, there has been a historic development of the Yugoslav idea regarding the unification of all South Slavs in one state. From the very beginning, this idea included both civic and ethnic nationalism, or political and cultural projects. Even now, in the new successor states of the former Yugoslavia, we can find both versions of nationalism inscribed in the various new constitutions. While all of the new states emphasized the ethnonational principle for citizenship, only the third Yugoslavia was founded as a civic state with an inclusive principle of citizenship for all its citizens. As well, article 1 of the Constitution of FRY from 1992 strictly prohibited state nationalism. Yet, in both cases we notice elements of both ethnic and civic nationalism. Even though the new constitutions of Slovenia, Croatia, Bosnia and Macedonia promote ethnic nationalism, there are also notable elements involving civic projects. For example, article 5 of the new constitution of the Republic of Slovenia from 1991 emphasizes both the inclusion and the protection of the rights of its two major national minorities: Hungarian and Italian. On the other hand, while Milosevic's Yugoslavia was a classic federal state based on the civic principle of political unity and equality of all its citizens, not only of members of the major national groups, armed conflict played out with the ethnic Albanian minority living in the province of Kosovo, whose status remains an unresolved question.

However, in Crnobrnja's and Djilas' terms, Yugoslavia was shaped by both centripetal and centrifugal forces: the former involves a project of building one modern Yugoslav nation promoted by the idea of Yugoslavism and most recently developed into a socialist multinational federal state, while the latter, centrifugal element involves separate national projects and struggles for independence.

Although the question of 'the Yugoslav nation' has been the biggest paradox of Yugoslav unity, given the fact that Yugoslavs never came into being as a 'nation' in the classic sense, nevertheless, the concept of supranational and civic Yugoslavism was both a viable and noble idea. To clarify this claim, it is necessary to mention at this point that the Federal Republic of Yugoslavia was formally abolished on February 4 of 2003 as both a state and the last country of the South Slavs or Yugoslavs, and was replaced with a loose transitional union between the Republics of Serbia and Montenegro. The European Union mediated and brokered this agreement, which also gave the right to both republics to hold referendums for full independence in three years. Not surprisingly, a large portion of people still consider themselves to be 'Yugoslavs,' rather than only Serbs or Montenegrins, or as the popular joke proposes: 'Serbo-Montenegrins.'

The whole changeover process of renaming the state was relatively easy, and everyone quickly adapted to this change, but not so with the sensitive issue of finding a new name for its perplexed citizens who have held onto the concept of Yugoslav national identity for so long. In fact Milosevic's Yugoslavia received the majority of Yugoslavs who became refugees or internally displaced persons in their own republics, and who sought shelter in this 'new homeland of the old Yugoslavs.' However, the fact that the name 'Yugoslavia' is now relegated to the past does not mean that the Yugoslav idea or Yugoslavs will disappear forever, nor does it mean that Yugoslavia was an artificial project from the start.

Given that all of the successor states of the former Yugoslavia are now harmonizing their economies motivated by their individual desires to join the European Union separately, who knows what the future holds? Perhaps economic, cultural and personal ties will one day bring together again what politicians tore apart in such a violent manner.

Although explained in more detail later on, I need to mention here the fact that only 6% of the total population of Yugoslavia formally declared their nationality as 'Yugoslavs' in the Census of 1981, which decreased to 3% in the final Census of 1991. Statistically speaking, this demonstrates that Yugoslavs were a national minority in their own state rather than a nation. The paradox surrounding the Yugoslav nation, which in practical terms was situated somewhere between a nation and a national minority, is also singled out by Djilas, who asserts that even though Yugoslavs "might well be considered the seventh South Slav nation of Yugoslavia," they were only "recorded separately in statistics but are not recognized as a nation."[43] This paradox of Yugoslav national identity is, in my view, historically rooted in the 'supranationality' of Yugoslav unity, developed especially by the so-called new Yugoslavism. In political terms, the supranationality of Yugoslavism implied that Yugoslav nationality referred only to citizenship, and not to one's ethnicity, meaning that people were simultaneously both Yugoslavs and Serbs, Croats, etc.

As Djilas points out, communists in particular promoted the new Yugoslavism in the aftermath of the conflict with Stalin in 1948. They specified that this new Yugoslavism aimed neither to create one hegemonic nation embracing all other nations, as promoted during the absolutist rule of King Alexander in the previous unitary monarchy (integral Yugoslavism), nor did it aim to form a new nation. Rather, the communists believed that the development of socialism and Yugoslavism would go hand in hand in accelerating the development of a modern Yugoslav community for all of its peoples. This new pro-Yugoslav orientation was different from the previous model created immediately after World War II, which became superfluous in further socialist development. In Djilas words, "on the basis of the common interest of the working people, and within the framework of an already developed and unified sociopolitical system, a 'unified Yugoslav community' was coming into being. *This new community was overcoming the national consciousness of individual nations without at the same time becoming a nation in the 'old sense'*."[44] One might even say that to some extent a multinational Yugoslavia was, to use Motyl's analogy, a 'supranational,' or post-national, community before such a community was even 'invented.' That is, Yugoslavia was Europe in miniature in terms of the variety of nations and nationalities composing it, before the European Union was even 'imagined' let alone created. As such, the new concept of Yugoslavism was based on this 'supranational' principle, even though its driving force was socialism and not capitalism. Just as the post-national European Union is composed of Europeans who see themselves primarily as Germans, French and so on, socialist Yugoslavia was composed of Yugoslavs who were simultaneously Serbs, Croats, Muslims, etc.

I need to also stress that prior to this new Yugoslavism of the 1950s, there were two other forms of nationalism that were more ethnic than civic and, as such, led to the emergence of the new Yugoslavism. After World War II and the victory of the socialist revolution, the new idea of multinational federalism and Yugoslavism was indeed a great step forward, in comparison with pre war Serbian hegemony and the bloody civil war (1941-1945). The first wave of post war nationalism, which was inspired by a victorious socialist revolution and the defeat of Nazism, ignited mistrust and violent behaviour against non Slavic national minorities, particularly against Hungarians and Albanians because of their collaboration with the German and Italian occupying authorities. According to Djilas, the worst forms of retaliation were particularly directed towards German and Italian national minorities, who left Yugoslavia either because of fear or coercion. The second form of post war nationalism was in Djilas' words "a peculiar version of supranational nationalism...revived... [by] Soviet leaders...[at] the end of the war" that resembled a version of "traditional pan-Slavism."[45] However, after the duel with Stalin in 1948, this neo pan-Slavism ceased to exist in Yugoslavia, being superseded by the new Yugoslavism of the 1950s, which continued to flourish in the form of supranationality that still exists in the minds of many of its citizens even after the disappearance of both the name and the country. It is worth pointing out that this version of the supranationality of imperialist pre- and post-war Soviet pan-Slavism has nothing in common with my analogy between the former Yugoslavia and the European Union. The supranationality of the new Yugoslavism was based on the equality of nations and national minorities of Yugoslavia, meaning that all the various national identities were simply enriched by this supranationality of Yugoslavism and Yugoslav citizenship.

We will see in the fourth chapter that people who saw or declared themselves to be 'Yugoslavs' were among the first targets, particularly in the new states of Croatia and of Bosnia, of both forms of ethnic cleansing: the massive displacement of people, or uprootedness, and bureaucratic ethnic cleansing or constitutional nationalism in Hayden's terms. For this reason, I argue that the disintegration of the former Yugoslavia should be seen as a transition, or more precisely, a regression, from peaceful civic nationalism to violent ethnic nationalism. That is, a socialist supranational Yugoslavism that was motivated by civic nationalism and built on the idea of political unity and community of all of its citizens and nationalities regressed to the recent ethnic, aggressive and chauvinist, nationalism of the 1990s, which is based on the building of homogenous nation-states in ethnically heterogeneous or 'mixed' territories. This over-night transformation of 'the individual' to 'the national' is best described by Slavenka Drakulic, who states that she can no longer be "a person," since her personality has become completely reduced to her nationality (see Introduction). Accordingly, I agree with Kai Nielsen's argument that ethnic nationalism is bad because it is violent, barbaric, nonliberal and often includes, as in Yugoslavia's case, vicious forms of ethnic cleansing. In this sense, I have to agree that there is a crucial difference between civic or non-violent nationalism as is the case in Quebec or Scotland and ethnic or violent nationalism as experienced in the former Yugoslavia, since the former implies, in Kai Nielsen's terms, "words and votes" and the latter "guns and tanks." However, I disagree with a priori radical division between good and bad nationalism since nation-building projects usually involve both elements: ethnic claims and political participation.[46]

In this regard, the labyrinth of the disintegration of Yugoslavia is more complex than assumed by both primordialist and constructivist schools of thought. It is of up-most importance to note that the violent collapse of Yugoslavia was avoidable on both internal and external levels. Although the external, or foreign, dimension will be discussed in the next chapter, it is worth citing Gerard Baudson, a French diplomat, who argues that the International Community, led by EU and UN respectively, and influenced by Germany and the U.S., bears a direct responsibility for the outbreak of the civil war in Yugoslavia. Baudson demonstrates that the violent destruction of the country was avoidable and could have been prevented up to the last moment if the International Community had 'frozen,' or delayed, the international recognition of the new republican borders until the protection of national minority rights in the new successor states had been assured. He eloquently argues that Yugoslavia was sacrificed for the sake of the unity of the European Community, because none of the European nations wanted to challenge Germany's premature and thoughtless international recognition of Slovenia and Croatia within their republican borders (the latter being a bi-national republic with a large Serbian population). Baudson notes that the expectation that Serbs should accept the independence of Croatia would be similar to asking of Jews who survived the Holocaust to return to Germany or Austria re-surrected under Nazi symbols. Franjo Tudman, the President of Croatia at the time, "encouraged the usage of symbols, songs and uniforms as well the adoption of the national flag almost identical to the Ustashi chess-board flag [the official flag of the Nazi Ustashi regime in the 'Independent State of Croatia' existing from 1941-1945]."[47]

Moreover, the Badinter Commission that was established to investigate the suitability of the Yugoslav republics to become independent states largely ignored questions of the 'newly created' national minorities or the core problem of borders between republics, which were never identical to the 'invisible' borders between nations. This arbitrary commission completely overlooked existing international law about the immutability of internationally recognized borders of Yugoslavia, and recognized the republics within their existing borders, knowing that these had been drawn exclusively for administrative purposes and never according to national structures and distribution. This *a priori* and then official international recognition of the new successor states in their republican borders is the primary reason for the violent break-up of Yugoslavia. While Germany and the Vatican gave the green light for Slovenia's and Croatia's unilateral declaration of independence on June 25/26 of 1991 (which resulted in the outbreak of the civil war the next day) and granted them early international recognition, the U.S. provided the necessary go ahead for Bosnia's 1992 declaration of independence to be officially recognized by the European Community on April 6 and then by the U.S. on April 7, resulting immediately in the declaration of a state of emergency in Bosnia on April 8. This made civil war irrevocable. Since Slovenia was the most homogeneous republic without any significant South Slav national minority, there was no issue with respect to the minority question or its state borders and, for this reason, the so-called 'mini' or 'phony' civil war ended within ten days with minimal military causalities, followed shortly after by the acceptance of its independence and the retreat of the Yugoslav Army from Slovenia.

According to Baudson, the civil wars in Croatia and Bosnia were avoidable, right up until the very last moment, had the International Community only accepted the French diplomatic initiative and the recommendation of President Mitterand to freeze the recognition of the republics of the former Yugoslavia until the rights of national minorities had been established.[48] With regard to the civil war in Bosnia, which was avoidable and could have been prevented for the same reasons as in Croatia, the Lisbon Agreement of early March 1992 proposed the ethnic 'cantonization' of Bosnia (a model similar to Switzerland), and was signed prior to the eruption of the war by all three constitutive national groups: the Serbs, the Croats and the Muslims. The plan then failed because Alija Izerbegovic, the Bosnian Muslim leader and the acting President of Bosnia at the time, reneged his approval of the plan after consultation with, and encouragement by, Warren Zimmerman, the former American Ambassador for Yugoslavia.[49]

In the next chapter, I will show that the ethnic divisions and struggles over borders and territories of Yugoslavia, what I call 'internal' Balkanization, are a direct consequence of a previous 'external' Balkanization. That is to say that the territorial division of Yugoslavia, and the subsequent turning of its peoples against each other, has historically and continues to be propelled by diverse foreign powers, all of which have their own economic and geopolitical interests in the Balkans. The military strategic importance of the Balkans is also acknowledged in popular board-games, such as, "Risk" and "Diplomacy" as well as in the operational war-games like, for example, the GDW's "Third World War: Southern Front," the SPI/Decision Games "Modern Battles II: Yugoslavia" or the Victory Games "Aegean and Strike."[50] The political instability of the Balkans then, is historically a product of outside intervention, or perpetual re-colonialization. It operates through the historical and current politics of 'Divide and Rule.' It is crucial to note that prior to the recent civil wars, there were massive and multinational demonstrations of working people across Yugoslavia, provoked by a deep economic and socio-political crisis that was induced by the macro-economic structural adjustment reforms of the International Monetary Fond (IMF) and the World Bank. Michel Chossudovsky rightly points out that in 1990, these new economic reforms of both international financial institutions had, on the one hand, enflamed the separatist nationalist movements while, on the other, they also provoked a multinational worker resistance of Serbs, Croats, Bosnians, Slovenians and so on who mobilized across the country to protest against the rapid impoverishment of the Yugoslav population.[51] These economic reforms were first introduced in Yugoslavia in 1980 with catastrophic consequences; this period is known to the Yugoslav public as the decade of so-called 'stabilization' which implied the overall shortage and restriction of basic goods and services, as well as rampant inflation and devaluation of national currency. We will see further in the next chapter that the external factors, primarily the economic and geopolitical interests of the Western countries, U.S. and Germany in particular, are crucial figures in the Yugoslav tragedy.

Returning now to the debate on nationalism that is central to this chapter, it is important to further stress the fact that the war was also avoidable at the internal level, or within the Yugoslav federation. There was a civic, political solution to the ethnic division of the country and the fraternal war. Indeed, prior to the war and dissolution of the country at the final 14th Congress of the Communist Party of Yugoslavia, held in Belgrade in January 1990, the Slovenian communists, backed only by the Croatian delegation, had proposed a model of confederation as the new step that would keep the Yugoslav community together. Since Slobodan Milosevic and the rest of the republican leaders arrogantly refused this proposal, Slovenian and Croatian delegations immediately abandoned the Congress in a sign of protest, and walked out of the Communist Party of Yugoslavia. This was the beginning of the end for the multinational Yugoslav federal state. For this reason, I agree with Calhoun that ethnic claims are intertwined with the civil projects of political participation, or in Greg Nielsen's terms there is always an open-ended or unfinalized two-sided answerability between 'ethnos' and 'demos.'

Accordingly, Will Kymlicka is right to state that even though "a multi-nation model of federalism" that is advocated by the Quebecois and Aboriginal people in Canada, might be the "only chance to keep Canada together," there are "no guarantees" that, even if the proposed multinational federalism would be accepted by Anglophone Canadians, "it would not be simply a stepping-stone to the inevitable dissolution of Canada."[52] Since socialist Yugoslavia was founded on such multinational principles, it is a good example of both a successful model of multinational federation and the dissolution of such an advanced federal model, which does not mean in any way that disintegration is an inherent component of federation or confederation. The collapse of Yugoslavia was, among other reasons, also a result of the rejection of the confederation that would have been the next logical step in solving national issues and developing a multinational confederate state as the apparent solution for avoiding civil war. In fact, as we have seen in this chapter, Yugoslavia was actually somewhere between a federation and a confederation. This is to say that the republics were behaving as states within the state of Yugoslavia, which was constitutionally a state founded on dual sovereignty: that of nations and nationalities as well as of working people. In reality, it was a distinct socialist self-managed community of working people and citizens, as well as that of equal nations and national minorities that, together, developed a unique model of (successful) market socialism.[53]

In contrast to Canada, the former Yugoslavia was not a country of immigration, and therefore, it had no immigrant minorities in Kymlicka's terms, even though all of Yugoslavia's national minorities, in particular the Albanians,[54] could also be defined as both immigrant and ethnic groups. The former socialist Yugoslavia was a federal republic formed as a community of voluntarily united nations and national minorities (narodi and narodnosti in Serbo-Croatian). Thus, neither in Yugoslavia's constitutions nor in the official terminology or public usage can we find terms that are in Canadian daily usage, namely, 'immigrants' or 'ethnic minorities'. Contrary to Canada, the former Yugoslavia was initially composed of five constitutive and sovereign nations (Slovenes, Croats, Serbs, Montenegrins and Macedonians) that were joined by the Muslims as the sixth nation, formally recognized by the constitution of 1963. Arguably, the 'Yugoslavs' were 'the seventh nation,' or at least a paradoxical national minority in their own country. As I argue in the following chapters, this seventh South Slav nation of Yugoslavia, including 'the Bosnians,' 'the Eskimos' or 'the others,' is unjustifiably excluded from official reports about refugees with respect to their national identities. Ironically, those people who declared themselves 'Yugoslavs' in the latest census were among the first uprooted peoples, regardless of whether they were counted as internally displaced persons or refugees. Moreover, the new successor states of the former Yugoslavia abolished the usage of the word 'Yugoslav.' Officially, neither the term nor the concept exists any longer. The Yugoslavs thus disappeared from official terminology and vocabulary, as well as in the statistical categories of national identity, within and outside the former Yugoslavia.

In terms of national minorities, socialist Yugoslavia was a treasure of various nations and national minorities whose diverse cultures and traditions represented Europe in miniature. Since Yugoslavia was a republic based on group rights, these numerous and various national minorities had extensive and well-protected rights, in particular the two largest groups, the Hungarians in Vojvodina and the Albanians in Kosovo, both autonomous provinces of Serbia. Their two distinct languages, besides the three major Slavic languages (Serbo-Croatian, Slovenian and Macedonian), were also in official and active use. According to Crnobrnja, "the other minorities—Italians, Slovaks, Rumanians, Bulgarians, Turks, Roms (Gypsies), Rusines, and so on" strongly contributed to "the complexity and richness of the Yugoslav linguistic cocktail [as all of them] were entitled to education and cultural communication" in their own languages.[55] In this sense, like Canada, Yugoslavia was a multicultural state with a completely open and inclusive agenda based on the multicultural coexistence of various ethnocultural groups. More specifically, Yugoslavia, similar to Quebec, promoted a policy of interculturalism or active cooperation between its diverse ethnocultural groups, their cultural convergence and mutual influence through interactions, exchange and intermingling. In contrast to Canada, which is founded on liberal, thus, individual rights, Yugoslavia was a republic that, as such, embraced all of the large and the small 'ethnocultural' or 'ethnonational' groups. As we will see in the last chapter, this is one of the reasons why 'Yugoslavs,' like Salvadorans, are seen as too small an ethnic group to be included in Canada's multicultural agenda. Yugoslavs are also, for different reasons, excluded from the Western political agendas and media reports, and are therefore basically 'invisible' war victims and 'non-existent' refugees.

Although socialist Yugoslavia was a country of the South Slavs, all of its national minorities were, regardless of whether they were Slavic or not, considered equal with the same duties and rights as the Yugoslav nations. For this reason, there were no meaningful disputes or confrontations between the Yugoslav state and national minorities, except in the Albanian case that can be to some extent defined as a 'minority nationalism' in Kymlicka's terms, or the 'irredentism' as defined in Yugoslavia's official terminology. As Crnobrnja explains, the dispute was the result of Albanian demands to be treated as a constitutive nation of Yugoslavia, which ultimately implied political independence of the already autonomous Serbian province of Kosovo and Metohija. Ethnic Albanians argued that they were more numerous than Slovenians, Macedonians and Montenegrins, who had their own republics. The official counter-argument of the Yugoslav Government was that the Albanians "cannot be a nation within Yugoslavia since there is an Albanian national state adjacent to Yugoslavia, so they must be satisfied with the status of a national minority, regardless of their number."[56] However, following recent events, ethnic Albanians may succeed in creating their 'Independent State of Kosovo,' and perhaps even enlarge it by claiming sections of Macedonia.[57]

Although Canada and the former Yugoslavia both had in common federal and multicultural states, their political and social systems differ significantly; for my purposes, with respect to group rights: the former was founded as a liberal democracy, and the latter as a socialist republic. Yugoslavia's national minorities could nonetheless be defined as immigrant groups and as ethnic groups, because all of them 'immigrated' at some point in history, even if it was mainly through the act of conquest. Differing from Canadian ethnic or immigrant groups, and similar to the Quebecois and Aboriginal national minorities in Canada, all of Yugoslavia's national minorities consider themselves to be *starosedeoci*, meaning aboriginals, indigene or autochthonous peoples. In Kymlicka's terms it would correspond to his notion of 'the old settlers' or 'the colonial settlers.' However, in Yugoslavia's terminology these ethnic minorities were defined as national minorities.

As a result, I would argue that if socialist Yugoslavia, which was an exceptionally advanced multinational federation, was an artificial community then, by the same logic, every country that is officially, or sociologically speaking, composed of more than one nation is under imminent threat of dissolving into smaller units, or new states, including Canada.[58] In this sense, if Yugoslavia was artificial, then Yugoslavia is everywhere, and what happened in Yugoslavia could happen anywhere in the world. Although I present in the fourth chapter Hayden's remarkable analysis of the ethnic cleansing and nation-building of the homogenous states in heterogeneous territories, his argument would be more attractive and powerful if it was less constructivist and included more historical, economic and political explanations, particularly in terms of the multitude of external factors that contributed to the disintegration of Yugoslavia. In further contrast to the constructivist claim that Yugoslavia was an artificially 'imagined community,' I argue that there was a strong multinational resistance across Yugoslavia against the dissolution of the Yugoslav state and approaching civil war. This claim will be elaborated in the fourth chapter, which examines elements of popular and political resistance, particularly in multinational Bosnia. For now, I close with a statement of one of my survey respondents (a Serb), who asserted that "Yugoslavia certainly needed changes, but in a peaceful way, and in no case by war."

## Summary

We have seen that the Yugoslav idea regarding the formation of one common state for all South Slavs has a long history. Yugoslav nations are old nations that voluntarily united in the first, then in the second, and finally in the third Yugoslavia. The former Yugoslavia was a viable political community that developed an advanced multinational federation and a distinct form of socialist self management. Therefore, key questions raised in this chapter were: If the idea of Yugoslav unity and formation of a common state was an artificial social construct as constructivists argue, how do they account for the long struggle of the South Slavs for a common statehood? Even if we ignore history, it still begs the question: What precisely was artificial in the past hundred years of the emergence of the Yugoslav state? Was socialist Yugoslavia artificial due to its multiethnic or multinational composition or due to the artificiality of socialism, or both? And finally, if it was an artificial country from the beginning, why was this same artificiality, or the same mistake, repeated not only once, but three times within the twentieth century resulting in the creation of three Yugoslavia?

In the following pages we will see that the complexity of the collapse of the former Yugoslavia far exceeds the primordialist thesis of ancient ethnic hatreds and the constructivist claim of the artificiality of its imagined community. The 'Yugoslav dilemma,' its disintegration, cannot be reduced only to internal Balkanization as both schools have done. The next chapter deals with external Balkanization, challenging both theories of nation and nationalism, and showing that the political instability of the Balkans, and specifically Yugoslavia, was caused primarily by foreign interference, or conquest, and not by centuries old ethnic hatreds. I conclude this chapter with a key claim that I will take up in the coming pages: that Yugoslavia was definitely a noble experiment that resulted in a successful, internationally respected socialist country, that developed a unique system of market socialism based on a not-for-profit oriented economy. For this very reason, Yugoslavia was an obstacle to the neoliberal 'diktat' of the free-market policy of the New World Order that emerged from the ruins of the Cold War division of the world.

## NOTES

1. Mihailo Crnobrnja. *The Yugoslav Drama*. Montreal: McGill-Queen's University Press. 1994, p. 9.

2. Mihailo Crnobrnja. "Intelligentsia and Nationalism in the Yugoslav Drama." *Europe: Central and East (Critical Perspective on Historic Issues, Volume 6)*. Marguerite Mendell and Klaus Nielsen (eds.). New York: Black Rose Books, 1995, p. 131.

3. Crnobrnja, 1994, *op. cit.*, p. 6.

4. Crnobrnja, 1995, *op. cit.*, p. 131.

5. Crnobrnja, 1994, *op. cit.*, p. 3.

6. Indeed, even though all of the Yugoslav nations were medieval states (Slovenia only for a very short period of time), only the Kingdoms of Serbia and of Montenegro entered into the Yugoslav state in 1918 as internationally recognized states. Both countries had achieved *de jure* statehood at the Berlin Congress in 1878. See more details in Baudson 1996, Crnobrnja, 1994 and Djilas, 1996.

7. Crnobrnja, 1994, *op. cit.*, p. 4.

8. *Ibid.*, my emphasis.

9. For more details about the shift from state socialism to state nationalism that was performed by the same persons who just changed their shirts, see Zarana Papic et al. "From State Socialism to State Nationalism: the Case of Serbia in Gender Perspective" in *What Can We Do for Ourselves: East European Feminist Conference, Belgrade 1994*. Marina Blagojevic, Dasa Duhacek and Jasmina Lukic (eds.). Belgrade: Center for Women's Studies, Research and Communication, 1995. See also Hayden, 1996 and Samary, 1995.

10. Crnobrnja, 1994, *op. cit.*, p. 7.

11. Crnobrnja, 1995, *op. cit.*, pp. 131, 132.

12. *Ibid.*

13. *Ibid.*, pp. 133, 139.

14. *Ibid.*, p. 139.

15. I stress again that in Crnobrnja's sense, the primordialist approach is incorrect, because there was not a long Yugoslavian history of nationalist struggle against each other. On the contrary, "mutual antagonism and aggression is of a relatively recent nature" (Crnobrnja, 1994, p. 6). For this reason, I find his argument closer to constructivism even though Crnobrnja's overall analysis is more complex and thus surpasses its theoretical framework, as we will see in the following pages.

16. Crnobrnja, 1994, *op. cit.*, p. 6.

17. Robert Hayden. "Imagined Communities and Real Victims: Self-determination and Ethnic Cleansing in Yugoslavia" in *American Ethnologist*. Vol. 23 (4), 1996, p. 788.

18. Aleksa Djilas. *The Contested Country: Yugoslav Unity and Communist Revolution 1919-1953*. Cambridge Massachusetts: Harvard University Press, 1996 (1991), p. 15.

19. *Ibid.*, p. 36.

20. While Slovenian language is distinctive it is nonetheless very similar and closely related to Serbo-Croatian language. At that time, Macedonian language and nation were not officially recognized. Indeed, the first Yugoslavia (1918-1941) was founded as the unitary

monarchy, known as the 'Kingdom of Serbs, Croats and Slovenes, thus excluding other peoples.

21. Djilas, *op. cit.*, p. 44, my emphasis.

22. This conference was important for several reasons. First of all, the idea that the workers and their socialist party, later renamed the Communist party, "could be the creators of the Yugoslav nation" was a completely "new idea" (Djilas, *op. cit.*, p. 46). Before the conference, Yugoslavism was advocated by the intelligentsia and it was assumed that the spirit of Yugoslavism, like literacy, would penetrate the lower classes "from above." According to Djilas, "the Tivoli resolution" drafted at the end of the conference, among other decisions, addressed the national question stating that "Austria-Hungary should, through constitutional changes and reform of the electoral law, become a *confederation*, with democratically elected political parties that would represent *the nations* rather than the sovereign states" (*ibid.*, p. 47, my emphasis). Djilas explains that socialists argued that as "sovereignty was within nations...the unity of the South Slavs should first be achieved through one literary language." Even more importantly, "the Ljubljana conference and the Tivoli resolution showed on the eve of the First World War that socialists of the different Yugoslav nations had no great difficulty in working together in the *spirit of Yugoslavism*" (*ibid.*, my emphasis).

23. Djilas, *ibid.*, p. 46.

24. *Ibid.*, p. 62.

25. *Ibid.*, p. 72.

26. *Ibid.*, pp. 161, 162.

27. One illustrative example of the foremost difference between the communist bloc led by USSR and socialist Yugoslavia was the fact that Tito, in contrast to Stalin, never declared to reach the final destination of communism. In this sense, socialist Yugoslavia under Tito and later Milosevic was officially in transition from socialism to capitalism. Another important difference between Eastern Europe and the former Yugoslavia is that the latter was never a member of the Warsaw's Pact and there was neither Russian nor American military presence on its territory.

28. Djilas, *op. cit.*, pp. 178, 179.

29. "Introductory Part, Basic Principles" of *The Constitution of the Socialist Federal Republic of Yugoslavia with Explanation*. Ljubljana: Center za samoupravno normativno dejavnost, 1974, my translation from Slovenian language and my emphasis.

30. See article 1 and 3 of the constitutions of SFRY and of Slovenia, or of any other Yugoslav republic.

31. Hayden, *op. cit.*, p. 787.

32. *The Constitution of Federal Republic of Yugoslavia with Ten Special Appendices*, Belgrade: Savremena Administracija, 1992, my translation from Serbo-Croatian.

33. Hayden, *op. cit.*, 793.

34. See, for example, Branislav Grujic. *Dictionary: English-SerboCroatian*. Beograd: Narodna Knjiga, 1981, and Milan Drvodelic. *English-Croatian or Serbian Dictionary*. Zagreb: Skolska Knjiga, 1973.

35. Djilas, *op. cit.*, p. 1.

36. See an interesting website about media reports entitled "Balkan Mediations" at www.pomgrenade.org.

37. Crnobrnja, 1994, *op. cit.*, p. 66.

38. Djilas, *op. cit.*, p. 189, note 1.

39. Alexander Motyl. *Revolutions, Nations, Empires: Conceptual Limits and Theoretical Possibilities.* New York: Columbia University Press, 1999, p. 78.

40. Craig Calhoun. *Nationalism.* Buckingham: Open University Press, 1997, p. 62, my emphasis.

41. In Djilas, *op. cit.*, p. 232, note 3. Djilas is referring to Smith's account of Yugoslavia in Anthony Smith. *State and Nation in the Third World,* London: Brighton, 1983, p. 123.

42. Djilas, *ibid.*, pp. 181, 182, my emphasis.

43. *Ibid.*, p. 1.

44. *Ibid.*, p. 180, my emphasis. Djilas is referring to Edvard Kardelj's account (in 1953) of new Yugoslav federation and its future in general.

45. *Ibid.*, p. 170.

46. Even the case of Quebec reflects both versions of nationalism since there was a short period of violence during the so-called FLQ crisis of the 1970s (FLQ stands for "Front de Liberation du Quebec"), which resulted in the imposition of an emergency state in Quebec. Also, after the last referendum for the independence of Quebec in 1995, Jacques Pariseau, then leader of Partie Quebecois (PQ) and Premier of Quebec, commented that the referendum failed primarily because of "the ethnic vote" implying obviously both the immigrant cultural communities and the Anglophone national minority. However, he also stated that "the money vote" of the business community was another decisive factor. Nevertheless, this divisive and exclusionary remark of "the ethnic vote" should not be understood as a racist or an anti-democratic statement, because the Quebec's 'demos' or political community is indeed composed of many 'ethnos' or ethnic groups, as is also the case in almost all known countries in the world, especially since they are becoming more and more multicultural due to the unprecedented mass migration of peoples around the globe.

47. Gerard Baudson. *Novi Svetski Poredak i Jugoslavija.* Beograd: ING-PRO, 1996. Translated from French by Dimitrije Radovanovic (Original version: *Le Nouvel Ordre Mondial et la Yugoslavie.* Paris: Gill Wern Editions. 1996), p. 152, my translation.

48. *Ibid.*, p. 155. For a more detailed explanation see the subsection "The Responsibility of the International Community" pp. 153-157 in the chapter entitled "Danke Deutschland or Croatian Independence."

49. See also Baudson, *ibid.*, pp. 87, 88.

50. I am grateful to Robert Hingley for bringing this information to my attention.

51. Michel Chossudovsky, *The Globalization of Poverty: Impacts of IMF and World Bank Reforms.* London and New Jersey: Zed Books, 1997, p. 246. Chossudovsky is referring to Sean Gervasi's article "Germany, U.S. and the Yugoslav Crisis" in *Covert Action Quarterly.* No. 43, Winter 1992-93, p. 44 and to Ralph Schoenman "Divide and Rule Schemes in the Balkans" in *The Organiser,* September 11, 1995.

52. Will Kymlicka. *Finding Our Way: Rethinking Ethnocultural Relations in Canada.* Oxford: Oxford University Press, 1998, p. 11.

53. See Article 3, *The Constitution of SFRY*, 1974, *op. cit.*

54. The large portion of ethnic Albanians who live mostly in the Serbian autonomous province of Kosovo and Metohija are recent post-World War II immigrants who were massively running away from impoverished and Stalinist Albania to Tito's more liberal Yugoslavia. Although 'Albanian occupation of Kosovo' in Baudson's terms has a long 'immigration' history (*op. cit.*, pp.127-133), it is important to mention that the Albanians were the largest and most recent immigration group in socialist Yugoslavia.

55. Crnobrnja, 1994, *op. cit.*, p. 20.

56. *Ibid.*, p. 21.

57. The current project of building an ethnically pure Albanian Kosovo apparently includes the abolition of the very name of this Serbian province. For clear political purposes, the official and historic name of "Kosovo and Metohija" is represented to the world public either as only "Kosovo" or as recent Albanian neologism "Kosova." The reason why the name of the province included "Metohija" was that, in fact, this territory was the medieval property of the Serbian Orthodox Church. This word is a derivation from the Greek term "Metohi" which means the agricultural feudality of the Orthodox Church or Monastery. This historic fact is probably the main reason why the Albanian Kosovo Liberation Army (KLA) in the aftermath of "the liberation" of Kosovo in 1999, backed by UN and NATO troops, burned to the ground almost all Serbian Orthodox churches and monasteries as well as other ancient cultural monuments, deliberately destroying every trace of the existence of Serbian culture or people, and various other national minorities.

58. In fact, Baudson points out that "the Yugoslavian virus of fragmentation has already arrived in the West," *op. cit.*, p. 156. Similarly, Catherine Samary meaningfully entitled her conclusion "Today Yugoslavia, Tomorrow Europe..." in *Yugoslavia Dismembered.* Translated from French by Peter Drucker. New York: Monthly Review Press, 1995.

# Chapter Three
# 'Divide and Rule' Politics of External Balkanization

The following concise historical and political retrospective of external Balkanization will provide new insights about the origins and legacy of 'ancient ethnic hatreds' in the former Yugoslavia, a primordial thesis that is passionately promoted by Western media and politicians, yet, does not stand up to historical scrutiny. This analysis of the historical context of external Balkanization, or the foreign dimension, will enrich our understanding of the disintegration of Yugoslavia and its impact on the past and present life experience of refugees from the former Yugoslavia and, more specifically, from Bosnia. This chapter demonstrates how, historically, various Great Powers and Empires divided the territories of the future Yugoslavia, and how, by constantly redrawing the borderlines, they often divided the territories along a 'Western and Eastern' partition. These external divisions and continuous re-making of borders often, but not always, partitioned Yugoslavia in half by cutting through or around Bosnia. For this reason, I argue that the geopolitical and military strategic importance of the Balkans, combined with the economic interests of powerful Empires or countries, were, in both historic and current conditions, actively involved in the political fragmentation of the Balkans and the consequent civil war in the former Yugoslavia. In other words, external Balkanization led to the internal one, and not vice versa. The complexity of 'Balkanization' far exceeds common media representations of an exclusively internal Balkanization expressed in the form of 'barbaric' ethnic wars and cleansing. This religious and national fanaticism is, by and large, over-represented in media reports within and outside the former Yugoslavia.

The arguments presented in this chapter, and throughout the book, are neither a denial of internal Balkanization nor of the committed atrocities. Rather it is an attempt to illustrate the other side of the coin. The history of Yugoslavia reflects the record of both the 'old and new' world orders, whereby a long tradition of 'Divide and Rule' politics in the Balkans, or 'Divide et Impera' in the original ancient Roman version, has been executed by external occupying forces. The division of territories and changes made to the borders within Yugoslavia were, and still are, primarily due to foreign intervention in the Balkans. The territorial divisions created by internal forces are a consequence of a prior external Balkanization. In other words, once the territories of the future Yugoslavia were occupied and divided between often mutually hostile Empires, such as the Ottoman and Austro-Hungarian, the South Slavs were turned against each other and had to fight on opposite sides. For instance, during both world wars they fought against each other. In World War I, the Slovenes and Croats were Austro-Hungarian soldiers, while the Kingdoms of Serbia and of Montenegro were allies with the Entente. Moreover, the Nazi occupation and division of Yugoslavia resulted in a bloody fraternal war and the genocide of the Serbs, Jews and Gypsies. I argue in this chapter that ethnic nationalism is the product, or the 'offspring,' of external Balkanization. For the purpose of this book, my focus is the Yugoslav part of the Balkan Peninsula (which also includes Turkey, Bulgaria, Greece and Albania).

## The Old World Orders in the Balkans

The history of the Balkans, particularly that of Yugoslavia, is primarily a history of continuous struggle for liberation from foreign occupation. The 'Divide and Rule' politics of powerful Empires, particularly of the Roman, Ottoman and Austro-Hungarian Empires, resulted in various divisions of territory of the future Yugoslavia in the aftermath of the subjugation of the indigenous Illyrians and, subsequently, of the South Slavs or Yugoslavs. Thus, the history of the Balkans reflects the history of all major 'World Orders,' as established by the Roman Empire, Holy Christendom, the Ottoman Empire, Napoleon's Rule, German 'Drang nach Osten' (drive to the east) and the Hitler-Mussolini's World Order—to list the foremost ones. Besides division of the territories of Yugoslavia along religious lines (Roman-Catholic, Greek-Orthodox and Islam), the following Map 3 (a, b, c and d) illustrates several of the political schemes of external Balkanization, or its 'Divide and Rule' politics.[1]

As we can see from Map 3a, the division of the Roman Empire along Western and Eastern (Byzantine) Empires cut the future Yugoslavia in half: the borderline is similar to the present-day one between the Republics of Serbia, Montenegro and Macedonia on the East side with Bosnia, Croatia and Slovenia

Map 3:  'Divide and Rule' Schemes in the Balkans, or External
         Balkanization

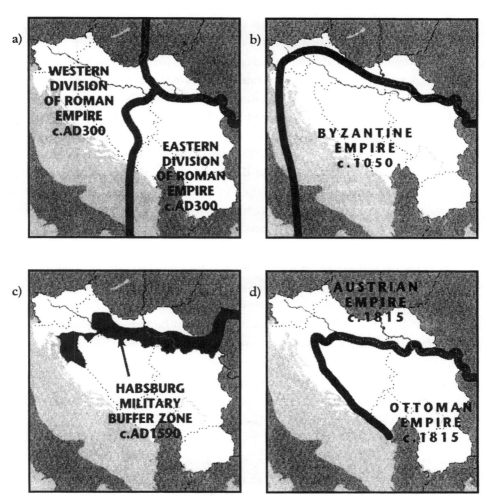

Source: Crnobrnja, Mihailo. *The Yugoslav Drama*, 1994, p. 18.

remaining on the West side. The second Map 3b, shows a west-east division of
the future Yugoslavia along similar borders of by Byzantine Empire, from the
early eleventh century. Again, the Roman Catholic and the Greek Orthodox
Churches drew a similar borderline after the Schism of the Christian Church in
1054. Another significant division of the future Yugoslavia occurred during the
Ottoman Empire and its invasion of Europe, which, in particular, shows the importance of geopolitical and military strategic factors in the Balkans. As Maps 3c
and 3d also show, the Yugoslav territories had for centuries played a major role
in the European Defence System as a 'Military Buffer Zone,' or 'Vojna Krajina'
in the Serbo-Croatian language (literary translated means 'Military Frontier').
The Habsburg Monarchy established 'Krajina' in the fifteenth century on the
territory between today's Croatia and Bosnia to protect itself and Europe at
large from the further advancement of the Ottoman Turks. In return for manda-
tory military service, the settlers of Krajina, mostly Serbian and Croatian refugees who were fleeing from the Ottomans, were granted land along with an
autonomous, special status for this territory.[2]

The result of centuries long Ottoman rule in the region was the Islamization
of some parts of the Balkans, as well as a century long division of the South Slavs
and occupation of their territories. This division of the territories of the future
Yugoslavia between Ottoman and Austro-Hungarian Empire on the west and
east sides of the country is another key case of external Balkanization. Map 3 (a,
b, c, and d) show several of the 'Divide and Rule' schemes in the Balkans that left
a legacy of internal conflicts over the territories later known as Yugoslavia. For a
better understanding of the impact of external Balkanization, it is noteworthy
that the South Slavs were nomadic tribes and pagans when they settled the Balkans in sixth and seventh century CE. The Islamization of the Balkans occurred
centuries after the Schism between the Catholic and Greek Orthodox
Churches, which cut the territory of what would become Yugoslavia almost in
half and divided the South Slavs between Catholics and Orthodox Christians
(eventually Protestant sects would also appear).[3] In this regard, Crnobrnja best
summarizes the origins of Islam in the former Yugoslavia and particularly in
Bosnia, its main homeland:

> The Turkish invasion and the domination of most of these territories [of
> the future Yugoslavia] by the Ottoman Empire brought with it the Is-
> lamic religion. The original Islamic believers were Turks who came and
> settled in conquered territories. But a portion of the indigenous popula-

tion converted to Islam. The converts were relatively few among Ortho-dox Christians, even fewer amongst Catholics. The largest conversion to Islam occurred among the Bogumils, a heretical religious sect that occu-pied Bosnia, the central part of what was later to be Yugoslavia.[4]

External Balkanization is then at the heart of historic divisions among the South Slavs. On the one hand, once divided, they often were pitted against and had to fight against each other. On the other hand, the peoples or nations of Yugosla-via share a history of mutual and separate struggles against various foreign occu-pying forces. History also reveals that there have always been people who sided with the occupying authority to try and profit from the occupation, just as there have always been people who fought against it. This duality was the most obvi-ous during the long Turkish occupation, from which time there still exist his-toric remains of fortresses (and many other traces) held by the South Slavic warriors fighting against the Ottoman Turks (know as *uskoci* and *hajduci* in Serbo- Croatian).[5] One illustrative and tragic historic example of this paradoxi-cal plight of being forced to fight for an occupying force while fighting against, not only neighbouring South Slavs but also against one's own people, even fam-ily, occurred during the terrifying Ottoman practice of so called 'taxation in blood' (*danak u krvi* in Serbo-Croatian). It is remarkably described by famed Bosnian writer Ivo Andric, who won the Nobel Prize for Literature in 1961.[6] Andric authentically depicts this 'bloody tribute' which involved the removal of Christian male children from their Bosnian and Serbian parents who, to save their children, would hide them in the forest, teach them to pretend to have dis-abilities, and some would even maim them by cutting off a finger, since only healthy, bright and good-looking boys were selected and brought to Istanbul. Once in Istambul, they would then be converted to Islam and trained to join the *corps d'elite* of Turkish troops called 'Janissaries,' organized in the fourteenth century and abolished in 1826. Some of these boys would later return to Bosnia as Janissaries representing the Turkish authority, ruling over their own people and fighting against other South Slavs, the future nations of socialist Yugosla-via.

A popular saying among Yugoslavs best illustrates public opinion about their 'bloody' history of fighting for foreign interests: "We died for Emperors playing war games!" The two Balkan wars that occurred in 1912 and 1913 are a most powerful example of how external Balkanization produced internal divi-sion. Indeed, while the first Balkan war was fought by the 'Balkan Alliance,' composed of Serbia, Montenegro, Bulgaria and Greece for the liberation from Ottoman Turkish rule, the second Balkan war was initiated by Bulgaria against Serbia and Greece over the territories of Macedonia, which then spread further to involve Montenegro, as well as Turkey and Romania.[7] Once liberated from foreign domination, the Balkan countries ended up in a second Balkan war over the disputed territory of Macedonia, claimed by each of them as their historic territory, and therefore, retaining a 'legitimate right' to occupy and dominate it. Immediately after the Balkan Wars, Yugoslav nations had to again fight each other during World War I, since the territories of Slovenia, Croatia and Bosnia were all part of the Austro-Hungarian Empire, while Serbia and Montenegro were allied with the Entente. Finally, in World War II, there was a civil war in Yugoslavia provoked by the Nazi occupation and its continuation of the legacy of 'Divide and Rule' politics in the Balkans.

I suggest that in light of this legacy of 'Divide and Rule' politics of external Balkanization, which ultimately divided the Yugoslav peoples and turned them against each other, one should understand Andric's short story entitled Letter from 1920. In it, he acknowledges the existence of 'latent or dormant hatreds' in Bosnia after World War I through the main Bosnian Jewish protagonist who decides to leave Bosnia forever because he is unable to deal with the surfacing hatreds.[8] We will see in the last chapter that political reconfiguration of the Balkans has always been followed by mass migrations, or the 'ethnic unmixing' of peoples in Rogers Brubaker's terms. For now, in order to further illuminate the complexity of the history of Yugoslavia, especially of Bosnia, and the paradoxical struggle against both foreign occupation and one another, it is worthy considering the context of World War I. While the Great War was triggered by the assassination of Archduke Ferdinand in 1914 in Sarajevo, the South Slavs had to fight against each other throughout World War I, since they were on the opposite sides. For the purpose of my analysis, this assassination was a direct response to the Austro- Hungarian annexation of Bosnia committed by Gavrilo Princip who was a Bosnian Serb born in Bosnian Grahovo and was a member of a multinational revolutionary Bosnian organization called "Young Bosnia," composed of Bosnian Serbs, Croats and Muslims. The organization's political agenda and goals were based on a pro-Yugoslav orientation calling for the national liberation of Bosnia and all South Slavs from foreign rule. 'Young Bosnia' particularly emphasized the importance of struggle against further internal national and religious divisions between both Bosnian and Yugoslav peoples. As detailed in the previous chapter, this early link between national radicalism and progressive ideas was at the heart of the origins of Yugoslavism and the unity of all South Slavs in a common state. This ultimately implied both the destruction of the Austro-Hungarian Empire, and the creation of an independent Yugoslav state.

With regard to external Balkanization, Gerard Baudson[9] points out that, in the aftermath of World War I, France influenced the creation of the first Yugoslavia in 1918 in order to surround Germany with a "security zone," that is, with the "creation of three new states: Poland, Czechoslovakia and Yugoslavia."[10] Baudson further notes that Hitler's vision of the 'New World Order,' as also written in *Mein Kampf*, implies that all the countries that emerged from the Versailles Agreement are an insupportable insult. For Hitler, "Yugoslavia is one of these countries."[11] In World War II then, Yugoslavia was once again a victim of Hitler's world order and his 'Divide and Rule' politics in the Balkans.

Similarly, Tito's Yugoslavia (SFRY: 1945-1991) was *de facto* created, or given a rubber stamp, by Churchill, Stalin and Roosevelt at the Yalta Conference in February of 1945, where they established the post-war 'World Order.' This Conference made some important compromises, known as "the fifty-fifty politics that hit the Balkans particularly hard, especially Yugoslavia whose territory became a sphere of interest divided between the USSR and Western powers."[12] Although Yugoslavia was liberated by its own forces, the Yugoslav People's Army (JNA), the Yalta Conference recommended an agreement between Tito's National Committee and the Government in exile living in London from the onset of the war in 1941. However, the Communist Party led by Tito won the first free post-war elections in 1946, which led to the establishment of socialist Yugoslavia as the federation of five constitutive nations. To avoid over-simplification of these historical events, it is important to point out that World War II in Yugoslavia simultaneously included Nazi occupation, civil war and a socialist revolution. After the bloody fraternal war and Nazi occupation, which together resulted in the genocide of 750,000 Serbs, 50,000 Jews and 25,000 Gypsies,[13] the Yugoslav nations and nationalities united voluntarily in a socialist and multinational federation under Marshall Tito, its life-long President. As noted previously in Djilas' analysis, the idea of the unification of the South Slavs in a common state has a long history. The development of both Yugoslav Unity and Yugoslavism has been on the agenda of the Yugoslav radical intelligentsia and socialists since the Enlightenment. The complexity of the national question in the first and second Yugoslavias involved tension between those who advocated Yugoslavism and those who promoted separatism and ethnic nationalism, as well as the progressive role of socialist revolution, and the subsequent creation of the multinational and multicultural Yugoslavia.

The aforementioned historic events, and especially the decisive role of out-side colonizing powers, demonstrate that external Balkanization reflects the 'Old' and the 'New World Orders' in the Balkans, based on a politics of 'Divide and Rule' that often divided the territory of Yugoslavia along its western and eastern borders. External Balkanization and its division of the South Slavs led to their internal conflicts, particularly with regard to historically disputed territo-ries. I argue that ethnic nationalism is an offshoot of external Balkanization, that culminated in two Balkan Wars, World War I and World War II, as well as in the recent civil war of the 1990s. Despite ethnic nationalism and civil wars in Yugoslavia's recent history, there remains an even stronger sense of national and religious tolerance and mutual respect. In particular, once liberated from Nazism and its domestic ultra-nationalist collaborators—the Croatian 'Ustashi', Serbian 'Chetniks', Bosnian 'Young Muslims' and Albanian 'Balists,' to name a few—the peoples of Yugoslavia united in a socialist and multinational country which developed a strong sense of national tolerance and cultural diversity. In-ternally and externally, Tito's Yugoslavia initiated a remarkable politics of 'ac-tive and peaceful coexistence', a landmark of the Non-Alignment Movement, a noble alternative yet not influential enough to counter the Cold War division of the world. However, the disintegration of the former Yugoslavia also meant the end of its membership in this peaceful movement of mainly Third World coun-tries. Today this movement is seen in the West as an international movement of 'Rogue States,' in reference to individual cases of human rights violation or nu-clear proliferation.[14]

## Yugoslavia and the New World Order

With regard to the emergence of the 'New World Order,' Noam Chomsky main-tains that at the end of the Cold War there were two almost simultaneous yet op-posing calls for a New World Order. Which call that would succeed was obvious from the very beginning. The nongovernmental South Commission composed of prominent Third World economists, planners, religious leaders and others made a call for a more just, equal and democratic 'New World Order,' a plea that "passed silently into oblivion."[15] Not so regarding the call from U.S. President

George Bush Senior shortly thereafter for a 'New World Order' that was, as Chomsky explains, not only "a rhetorical cover" for the Gulf war in 1990, but also a call that resonated and pushed aside "the plaintive plea of the South, unreported and unheard," clearly indicating that such a "reaction to the two near-simultaneous calls for a New World Order reflects, of course, the power relations [between a rich North and a poor South]."[16] At that time, as Chomsky reminds us, George Bush Senior proclaimed that the U.S. "would lead a new world order—where diverse nations are drawn together in common cause, to achieve the universal aspirations of mankind: peace and security, freedom and the rule of law."[17] While the main objective and justification for the first Gulf War were the protection of international borders between sovereign countries (specifically protecting Kuwait from Iraq's invasion in order to avoid future chaotic situations leading to international anarchy), the key issue, however, was that "America's victory in the cold war was...a victory for a set of political and economic principles: democracy and the free market...the free market is the wave of the future—a future for which America is both the gatekeeper and the model."[18] The most recent version of this new world order is already being called a 'new' New World Order, reflected in George Bush Junior's Gulf War II of 2003, and his unilateralist way of imposing his vision of democracy and the free market around the world. The paradox, and irony, of both new world orders, of Bush Senior and Junior, is not only that Iraq is now, in the aftermath of the 'U.S. liberation,' experiencing both chaos and anarchy, but that the former Yugoslavia has been dismembered because this same international law about the immutability of international borders was not respected. Moreover, Milosevic's Yugoslavia was massively bombed by NATO in 1999, despite the fact that did not have any nuclear weapons, nor did it pose a threat to the world nor any neighbouring or NATO country.

Regarding the 'New World Order'[19] and its neoliberal ideology of the free market, Canadian and internationally renowned economist Michel Chossudovsky eloquently argues that the former Yugoslavia is just another country on the long list of victims of what he accurately calls the 'Globalization of Poverty.' He claims that the worldwide imposed macro-economic structural adjustment reforms of the International Monetary Fund (IMF) and World Bank has brought about global economic devastation to over a hundred Third World countries. As these reforms were also applied to all the former communist countries, including socialist Yugoslavia, with the same devastating economic results,

Chossudovsky names this process the "thirdworldization of Yugoslavia."[20] In discussing a direct relationship between these macro-economic reforms and the strategic interests of Germany and the U.S., he maintains that both were at the heart of the Yugoslav conflict, constituting the real, deep-seated cause of the socio-political crisis that ignited separatist ideas leading to the war. According to Chossudovsky, this intimate link between the imposition of free-market reforms and U.S. geopolitical goals is obvious in a U.S. National Security Decision Directive (NSDD 54) from 1982 regarding Eastern Europe, whose objectives explicitly refer to "expanded efforts to promote a 'quiet revolution' to overthrow Communist governments and parties while reintegrating the countries of Eastern Europe into a market-oriented economy."[21] A more specific version pertaining to Yugoslavia was written in 1984 in NSDD 133, entitled "United States Policy towards Yugoslavia labelled SECRET SENSITIVE."[22] As Chossudovsky concludes, "Washington's strategic objective was to integrate the Balkans into the orbit of the 'free market' system."[23]

While these macro-economic reforms undermined the Yugoslav economy throughout the 1980s, the worst crisis was initiated in January of 1990, when the IMF imposed 'shock therapy' on Yugoslavia and took a successful control of its Central Bank. This effective control resulted in a diversion of state revenues away from the usual transfer payments to the republics and into payments on Yugoslavia's external debt with the IMF's Paris and London clubs. As Chossudovsky states: "By cutting the financial arteries between Belgrade and the republics, the reforms fuelled secessionist tendencies that fed on economic factors as well as ethnic divisions, virtually ensuring the de facto secession of the republics."[24] The main goal of these reforms was to massively privatize the public sector leading to massive bankruptcy and liquidation of socially owned businesses and the banking system—the core of Yugoslavia's noble and successful experiment in market socialism with its unique form of socialist (workers') self-management. This massive privatization led to massive unemployment, a result of massive layoff of redundant workers. However, the crucial role of these reforms in the disintegration of Yugoslavia, with their devastating economic, social and political impact, is absent from Western media representations of the crisis. Instead, the focus of media reports is on how internal ethnic and religious divisions and hatreds caused the crisis and the war. Chossudovsky also rightly maintains that "while local leaders and Western interests share the spoils of the former Yugoslav economy, they have entrenched socio-ethnic divisions in the very structure of partition. This permanent fragmentation of Yugoslavia along ethnic lines thwarts a united resistance of Yugoslavs of all ethnic origins against the recolonization of their homeland."[25]

Commenting on the question of Bosnia, Chossudovsky asserts that the Dayton Peace Accords, signed at the end of 1995 and officially ending the civil war, represents "a full-fledged Western colonial administration in Bosnia," imposed by both the EU and the U.S. He argues that:

> With a Bosnian peace settlement holding under NATO guns, the West has unveiled a 'reconstruction' program that strips that brutalized country of sovereignty to a degree not seen in Europe since the end of World War II. It consists largely of making Bosnia a divided territory under NATO military occupation and Western administration.[26]

According to the Dayton Peace Accords, the appointed High Representative for Bosnia is the ultimate civil authority, holding absolute executive power, including the right to rule against decisions of both legal entities: the Croatian-Muslim Federation and the Serbian Republic. The new constitution of Bosnia is not only written on behalf of Western creditors, but it gives over control of economic policy to the Bretton Woods institutions (IMF, World Bank, World Trade Organization, UN) and European Bank for Reconstruction and Development (EBRD). Accordingly, as Chossudovsky aptly puts it,

> The IMF is empowered to appoint the first governor of the Bosnian Central Bank, who, like the High Representative, 'shall not be a citizen of Bosnia and Herzegovina or a neighbouring State.' Under the IMF regency, the Central Bank will not be allowed to function as a Central Bank...it may not extend credit by creating money...neither will Bosnia be allowed to have its own currency...nor permitted to mobilize its internal resources...While the Central Bank is in IMF custody, the EBRD heads the Commission on Public Corporations, which supervises operations of all public sector enterprises, including energy, water, postal services, telecommunications, and transportation.[27]

Under the Dayton agreements, Bosnia, besides being divided into the Federation of Croats and Muslims versus the Serbian Republic, is also divided into three basic zones of NATO military control. These, in turn, are ruled by each of the main allies: the United States, Britain and France. These divisions, including NATO's military occupation, are indispensable elements of the, in

Chossudovsky's words, "neocolonization of Bosnia" that emerged in the aftermath of the dismantling of the former Yugoslavia. In my account, this redrawing of borders and military occupation is another instance of external Balkanization in Bosnia and the former Yugoslavia at large. At the core of the New World Order is a mixture of Western/U.S. geopolitical and economic interests, where the IMF's imposition of neoliberal free market reforms plays a crucial role in devastating the socio-economic and political landscape, not only in the former Yugoslavia, but around the globe. The social and political impact of these restructuring reforms is behind the 'ancient ethnic hatreds,' and this helps us to understand what really went wrong in the only socialist country in the world that was an economic success. As Chossudovsky explains:

> The neocolonization of Bosnia is the logical culmination of long Western efforts to undo Yugoslavia's experiment in market socialism and workers' self-management and to impose the *diktat* of the free market. Multiethnic, socialist Yugoslavia was once a regional industrial power and economic success. In the two decades before 1980, annual gross domestic product (GDP) growth averaged 6.1 percent, medical care was free, the literacy was 91 percent, and life expectancy was 72 years. But after a decade of Western economic ministrations and five years of disintegration, war, boycott, and embargo, the economies of the former Yugoslavia are prostrate, their industrial sectors dismantled.[28]

In his analysis of the aftermath of NATO's bombing campaign against Yugoslavia in 1999, Michael Parenti, an American political scientist, also points out that 'the rational destruction of Yugoslavia' by the U.S. and other Western powers ultimately aimed at privatization and the 'thirdworldization of Yugoslavia.' Parenti argues that the former Yugoslavia was dismantled because it was an obstacle to the new economic and political world order. Although socialist Yugoslavia was certainly not a country that global capitalism could accept to exist as such, it was permitted to exist for so long because of its strategic geopolitical importance for the West. That is, it was seen as a buffer zone between the NATO and the Warsaw Pact countries. For Parenti, there is no doubt that "the dismemberment and mutilation of Yugoslavia was part of a concerted policy initiated by the United States and the other Western powers in 1989. Yugoslavia was the one country in Eastern Europe that would not voluntarily overthrow what remained of its socialist system and install a free-market economic order."[29] Noting how proud Yugoslavs were of their distinct socio-economic and political system that focused on sustained development and represented their independence from both NATO and the Warsaw Pact, Parenti argues that the disintegration of Yugoslavia was rooted in the disastrous impacts of free market reforms under the guise of democracy. In particular, it was due to the direct interference of the U.S. in the internal affairs of Yugoslavia, including financial support of ultra right-wing nationalist parties. He states that there is a "public record" of U.S. direct involvement in the disintegration of Yugoslavia:

> In November 1990, the Bush administration pressured Congress into passing the 1991 Foreign Operations Appropriations Act, which provided that any part of Yugoslavia failing to declare independence within six months would lose U.S. financial support. The law demanded separate elections in each of the six Yugoslav republics, and mandated U.S. State Department approval of both election procedures and results as a condition for any future aid. Aid would go only to the separate republics, not to the Yugoslav government, and only to those forces whom Washington defined as 'democratic', meaning right-wing, free-market, separatist parties.[30]

A multinational, socialist Yugoslavia and its successful non-profit economy that (almost) equaled Western European living standards was antithetical to the process of free market globalization, or to the designs of the 'New World Order' for the Balkans. In line with Parenti, Chossudovsky, Baudson, Samary and others, I argue that Western geopolitical and economic interests, in particular that of Germany and the U.S., were key factors and players in dismantling the former Yugoslavia. In other words, once Yugoslavs were divided by 'new world order' politics whose ultimate goal was privatization and the 'dictate of free market,' it was easy to turn them against each other thereby lighting the fuse for the civil war. This is emphatically not to deny the atrocities of aggressive, ethnic nationalism committed between Serbs, Croats, Bosnian Muslims, Albanians and so on, but rather to criticize simplistic and misleading Western representations of the Yugoslav crisis that omit the indispensable role of external factors, particularly of the West, and of the International Community, that are directly responsible for the war. In this regard, Catherine Samary, a French economist, maintains that:

> The break up of a multinational country, Yugoslavia, is combined with the crisis of a (socioeconomic and political) system, in the context of a

world where the 'free market' is on the offensive...There will be no peaceful 'new world order' founded on exclusion. *Antiliberal and fascist nationalism is the classical answer to such crises.*[31]

The importance of the geopolitical and military strategic location of the Yugoslav territories is based in their historical and geographical positioning as the
'Golden Door between the West and the East,' or between Europe, the Middle
East and Asia. As Baudson notes, Winston Churchill called Yugoslavia the
"tender belly of Europe."[32] Crnobrnja also singles out the geopolitical importance of the Balkans and the role of external factors in the creation and destruction of Yugoslavia. He states that "as with most countries, and certainly every
European country, the international context was and is extremely important.
The territories of Yugoslavia, central in both geopolitical and strategic terms,
have been of interest to large powers for centuries."[33] To nuance his argument,
Crnobrnja recognizes the importance of the foreign dimension, as one of many
factors that led to the creation and destruction of Yugoslavia. He argues that
while it would be "an exaggeration to say that Yugoslavia was imposed on the
Yugoslavs by foreign powers... it would not be an exaggeration...to say that Yugoslavia was to a considerable degree moulded by influences from without...[therefore] If Yugoslavia was not created by external forces alone, it
certainly found one of its important reasons for staying together in the hostile
environment of the Cold War."[34]

Besides ethnic nationalism and an inappropriate political system, for
Crnobrnja, the broader international environment was indeed an important
factor in the recent Yugoslav conflict. He emphasizes that neither different "national characteristics" nor "the history of mutual aggression" were determining
factors in the recent war, because while it is true that "there have been bloody
confrontations among the Serbs, Croats, Muslims and Albanians...we are not
talking about a millennium-old history of hatred and fighting, as is sometimes
claimed."[35] According to Crnobrnja, the mutual hostility and violent conflicts
among Yugoslav nations are recent, occurring within the twentieth century. For
him then, ethnic nationalism was an indispensable component, but not a determining factor in the disintegration of the former Yugoslavia. Other crucial elements include "the state of the political system, the international environment,
economic conditions, history, tradition, and national characteristics."[36] In discussing the complexity of the development of the Yugoslav state and its ultimate
viability as opposed to its artificiality, Crnobrnja poses a logical question by not-

ing that, if the first Yugoslavia (1918-1941) was a mistake, then "why was the same mistake repeated in 1945? [and]...how was it possible for Yugoslavia to reach the level of international respectability and internal stability that it enjoyed for almost thirty years?"[37]

With regard to the political system, Crnobrnja notes that some form of totalitarian, or rather authoritarian, rule governed both Yugoslavias. While the first Yugoslavia, or "The Kingdom of Slovenes, Croats and Serbs" (1918-1941), was principally "an absolutist non-parliamentary monarchy," the second Yugoslavia, or "Socialist Federal Republic of Yugoslavia" (1945-1991), was under "the quasi-parliamentary rule of the Communist Party and Tito personally."[38] In these regimes, Crnobrnja sees both a lack of democratic political culture and the suppression of the national question as the main unresolved issues in both Yugoslavias (1918-1991), which also contributed to the onset of the war. He states that "the national issues, masterfully guided through the media by the 'patriots,' rapidly turned into nationalism and then into its aggressive variety, pushing the problem of the democratic deficit to the sidelines."[39] I agree then with Crnobrnja's claim that the main cause for the violent collapse of Yugoslavia was unsolved key issue of borders, that is, the incompatibility of ethnic borders with republican borders, which were drawn only for administrative purposes. These administrative borders were, in Crnobrnja's words, "a major issue" of national disputes and conflicts, being thus "one of the principal causes of the current blaze of the nationalist fire."[40] As mentioned in the previous chapter, the republics of the former Yugoslavia were indeed bi- or multi-national, especially Bosnia.

In line with these authors, I argue that the former Yugoslavia was dismantled primarily by external, Western, powers, since they gave the political 'go ahead' to right-wing nationalist separatist forces in Yugoslavia. This *de facto* encouragement was soon followed by formal, *de jure* international recognition, first by the Vatican and Germany, and followed by the European Community and the United States. They recognized the new successor states of the former Yugoslavia within their republican borders, that covered ethnically heterogeneous or mixed regions since they were drawn according to administrative purposes. In Baudson's words, this sounded "a death knell" for national minorities and human rights across the former Yugoslavia. As a consequence, as Baudson explains, all parties to the civil war sought to avoid the status of national minority, particularly the Serbs, of whom over 2 million lived outside Serbia. Also, Samary and Hayden accurately claim that multi-ethnic Yugoslavia had an ever-increasing rate of mixed marriages and the number of people who declared themselves Yugoslavs was on the increase, particularly in Bosnia. Central to my argument then is the obvious fact that the vast majority of victims of ethnic cleansing were ethnically 'mixed people' and the 'newly created' national minorities, the original constitutive nations of Yugoslavia. This includes the most paradoxical national 'minority,' the Yugoslavs, as I will further demonstrate in the next chapter.

In his excellent historical and political analysis of the dismemberment of Yugoslavia based on the 'New World Order,' Baudson argues that never in the history of the world were so many borders changed in such a short period of time, from the Adriatic coast of the Mediterranean Sea to the borders of China. In discussing the question of whether Yugoslavia was dismembered due to internal factors (ethnic nationalism) or external factors (International/Western intervention) for the sake of the new world order, Baudson lucidly depicts the image: "At last, what is Yugoslavia—'a suicide of one nation' or 'a homicide of one country'? Let's say that *the victim was found hanged after shooting itself from behind*."[41] For him, it is obvious that Yugoslavia was a clear victim of the 'New World Order,' with an undesirable 'boomerang effect'. In Baudson's words:

> It is a madness to destroy, in a couple of months, a country which has existed for 80 years and has 24 million people...It is a madness to transform nations into national minorities as the Badinter Commission did. It is a madness to aspire to create a Europe constituted by different nations, nationalities and religions, different languages, cultures and customs; and at the same time, to destroy Yugoslavia which was already Europe in miniature constituted of multiple nationalities, religions and customs. The dismemberment of Yugoslavia is a 'death knell' for the European Unity as a common homeland of diverse nation- states.[42]

Central to Baudson's logical argument is the crucial point that, at the heart of the Yugoslav conflict, all the warring parties tried to avoid relegation to the vulnerable status of national minority by attempting to eliminate or cleanse 'the others.' It is therefore impossible to classify them as 'good and bad guys', as the Western, especially American, media and politicians have tended to frame such a multifaceted civil war. It is noteworthy to mention the following statements by two (American/UN) generals regarding both the attempt of all involved parties to avoid becoming minorities, and the American involvement in the war in Bosnia:

We, Americans, say that we want peace, but we have encouraged the spread of the war...all parties in the former Yugoslavia had the same goal: to avoid the status of minority in Yugoslavia or any of the successor states. The U.S. supported all these ambitions except the Serbs in Bosnia (General Charles Boyd)...There are no good guys on the one side and bad guys on the other side (General Brickmon).[43]

Baudson similarly comments, but with greater sarcasm, regarding the Holly-wood-like scenario of 'good and bad' guys in the war in Bosnia, particularly ob-vious in the data of the recently established UN International justice system for war crimes in Yugoslavia, the International Criminal Tribunal for the former Yugoslavia (ICTY):

In mid-November 1995, there were 52 sentenced persons, of which 45 were Serbs. When we encounter the barbarism of all civil wars; when we know that in Bosnia there are three conflicting sides which are from time to time both allies and enemies, as is the case with Croats and Muslims; it is incredible that the other seven are Croats from Bosnia sentenced for the massacres of Muslim civilians! There is no sentence for the war crimes against Serbs. Thus, there are evil Serbs, good Muslims and mainly cor-rect Croats.[44]

This is in no way to deny or diminish the responsibility of the Serbian side. It is, however, to challenge the ways in which 'Serbs' have been unjustifiably labelled and accused of being the only 'bad guys' in the drama of the disintegration of Yugoslavia. Instead, I advocate the careful allocation of shared responsibility for the war crimes indiscriminately committed by all warring parties in the former Yugoslavia. This includes the responsibility of outside powers that gave silent permission for ethnic cleansing, along with foreign paramilitary forces, who di-rectly committed crimes, ranging from various European neo-Nazi Skinheads to Mujahideen mercenaries, the Islamic 'holy warriors or freedom fighters.' Of course, the International Community, led by the EU and UN both strongly in-fluenced by Germany and the U.S., is also responsible and should be held ac-countable for its direct involvement in the war. Not only were crimes committed by all sides involved in the war, but also the civilian victims, those the killed and the banished or displaced, were consequently persons of diverse ethnic origins including many of various Yugoslav nations and nationalities. In general, the ci-vilian victims of such violent destruction of the country included all 24 million of the former Yugoslavs who lost a sense of the 'normality' of everyday living overnight, and whose life since 1991 has become, to varying degrees, a nightmare. In particular, the most immediate and direct victims were those designated 'undesirable elements' composed of the newly created national minorities, who previously made up the constitutive nations of Yugoslavia, people of mixed national origins and the 'Yugoslavs.' Consequently there are no winners in this war(s) of losers! In terms of a completely ethnically mixed Bosnia, Robert Hayden, similarly to Baudson, notes that the result of civil war "as of late 1994 was the more or less complete exchange of populations" among Serbs, Croats and Muslims.[45]

Crimes committed against the Serbian population in Croatia, Bosnia and are not only under-reported by Western media and politicians, but also downplayed by the ICTY, thus falling into oblivion. While the crimes committed by Serbs are central to media reports, crimes committed against Serbian civilians are barely reported, especially in newspapers. However, my modest collection of this obscure information includes the following brief update of Baudson's data from the ICTY showing that the pattern of exclusively Serbian 'bad guys' continues in spite of the fact that the Serbs were also victims of atrocities, having also suffered in the prison and 'concentration' camps. Thus, a year later, in 1996, the Hague Tribunal for Yugoslavia for the first time sentenced three Bosnian Muslims and one Croat as responsible for war crimes against Bosnian Serbs committed at the beginning of the war, in 1992, in the Celebici camp in central Bosnia.[46] In February of 2003, also for the first time, the ICTY acted against ethnic Albanians and indicted three soldiers of the Western-backed Kosovo Liberation Army (KLA) for war crimes against both Serbian and Albanian civilians committed in May and July of 1998 in a prison camp in Glogovac, Kosovo.[47] Given that these crimes happened in a camp, they were clearly committed in a well organized and systematic manner. This occurred a year prior to NATO's air strikes against Yugoslavia in 1999, designed and justified as a humanitarian intervention for the protection of ethnic Albanians from Serbian ethnic cleansing. Again, this is not to say that Serbian forces were innocent in the Kosovo conflict, but, rather, to expose the other side of the coin, especially biased media reporting and the justice system, and to acknowledge the crimes committed against Serbian population as well as against other nationalities.

The Canadian Broadcasting Corporation (CBC) televised documentary entitled "The Battle of Medak Pocket"[48] is a notable exception in media reporting of the civil war. This battle was the biggest combat Canadian forces engaged in since the war in Korea and for which Canadian Peacekeepers (from the Princess Patricia's Canadian Light Infantry) were finally honoured by Ottawa in December of 2002.[49] This unknown, or until recently unreported, battle between Canadian and Croatian troops occurred in September 1993 in Southern Krajina, a part of Croatia inhabited by Serbs. Croatian forces attacked an area called "Medak Pocket" where the Serbs lived in many dispersed villages that Canadians tried to protect. After the battle, in which Canadians killed 27 Croatian soldiers without any casualties on their side, the Croat forces finally let the frustrated Canadians inside the villages. It was, however, too late for the Serbian civilians. These Peacekeepers say they are still haunted today by what they saw: villages burned to the ground, all livestock killed and decomposing, rotting human corpses. Canadians found 16 mostly mutilated bodies, some unidentifiable as they were burned beyond recognition, whose remains the soldiers put into plastic body-bags that melted around the still smouldering corpses. The ethnic cleansing was so successful that no one to this day lives there. The utter lack of recognition of these crimes is clearly unjust for both the Serbian civilians and the Canadian Peacekeepers, particularly given their impunity and oblivion in the international justice system to date.

It is impossible, therefore, to make a division between good and bad crimes, or their perpetrators, since such atrocities cannot and should not be justified or left unpunished. One possible distinction might follow Dostoyevsky's suggestion that "crimes committed with extraordinary boldness are more likely to succeed than any others."[50] Hannah Arendt's distinction between limited and radical evil could offer another possible solution for distinguishing crimes. Commenting on the totalitarian radical evil crimes of Nazism and Stalinism, Arendt draws a distinction between murder and "the [totalitarian] radicalism of measures to treat people as if they had never existed and to make them disappear in the literal sense of the word," thus imposing the oblivion of victims.[51] Arendt further argues that "as we know today, murder is only a limited evil [because]...the murderer leaves a corpse behind and does not pretend that his victim has never existed; if he wipes out any traces, they are those of his own identity, and not the memory and grief of the persons who loved his victim; he destroys a life, but he does not destroy the fact of existence itself."[52]

As all conflicting parties tried to avoid the status of national minority and consequent expulsion, all of them fought 'defensive' wars based on a criminal strategy of ethnic cleansing to 'liberate' territories from 'the others.' Since the former Yugoslavia was a mini-Europe, containing an incredible cultural diversity on its small territory, it was both an absurdity and a crime to homogenize, by all forms of ethnic cleansing, originally heterogeneous territories. While the Western media largely focused their skewed reports on the portrayal of only 'bad guys' (Serbs) and their victims, the real situation, involving mutual ferocity inherent in any civil war, was in this sense similar everywhere: in Croatia, in Bosnia, in Kosovo and in Macedonia. This invisibility in the media of both the 'other' victims of the war and the responsibility of the International Community is aptly described by Sani Rifati who in May of 2002 as President of Voice of Roma led Western delegates for human rights, refugee assistance and peace activists to Kosovo to show them the impact of what he rightly calls "humanitarian ethnic cleansing." Rifati states:

> Since NATO's 'peace-keepers' arrived in Kosovo, more than 300,000 ethnic minorities have been 'cleansed' from the region by extremist Albanians...The ethnic cleansing of the Roma since UN peace-keepers arrived in June 12th of 1999 has resulted in more than 75% of this population (over 100,000 Romani people) fleeing Kosovo. Still the media and the international 'humanitarian' community are silent...The majority of the Roma who are left in Kosovo (25,000 out of a prewar population of 150,000) are internal refugees, but they do not have the official status of refugees. Instead these Roma are labelled 'internally displaced persons (IDPs), with fewer recognized rights than refugees, and are restricted to camps with very poor facilities...No other ethnic group is in the IDP camps, only Roma.[53]

This expulsion of 'other' national minorities, particularly Roma people (Gypsies), or their treatment as second class citizens in Kosovo, was never reported in the Western media. Nor was there any discussion of the real role of the International Community, with its 'humanitarian' institutions and reconstruction projects across the former Yugoslavia, particularly in Bosnia and Kosovo. These external, crucial players are clearly more preoccupied with promoting 'free market and democracy' while sharing the spoils of the war than with helping people to reconstruct their homes and country. Rifati accurately maintains that international relief agencies financed by development and investment corporations, including individuals such as Dick Cheney and George Soros,[54] are rebuilding Kosovo for the victorious ethnic Albanians while other numerous national minorities, such as the Roma, Serbs, Gorani, Bosnians, Turks and so on, are starving. Rifati asserts that "while most of these international institutions were bragging about 'free and democratic Kosovo', these people were forced to abandon their homes, suffering a 'humanitarian' supported ethnic cleansing that has been virtually invisible to the rest of the world. The ironic consequence of NATO/U.S. rescue of oppressed Albanians is that they then became oppressors themselves."[55] With similar criticism directed towards the misleading images presented by Western media and politicians, Michael Parenti comments in the aftermath of the NATO's bombing campaign against Yugoslavia in 1999: "Ironically, while the Serbs were repeatedly charged with ethnic cleansing, Serbia itself is now the only multi-ethnic society left in the former Yugoslavia, with some twenty-six nationality groups including thousands of Albanians who live in and around Belgrade."[56]

The multinational and cultural variety of socialist Yugoslavia is illustrated in Map 1: The Former Yugoslavia, Map 2: Ethnic Composition of Republics, and Map 6: The International Community on Trial, which best demonstrate the incompatibility of the Lebensraum of the constitutive national groups with the administrative republican borders of the former Yugoslavia. This obvious fact was a major issue in recent national disputes and conflicts, and is at the core of the recent internal Balkanization. Since Bosnia was the most 'mixed' republic, the absurdity of ethnic division and homogenization of such a multinational and multicultural territory resulted in an ugly fraternal war and numerous crimes. Since the majority of victims of ethnic cleansing in the former Yugoslavia were primarily from mixed territories, first of Croatia then of Bosnia, the subsequent outbreak of war in the Serbian province of Kosovo and, then, in Macedonia (both republics had mixed regions with large numbers of ethnic Albanians) can be seen as further steps in the 'ethnic unmixing' of peoples, or a continuation of the political fragmentation of the former Yugoslavia by both internal and external forces. This might eventually lead to the redrawing of the southern borders as well.

The complexity of the history of Yugoslavia and particularly the intricacy of its current violent demise as a common state of South Slavs, includes a multitude of external and internal factors: the powerful influences from outside and the internal centripetal and centrifugal forces that have shaped the country. On the one hand, although aggressive ethnic nationalism was seemingly defeated in World War II, it apparently was never completely uprooted, as the aforementioned events show and support. On the other hand, ethnic nationalism was a necessary but insufficient reason for the current tragic replication of civil war and bloodshed in the Balkans. As we have seen, the Yugoslav nations voluntarily united and created a socialist Yugoslavia, a viable political community that was far from being an artificially imagined country. Parenti accurately describes the origins of the viability of the Yugoslav idea: "Yugoslavia was built on an idea, namely that the Southern Slavs would not remain weak and divided peoples, squabbling among themselves and easy prey to outside imperial interests. Together they could form a substantial territory capable of its own economic development."[57] For these reasons, I share the opinion of many authors[58] who argue that socialist Yugoslavia was a noble example of a multinational and multicultural federal state with a pronounced sense of national and religious tolerance and mutual respect, in addition to economic success prior to the devastating effects of the IMF and the World Bank's first and second round of structural adjustment reforms in the 1980s and 1990s. Accordingly, Yugoslavia was dismembered primarily due to the external Balkanization, or the new world order's dictate of the free-market using the well known formula of 'Divide and Rule' politics in the Balkans.

In Samuel Huntington's extreme primordialist account of "the clash of civilizations" and the "kin-country syndrome" these economic, geopolitical and strategic factors are never mentioned. In a very contradictory manner with respect to the war in the former Yugoslavia, and in particular, Bosnia, Huntington acknowledges the international intervention in the Balkans, but exclusively as the "kin-country syndrome" that apparently justifies foreign, especially U.S. involvement. In Huntington's words,

> Western publics manifested sympathy and support for the Bosnian Muslims and the horrors they suffered at the hands of the Serbs. Relatively little concern was expressed, however, over Croatian attacks on Muslims and participation in the dismemberment of Bosnia-Herzegovina. In the early stages of the Yugoslav breakup, Germany, in an unusual display of diplomatic initiative and muscle, induced the other 11 members of the European Community to follow its lead in recognizing Slovenia and Croatia. As a result of the pope's determination to provide strong backing to the two Catholic countries, the Vatican extended recognition even before the Community did. The United States followed the European lead. Thus the leading actors in Western civilization rallied behind their coreligionists. Subsequently Croatia was reported to be receiving substantial quantities of arms from

Central European and other Western countries. Boris Yeltsin's government, on the other hand, attempted to pursue a middle course that would be sympathetic to the Orthodox Serbs but not alienate Russia from the West...By early 1993 several hundred Russians apparently were serving with the Serbian forces, and reports circulated of Russian arms being supplied to Serbia. Islamic governments and groups, on the other hand, castigated the West for not coming to the defence of the Bosnians. Iranian leaders urged Muslims from all countries to provide help to Bosnia; in violation of the UN arms embargo, Iran supplied weapons and men for the Bosnians; Iranian-supported Lebanese groups sent guerrillas to train and organize the Bosnian forces. In 1993 up to 4,000 Muslims from over two dozen Islamic countries were reported to be fighting in Bosnia...In the 1990s the Yugoslav conflict is provoking intervention from countries that are Muslim, Orthodox and Western Christian.[59]

Of course, Huntington's notion of the kin-country syndrome fails to explain how and why the Christian Western 'brotherhood' first supported Bosnian Muslims, and then ethnic Albanians in Kosovo and Macedonia who are predominantly Muslims. Above all, his analysis, and particularly his concept of 'kinship relations,' provides a justification for Western intervention and the expansion of NATO into the Balkans through the 'Partnership for Peace' project. For this very reason, Huntington omits to mention the geopolitical, strategic and economic interests of Western countries, in particular the energy crisis in the U.S. and its consequent 'friendship' (or war) with countries, particularly with Muslim ones, that possess rich oil fields. These Western economic and political interests are intertwined in the Balkans, especially due to the oil pipeline routes from the rich Caspian Sea basin to Europe through the Balkans.

Huntington's concept of the clash between civilizations has no historical legitimacy or relevance. Smilja Avramov eloquently argues for "historic morals" in the face of such grand ahistoric claims stating that while it is true that "the interactions between different civilizations played an important role in international relations; [nonetheless] different civilizations have existed for Ages and the conflicts had not occurred for this reason but rather because of confronting interests."[60] Huntington's notion of civilizational clash and the 'kin-country syndrome' in the former Yugoslavia is also highly problematic from a historical perspective: the South Slavs (Yugoslavs) and especially Bosnian peoples have most often fought together for the liberation of their territories from foreign invaders!

And as I have insisted, Yugoslavia was a mono-ethnic rather than a poly-ethnic country since it was founded as the multinational federation of the South Slavs who share the same ethnic origins, whose political histories and national development differ but cultural and linguistic similarities prevail. In this sense, the annexation of Bosnia by the Austro-Hungarian Empire resulted in the assassination of the Archduke in Sarajevo in 1914 leading to World War I, which was committed by the Bosnian multinational revolutionary youth organization "Mlada Bosna" ("The Young Bosnia"). At that time, and later, the Bosnian peoples opted for unification of all South Slavs in a common state rather than to division along cultural and religious lines. Finally, a popular Communist slogan "Brotherhood and Unity" dating from World War II ultimately meant: united we stand, divided we fall as easy prey to various imperialistic forces.

In contrast to Huntington, Ronald and Sir Alfred Sherman, among others, demystified the core of the 'kinship' relations as well as the clash of civilizations in Yugoslavia, particularly Bosnia. They do so by foregrounding the real reasons for U.S. intervention in the Balkans. In the "Foreword" of a collection of papers presented at the Lord Byron Foundation's Third Annual Conference devoted to U.S. policy in Southeast Europe held in Chicago in March 1997, Hatchett states that the U.S., like many nations,

> ...operate with hidden agendas in the international arena... According to Mr. Clinton and his administrators, American policy in the post-Cold War world is focused on expanding the community of free enterprise-based democracies and ensuring fundamental human rights for all peoples.[61]

Hatchett argues that U.S. foreign policy contradicts its own purpose and rules; it is allegedly based on the rule of law, respect for universal norms and international laws, as well for the sovereignty and equality of states, and in no case, so the argument goes, the U.S. wants to be a hegemonic super power. But this is clearly not the case, especially with regard to the war in Bosnia. Hatchett claims that Clinton's Administration portrayed a misleading picture of American aid going to "a small independent nation, called Bosnia, whose people are struggling to escape military conquest by an aggressive Yugoslav state dominated by the notoriously warlike Serbs, and led by an anachronistic, neocommunist, authoritarian regime."[62] Similarly, Sir Alfred Sherman comments on Bosnia by stressing that nobody seriously took into consideration the chauvinistic meaning and intention of the politically questionable book written by Bosnian President Alija Izerbegovic entitled *Islamic Declaration*.[63] While Izerbegovic advocated a 'united' and not a divided Bosnia under future Muslim rule, Sir Sherman emphasizes that prior to the crisis and the war, the majority of Bosnian peoples

> ...did not want to become 'Bosnians' in any political sense. The Croats, concentrated in western Herzegovina, sought secession from Yugoslavia in order to facilitate their union with an enlarged Croatia. The Serbs, for their part, wanted to remain linked to their brethren east of the Drina river [Serbs from Serbia], having suffered for centuries under alien misrule, including the clerico-fascist Ustas[h]a regime, which in 1941-1945 perpetrated genocide against the Serbs of Croatia and Bosnia with active Muslim participation.[64]

Commenting further on biased media reporting on Yugoslavia and why it is so, Hatchett argues that "the media...seemingly competing with each other in raising the level of sensationalism through selective reporting...provides a moral high ground for U.S. government actions in the Balkans" and simultaneously increases newspapers sales and TV ratings.[65] At the same time, the Clinton administration has created a 'myth' regarding the European inability to successfully manage and solve the crisis in the Balkans without American help and leadership. Hatchett states that anyone familiar with the history of Yugoslavia and the recent conflict in the Balkans knows that the accounts of U.S. media and politicians are highly deceptive. Hatchett critically questions the hypocrisy and double standard politics that are inherent to U.S. foreign policy in the Balkans:

> If America was so deeply committed to the concept of a 'multicultural' state in the Balkans, why did it so readily condone the dismembering of Yugoslavia?...If it prizes rule of law, why did America renege on its obligations under the UN Charter, and its agreement under the Helsinki Final Act of 1975 to 'respect the sovereignty and territorial integrity of all member states'—including Yugoslavia, a founding member of both institutions? If America places the right of self determination of peoples above the sovereignty and territorial integrity of states, why does it apply these principles to Slovenes, Croats, Bosnian Muslims and Skopje-Macedonians, but not to Serbs?...why is the desire of Serbs to come together into a single country...such a crime against humanity and a threat to world peace?[66]

In Hatchett's view, "the rights and aspirations of small nationality groups like the Serbs" are sacrificed for more important "U.S. geopolitical goals," such as: increasing cooperation with oil rich Muslim countries, finding a new *raison d'être* for NATO in the post-Cold War period as "the vehicle for continuing American 'leadership' in Europe," preventing "any 'resurgence' of Russia" as well as overseeing "the flow of oil from newly developing fields in the Caspian region."[67] However, as current events in the Middle East show, this cooperation with oil rich Muslim world can be achieved voluntarily or forcefully. Thus, in contrast to Huntington's extreme primordialist claim of the clash between civilizations, and similar media reports, the destruction of Yugoslavia involved the direct interference of the European Community, led by Germany, and the U.S., including crucial NATO's military intervention. It is not a cultural clash of civilizations in the Balkans but rather a clash of different economic and geopolitical interests, particularly of the West, but also of the East and of Islam—resulting in the Western recolonization of the territories of the former Yugoslavia.

Accordingly, Smilja Avramov points out that one of the main ideas of the 'New World Order' was expressed by U.S. President George Bush Senior with regard to the first Gulf War, when he stated on that ironic day of September 11 in 1990: "It is not only a war for Kuwait, but for the 'New World Order'...in which the 'Law of the Jungle' will be replaced by the 'Rule of Law'."[68] Apparently, the same reasoning was applied to justify the U.S. and NATO's intervention in Yugoslavia. Indeed, on September 11th, 1990, George Bush emphasized in his speech entitled "Towards a New World Order" that America and the world must defend common vital interests and support the rule of law as a guiding principle of the new world order. In his words:

> We stand today at a unique and extraordinary moment. The crisis in the Persian Gulf, as grave as it is, also offers a rare opportunity to move toward an historic period of cooperation. Out of these troubled times, our fifth objective—a new world order—can emerge: a new era—freer from the threat of terror, stronger in the pursuit of justice, and more secure in the quest for peace. An era in which the nations of the world, East and West, North and South, can prosper and live in harmony...Today that new world is struggling to be born, a world quite different from the one we've known. A world where the rule of law supplants the rule of the jungle. A world in which nations recognize the shared responsibility for freedom and justice. A world where the strong respects the rights of the weak...

Vital issues of principle are at stake. Saddam Hussein is literally trying to wipe a country off the face of the Earth...Vital economic interests are at risk as well. Iraq itself controls some 10 percent of the world's proven oil reserves. Iraq plus Kuwait controls twice that. An Iraq permitted to swallow Kuwait would have the economic and military power, as well as the arrogance, to intimidate and coerce its neighbors—neighbors who control the lion's share of the world's remaining oil reserves. We cannot permit a resource so vital to be dominated by one so ruthless.[69]

Ironically, never before the 1990s were there so many changes of borders worldwide: the collapse of the former Soviet Union and Yugoslavia alone created over 20 new countries with often disputable borders. Furthermore, there have never been so many armed conflicts and ever-increasing refugee crises since the new world order was heralded by Bush. Most recently, the replay of the Gulf War (II) and the subsequent sharing of the victor's spoils of war—Iraqi oil—show that control of the world's oil reserves is still a vital U.S. interest. Supplementing Hatchett's argument about U.S./NATO geopolitical goals, particularly in terms of control of the Caspian Sea 'oil route,' Avramov explains that in November of 1991 at the NATO Summit in Rome there were two zones named as "geostrategic" priorities: "the territory of former USSR and the Mediterranean basin."[70]

Avramov further argues that with "the disintegration of the Soviet Union and Yugoslavia, the territorial status quo was also broken up, and with the disappearance of the Eastern Bloc its essential function disappeared, too—the connection between the West and the East."[71] This connection between the West and the East, is illustrated on Map 4 that Avramov entitled "The Military Alliances and Countries of the Northern Hemisphere" where we can visualize the geopolitical importance of both the former Eastern European (Warsaw Pact) countries and particularly of the officially (neutral) non-aligned former Yugoslavia.

Avramov explains that in the post Cold War era, marked by the end of hostile bipolarity of the world, the concept of neutrality has also lost its purpose. This is why NATO's expansion to the East through the 'Partnership for Peace,' or 'Security Partnership,' included, besides the territories previously controlled by the Soviet Union and Russia itself, the former neutral countries, like Finland and Sweden, who joined in 1994. It even considered the adhesion of Switzerland. By December of 1992, NATO defined this partnership as "the continuous extension of cooperation in the security sphere from Vancouver to Vladivostok."[72] As Avramov asserts, two

Map 4:    The Military Alliances and Countries of the Northern Hemisphere

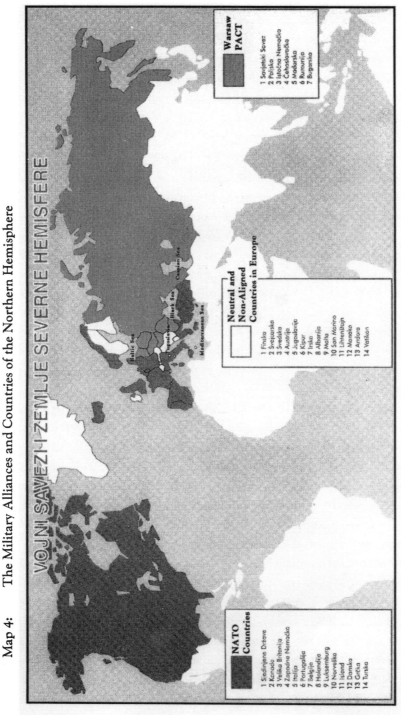

VOJNI SAVEZI-ZEMLJE SEVERNE HEMISFERE

**Warsaw PACT**

1 Sovjetski Savez
2 Poljska
3 Istočna Nemačka
4 Čehoslovačka
5 Mađarska
6 Rumunija
7 Bugarska

**Neutral and Non-Aligned Countries in Europe**

1 Finska
2 Švejcarska
3 Švedska
4 Austrija
5 Jugoslavija
6 Kipar
7 Irska
8 Albanija
9 Malta
10 San Marino
11 Lihtenštajn
12 Monako
13 Andora
14 Vatikan

**NATO Countries**

1 Sjedinjene Države
2 Kanada
3 Velika Britanija
4 Zapadna Nemačka
5 Italija
6 Portugalija
7 Belgija
8 Holandija
9 Luksemburg
10 Norveška
11 Island
12 Danska
13 Grčka
14 Turska

Baltic Sea

Caspian Sea

Black Sea

Mediterranean Sea

Yugoslavia

Source: Avramov, Smilja, *Postheroic War of the West Against Yugoslavia*, 1997, p. 110

Map 5:    The Expansion of the NATO to the East through the 'Partnership for Peace'

ŠIRENJE NATO-a NA ISTOK PREKO "PARTNERSTVA ZA MIR"

Country Members
of the
"Partnership
for Peace"

1 Švedska
2 Finska
3 Poljska
4 Češka Rep.
5 Slovačka
6 Mađarska
7 Rumunija
8 Bugarska
9 Albanija
10 Slovenija
11 Makedonija
12 Belorusija
13 Jermenija
14 Kazanstan
15 Kirgiston
16 Turkmenston
17 Azerbejdžan
18 Gruzija
19 Moldovija
20 Ukrajina
21 Litvanija
22 Letonija
23 Estonija
24 Irska

NATO
Countries

1 Sjedinjene Države
2 Kanada
3 Velika Britanija
4 Zapadna Nemacka
5 Italija
6 Portugalija
7 Belgija
8 Holandija
9 Luksemburg
10 Norveška
11 Island
12 Danska
13 Grčka
14 Turska

Source: Avramov, Smilja, Postheroic War of the West Against Yugoslavia, 1997, p. 111

key issues were raised with regard to NATO's treatment of Russia, who refused to be treated the same way along with all other countries demanding instead status of a Great Power, and of the former Eastern Warsaw bloc countries. Russia protested against the new current status of all Eastern Europe as a "buffer zone," a kind of "grey zone" instead of its previous (Cold War) important role of being "the bridge for connection between the West and the East," especially since Russia's new economic and political relations with these countries are of "vital interest."[73] By 1994, Russia finally joined NATO's 'Partnership for Peace' as its 21st member in spite of the disapproval of the Russian Parliament that saw it as 'a treason' since it gave Russia the demanded status of Great Power but without the right of veto or any power in decision-making process. This humiliating position was also strongly contested and condemned by many Russians, among them Gorbachev who stated that this plan of NATO expansion to the East "is short-sighted, leading to a new confrontation between the East and the West."[74]

As illustrated on Map 5, NATO with its 24 new country-members of the 'Partnership for Peace' now covers a huge Euro-Asian territory and is much closer to the borders of both Russia and China. We can see from these two maps (4 and 5) that NATO completely surrounded the territories of the former Yugoslavia, whose new successor countries are all, by now, either incorporated in this partnership or are under direct NATO's occupation. We can also see that these new states are on the 'oil route' that connects the East with the West, from the Caspian and Black Seas to both the Baltic and the Mediterranean Seas.

For this reason, the geopolitical and strategic importance of the former Yugoslavia's territories is still a key point of the Balkans' integration, or post-colonization (by agreement or by military force) into Western projects and plans. Also, it should be noted that by dismantling Yugoslavia (SFRY and FRY) both common goals of NATO/US and Germany are achieved: the Russians' access to all three Seas, the Black, the Mediterranean and the Baltic, is completely cut off, while Germany, as the American (now former) 'partner in leadership' finally dominates 'Middle Europe' by connecting the Baltic Sea through 'the Danube valley' (Serbia/Vojvodina) to the Black and Mediterranean Seas. Ironically, as Avramov points out in her concluding remarks, while Croatia celebrated its independence by singing 'Danke Deutchland', Germany celebrated its unification by singing the old hymn 'Deutchland, Deutchland über alles.' Accordingly, Avramov concludes her book entitled *Postheroic War of the West against Yugoslavia*—post-heroic because there is nothing heroic in the contemporary methods of modern war of sanctions based on international isolation or persecution of whole countries, punishing not only the whole nation (people) but also aiming at the destruction of the very state—with the statement that "one who had not learned from history becomes inevitably its victim."[75]

History also teaches us that political alliances and their geopolitical goals are not stable and permanent formations, they change through the time and sometimes yesterday's friends and allies become future enemies and warring parties. As Karl Polanyi[76] argued not long ago, the hundred years of peace in Europe (1815-1914), without precedent in European history, was possible due to many factors, of which, for my purposes, the most notable was the balance-of-power system that successfully prevented wars by changing alliances among the Great Powers at the time and, as well, by neutralizing the very causes of the war, particularly if small countries were involved in conflicts. The international disequilibrium of this balance was a prelude to both the Great War and the World War II. In our post Cold War times, the world is left with one victorious super power, the U.S., whose hegemony is not only at the heart of current conflicts but is also behind the destruction of old political alliances and the creation of new ones. This is particularly apparent now in the aftermath of the terrorist attack on the World Trade Centre. We are witnessing major geopolitical change that implies the breaking and the (re)making of the political and military coalitions. It is a matter of speculation to know or predict what the future will bring, however it is certain at this point that there is a rift in the Western and NATO alliance. While Germany, yesterday's U.S. partner in leadership, became an 'unfaithful' friend because of its refusal to follow the (new) Anglo-American coalition in the attack on Iraq in the Gulf War II, France similarly became an 'ungrateful' ally (not to mentioned U.S. 'disappointment' with its Canadian neighbour, a 'Northern brother' who also refused to join U.S. coalition against Iraq). In George W. Bush's vision of his New World Order, the twenty-first century is defined as the 'American Century' in which there is no alternative since Mr. Bush imposed a false dilemma on the whole world: "Either you are with us or you are against us." Not only did Bush alienate U.S. traditional allies with his unilateralist approach in re-arranging the map of the world, but also in a Huntingtonian way, he is indeed clashing with the Islamic civilization, besides clashing with the whole world and with the logical reasoning.

However, in his State of the Union speech given on the eve of the war against Iraq, George W. Bush stated that while "the technologies of war have changed, the risks and suffering of war have not" referring to eventual U.S. casualties since "the days of mourning always come" and for Bush, therefore, "no victory is free from sorrow."[77] As these casualties include in reality both innocent civilian victims and soldiers, and since this so-called 'collateral damage' is indeed inherent to modern war, one might only conclude that war itself is 'a politics of sorrow' and that now in the twenty-first century, and forever, the politics of sorrow of modern war entails the extermination of people.

In discussing the current "rivalry between America and 'Old Europe'," especially in terms of the competition between the U.S. dollar and the Euro, Chossudovsky accurately asserts that the world today is also divided along their respective currency zones of influence since "ultimately, control over national currency system is the basis upon which countries are colonized," and in this sense, "the war in Iraq pertains not only to control over oil reserves, but also the control over currency, money creation and credit."[78] He states further with regard to the Balkans that the U.S. and Germany have already divided the former Yugoslavia: "Germany has gained control over national currencies in Croatia, Bosnia and Kosovo where the Euro is King [while] the U.S. has established a permanent military presence in the region (i.e., the Bondsteel military base in Kosovo)."[79] Although the U.S. and the EU (led by Germany) financial interests are still struggling for the control of various national economies and currency systems, they apparently have agreed upon the division of their spheres of influence in the territories of the former Yugoslavia. This economic conquest of the Balkans is accompanied by military occupation making the post-colonization process complete. To paraphrase Parenti: the Balkans is once again Balkanized.

This continuous remaking of the borders or divisions in the Balkans is historically, and continues to be, primarily a product of external Balkanization, which in turn strongly encourages internal ethnic conflicts and wars. This is particularly true in the current crisis since the Western led International Community backed by NATO was and still is very active in redrawing the map, or the borders, of the former Yugoslavia. This fact is well illustrated by Map 6, meaningfully entitled by Samary "The International Community on Trial" showing Lord Owen's plan for his border-divisions of Bosnia (drawn together first with Vance in January of 1993 and then in August of the same year with Stoltenberg, all of them at that time appointed peace negotiators for Bosnia).

**Map 6:   The International Community on Trial**

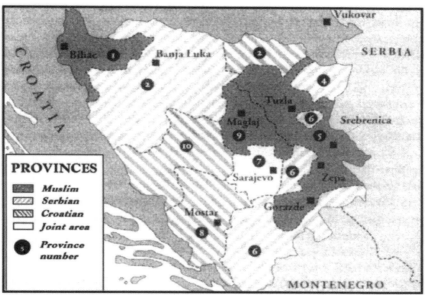

Vance-Owen Plan, January 1993.

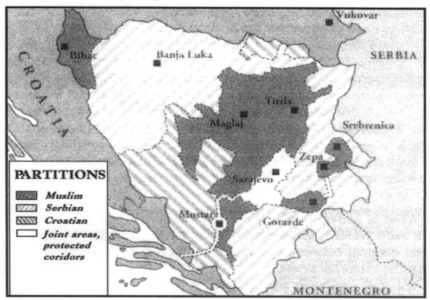

Owen-Stoltenberg Plan, August 1993.

Source: Samary, Catherine. *Yugoslavia Dismembered*, 1995, p. 117

I agree with Samary that the International Community should be held responsible and brought to trial for drawing such maps. The Dayton Peace Accord of 1995 imposed a similar division of Bosnia installing simultaneously a Western colonial administration and NATO's occupation, stripping Bosnia of any form of sovereignty. Finally, according to the neocolonial Bosnian Constitution, neither the High Representative, who is the final authority, nor the Governor of the Bosnian Central Bank can be a citizen of Bosnia or any other neighbouring Slavic state. Map 6 then, combined with the border-division of the Dayton agreement, explicitly demonstrates the current external Balkanization designed by the International Community, imposing new borders within Bosnia. Such redrawing of the contemporary borders of both Yugoslavia and Bosnia illustrate the direct Western led International interference as well as the continuation of the ancient 'Divide and Rule Schemes in the Balkans' as exemplify by the Map 3 (a, b, c, d). This external political reconfiguration of the Balkans is obviously still an ongoing process, especially since the armed conflicts spread to southern borders, inspiring Lord Owen in 2001 to call for further fragmentation of Yugoslavia by creating an independent state for Kosovo's Albanians, as well as by redrawing the boundaries of Bosnia along the lines he drafted in 1993.[80]

If we compare Maps 6 with Map 2 that shows the ethnic composition of the Yugoslav republics, we see that Bosnia was the most mixed region, which for this reason could not be homogenized without ethnic cleansing. Historically, all major border-divisions of the future Yugoslavia went through or around the territory of Bosnia, and in this regard, Map 2 illustrates the legacy of external Balkanization in both senses: as the inherited cultural diversity enhanced by further intermingling, as well as the potential for ethnic conflicts over historically disputed territories. One can also visualize by Maps 2 and 6 the emergence or the creation of 'new' national minorities whose status all three conflicting parties in Bosnia tried to avoid: the Serbs, Croats and Muslims. As we will see further in the next chapter, the transformation of the administrative borders into ethnic borders in historically and contemporary heterogeneous or 'mixed' regions of Yugoslavia, particularly with respect to the ethnic division of Bosnia, exemplifies the geographies of violence and of ethnic cleansing. As Hayden and Samary emphasize, the violence and ethnic cleansing occurred mainly in ethnically mixed regions of the new successor states since they were building homogenous nation-states in the heterogeneous territories of the former Yugoslavia.

The only legal force that could prevent or lately stop this 'purification' of the mixed regions of Yugoslavia was the Yugoslav People's Army (JNA), that was actually immobilized from the very beginning of the conflict for two main reasons: one external the other internal. Externally, the Yugoslav government was under extreme pressure from the International Community, especially from the EU and the U.S., to not use the JNA in any circumstances. Although the JNA was the fourth strongest military power in Europe, Yugoslavia was surrounded by NATO countries, and the consequences of the non-compliance could be even more catastrophic than the civil war itself. Internally, the Yugoslav Army had even less chances to act since it was paralyzed from the start, again for two basic reasons. The first is the fact that its very conception was grounded in the defense of the country from external enemies and never from internal, meaning that to fight against its own people was a completely foreign idea to the reasoning and to the mentality of its officers, not to mention the soldiers themselves. The second reason is the fact that the JNA was, since its emergence in World War II, a multinational Army composed of all Yugoslav nations and nationalities, being the main pillar of Tito's concept of "Brotherhood and Unity." When, on the eve of the war, the republican governments recalled their soldiers from the JNA, who then largely joined the newly created republican armies, the very *raison d'être* and the conception of the JNA was at stake and soon collapsed: it was no longer (so) multinational and its defense plan shifted towards internal affairs. However, with the Internationally/NATO enforced retreat of the JNA from Croatia and then Bosnia and more recently from Kosovo, the peoples of these regions were left at the mercy of domestic and foreign paramilitary formations and mercenaries, often mobilized from well known criminal circles or the underground world. Not surprising then that such bestial and bold crimes occurred. The fact that so many people were killed or displaced due to various *announced* schemas of ethnic purification of the country shows the irony of the war since the UN Peacekeepers, who by request of the West 'replaced' the JNA, were not able or willing to protect the diverse population of the former Yugoslavia.

## Summary

As we have seen in this chapter, nationalist conflicts and disputes over borders in Yugoslavia(s) are mainly outcomes of external Balkanization, or of the 'Divide and Rule' politics in the Balkans following 'Old and New World Orders.' The destiny of the Balkans was indeed too often shaped by powerful external, usually occupying, forces that left behind strong economic, political and cultural influences that became a part of the diverse ethno-cultural heritage of the future Yugoslavia. This multiethnic and multicultural legacy of the former Yugoslavia (Islam and Christianity or numerous ethnic minorities like Italians, Hungarians, Turks and so on) is thus primarily due to the 'Divide and Rule' politics of powerful empires, which at various points in history conquered the Balkans and divided the South Slavs. This external Balkanization, then, is at the core of the legacy of both contested histories and potential conflicts in the Balkans, since each nation or national minority may claim a disputed territory once belonging to them. That is, all of them might claim historical rights over conflicting regions. Although invading hordes, ambitious empires and their political and cultural divisions between East and West left the Balkan Peninsula with a legacy of potential conflicts and consequent massive migrations, socialist Yugoslavia surmounted ethnic nationalism and the unpleasant memories of the past by developing a remarkable sense of mutual respect and peaceful co-existence in such a multinational and multicultural country. External Balkanization indeed imposed on the former Yugoslavia a mixture of different cultural and religious traditions, including European Christianity, Slavic or Greek Orthodoxy and Islam.

These various cultures, historically and even more so in the contemporary period, intermingled and created a multiethnic and multicultural country, such as the socialist Yugoslavia was. But neither historically nor now can these cultural differences, which are primarily of a religious nature among the mono-ethnic South Slavs, be classified as a clash between civilizations. Instead, there were clashes between the economic and geopolitical interests of various Great Powers, clashes that usually ended in major wars. Although the territory of Yugoslavia, especially of Bosnia, is a crossroad of civilizations, there is rather a history of co-vivality instead of clashes between 'civilizations.' In the current conditions, the demise of the Berlin Wall and the Warsaw Pact was followed by the emergence of the New World Order and its rearranging of the economic and political map of the world. Multinational Yugoslavia with its distinct market socialism stood in the way of the victorious free market vision of the New World Order, enforced on a global scale by the imposition of the IMF and World

Bank's macroeconomic restructuring of the world. These structural adjustment reforms devastated more than one hundred Third World countries, including the former Soviet Union and Yugoslavia. Once again then, in the 1990s, the Yugoslav peoples were divided and turned against each other by both internal and external forces, or by domestic nationalists sponsored by the U.S. and Germany in accordance with the free market design of the New World Order for the Balkans. They were pushed to fight in absurd civil wars and to again die for the foreign interests of contemporary Emperors who in modern times play nuclear and other hi-tech war games. This now includes 'Star Wars' or the global satellite positioning system for missile guidance that enables so-called 'smart' bombs to destroy whole countries so effectively, contaminating them with known and unknown toxic agents for ages to come.

However, we have also seen that there is a long history of struggle by the South Slavs against foreign occupation as well as resistance to die in various imperialist wars fought in the Balkans. In closing, this fact of permanent resistance to colonization and the numerous wars fought in the twentieth century combined with the inherited legacy of cultural diversity is well illustrated by the popular song 'This is the Balkans' by the famous Yugoslav pop-rock star Bajaga:

*A country from a dream between the powerful forces of good and evil*
*.Here everyone can be a foe and a brother*
*Every 50 years a war breaks out*
*This country was created by warriors, poets and different Gods*
*This is the Balkans*
*A fragrant flower, warm but incomprehensible for all the world.* (My translation.)

In other words, in times of peace everyone is a brother while in war anyone can be a foe.

## NOTES

1. These Maps are from Mihailo Crnobrnja's The Yugoslav Drama. Montreal: McGill-Queen's University Press, 1994, Map 2: "The impact of empires on the future Yugoslavia," p. 18.

2. See more details about the history of Krajina in Radovan Samardzic (ed.) Istorija: Enciklopedijski Leksikon Mozaik Znanja (my translation: History. Encyclopedic Lexicon). Belgrade: Interpres, 1970, pp. 729, 730. For more details on Yugoslavia see Leo Gershoy (ed.) A Survey of European Civilization: Part One and Two. New York: Houghton Mifflin Company, 1969. See also Baudson, 1996; Crnobrnja, 1994; Djilas, 1996 and Samary, 1995.

3. As discussed above, all major world religions (Roman Catholic, Greek Orthodox and Islam) intersect the Yugoslav part of the Balkans, especially in Bosnia, where they were historically struggling for domination of these territories and peoples. See more about geographies of religions, in particular their conquest of the Balkans, in Refik Secibovic Uvod u opstu geografiju religije (my translation: Introduction to the General Geography of Religion). Novi Sad: Prometej, 1995.

4. Crnobrnja, 1994, op. cit., pp. 17, 18.

5. To my big surprise, one summer day in the new millennium while I was reading about the history of Yugoslavia in my apartment in Montreal, I heard a familiar sound of the fiddle and singing of very old South Slavic songs about their heroic fighting against the Ottoman occupation from which period this instrument similar to the violin and these popular songs date (Junacke Narodne Pjesme in Serbo-Croatian). When I looked through my window I saw the fiddler surrounded by a group of people from the former Yugoslavia singing and laughing together. I recognized the majority of them since they were mostly my neighbours or their friends, composed, not surprisingly, of Croats, Serbs, Bosnian Muslims and Montenegrins.

6. Andric's most internationally known book is The Bridge on the Drina (in original version Na Drini Cuprija) even though 'danak u krvi' is the theme of all his deeds dealing with this historic period. Another great Bosnian writer who authentically described the times of Turkish rule is Mesa Selimovic, notably in his books Dervis i Smrt and Tvrdava.

7. See History: Encyclopedic Lexicon, op. cit., p. 61.

8. Ivo Andric. "Pismo iz 1920" in Jevrejske Price (my translation: The Jewish Stories). Belgrade: Narodna Knjiga, 1991. This story is based on the letter of Andric's childhood friend, Dr. Maks Levenfeld (phonetically written) who was, in fact, an atheist of Jewish origins, whose family was long ago converted to Christianity. Levenfeld's mother was born in Italy (Trieste), a daughter of an Italian Baroness and an Austrian Navy Officer who was a descendent of French emigrants. Andric met his friend after the Great War at the train station where both were waiting for a train to leave Bosnia: Andric was going to Belgrade and his friend to Trieste. The doctor was planning to leave Europe forever and resettle somewhere in Latin America, like Argentina or Bolivia, because he was profoundly disgusted by the war and especially by the emergent hatreds in Bosnia. However, in his letter to Andric, he states that he is not naïve and he knows that hatreds exist everywhere in the world, particularly true for Europe after World War I. The doctor, in this sense, accurately predicted the future problems of the Yugoslav state(s): the latent national and religious ha-

treds. He acknowledges, nevertheless, his belief that the time of much needed deep social and spiritual change in Bosnia will come, even though the concept of so-called integral Yugoslavism did not seem to be an appropriate path at that time. While I agree with the doctor's analysis of the origins of hatred in Bosnia, which is almost identical with religious differences and which should be analyzed, diagnosed and cured as any other disease, I stress that this kind of irrational and murderous hatred is typical for war conditions, especially for civil wars, what World War I was for Yugoslav peoples.

9. Since the very beginning, Baudson was actively involved in the Yugoslav crisis as a part of the French diplomatic team. Besides Le Nouvel Ordre Mondial et la Yugoslavie (1996), he also published Europe of Lunatics (1993) and Europe of Apatrides (1994).

10. Gerard Baudson. Le Nouvel Ordre Mondial et la Yugoslavie. Paris: Gil Wern Editions, 1996, in translated Yugoslav edition Novi Svetski Poredak I Jugoslavija. Belgrade: Ing-Pro, 1996. All translations from Serbo-Croatian language are mine, p. 104.

11. Ibid., p. 105.

12. History: Encyclopaedic Lexicon, op. cit., p. 357.

13. Statistics according to Baudson, op. cit., p. 109.

14. Including Zimbabwe and some of those who George Bush Junior calls indiscriminately the 'Axis of Evil.'

15. Noam Chomsky. World Orders: Old and New. New York: Columbia University Press, 1994, p. 4.

16. Ibid., p. 7.

17. Ibid.

18. Ibid. Chomsky is referring and citing Thomas Friedman, chief diplomatic correspondent of New York Times, "Week in Review" June 2, 1992.

19. For more detailed explanation about the dismantling of Yugoslavia due to the 'New World Order' and/or International Intervention, in particular the leading role of Germany and the U.S., see more in-depth analyses in Avramov (1997), Baudson (1996), Chossudovsky (1996, 1997), Crnobrnja (1994), Hatchett Ronald and Sir Alfred Sherman et al. (1998), Parenti (2000) and Samary (1995).

20. See Michel Chossudovsky. The Globalization of Poverty: Impacts of IMF and World Bank Reforms. London and New Jersey: Zed Books, 1997, pp. 225-263.

21. Ibid., p. 244, Chossudovsky is citing Sean Gervasi "Germany, U.S. and the Yugoslav Crisis" in Covert Action Quarterly. No. 43, Winter 1992-1993, p. 42.

22. Ibid. Chossudovsky is citing Sean Gervasi, Ibid.

23. Ibid., p. 245.

24. Michel Chossudovsky. "Dismantling Yugoslavia Colonizing Bosnia" in Covert Action Quarterly. No. 56, Spring 1996, p. 33.

25. Ibid., p. 37.

26. Ibid., p. 32.

27. Ibid. Chossudovsky is referring to and citing Dayton Peace Accords, December 1995, respectively, "Agreement on High Representative," Articles I and II; "Agreement on Gen-

eral Framework," Article VII; "Agreement on Public Corporations," Article I, my emphasis.

28. Ibid., p. 33. See footnote 11 for statistics taken from the World Bank's "World Development Report 1991, Statistical Annex, Tables 1 and 2."

29. Michael Parenti. "The Rational Destruction of Yugoslavia" in Michael Parenti's Political Archive at http://www.michaelparenti.org/yugoslavia.html, 2000, accessed 24 May 2001.

30. Ibid.

31. Catherine Samary. Yugoslavia Dismembered. Translated from French by Peter Drucker. New York: Monthly Review Press, 1995, pp. 11, 14, my emphasis.

32. Baudson, 1996, op. cit., p. 83.

33. Crnobrnja, 1994, op. cit., p. 8.

34. Ibid.

35. Ibid., p. 9.

36. Ibid., p. 6.

37. Ibid., p. 10.

38. Ibid., p. 7.

39. Ibid., p. 8.

40. Ibid. p. 10.

41. Baudson, op. cit., p. 157, my emphasis and translation.

42. Ibid., p. 135, my translation. The citation is originally from an interview with Baudson for Quotidien de Paris, July 30, 1993.

43. Cited in Pierre Marie Gallois's 'Foreword' in Baudson's book Le Nouvel Ordre Mondial et la Yugoslavie, op. cit., p. 11.

44. Ibid., p. 210, my translation.

45. Robert Hayden. "Imagined Communities and Real Victims: Self-determination and Ethnic Cleansing in Yugoslavia." American Ethnologist. Vol. 23 (4). 1996, p. 795, see particularly Table 1 and 2.

46. See Le Devoir, Montreal, March 23/24, 1996.

47. See The Globe and Mail, "World in Brief" February 18, 19, 2003; also in National Post, February 19, 2003, p. A 13.

48. CBC News, "The National," July 14, 2003. See also an article written by Michael Snider "Firefight at the Medak Pocket" in Maclean's Magazine, Canada, September 2, 2002, and a book written by Scott Taylor and Brian Nolan Tested Mettle: Canada's Peacekeepers at War. Ottawa: Esprit de Corps Books. 1998.

49. Soldiers complained how upon their return to Canada, nobody in the country wanted to talk or listen about what happened there and what they went through. For political reasons, no publicity was given to this event, as it had simply never happened.

50. Fyodor Dostoyevsky. The Brothers Karamazov: A Novel in Four Parts With Epilogue. Translated from the Russian by Richard Pevear and Larissa Volokhonsky. New York: Vintage Books, 1991, p. 305.

51. Hannah Arendt. The Origins of Totalitarianism. New York: A Harvest/ HBJ Book. 1973 (1948), p. 442.

52. Ibid.

53. Sani Rifati. "The Roma and 'Humanitarian' Ethnic Cleansing in Kosovo" in Dissident Voice, October 13, 2002, accessed on Internet October 17, 2002 at http://www.dissident voice.org/Articles/Rifati_Kosovo.htm. Link also available at www.globalresearch.ca.

54. About the 'humanitarian or philanthropic' role of George Soros see the excellent article written by Heather Cottin "George Soros: Imperial Wizard" in Covert Action Quarterly, Number 74, Fall 2002, available at www.canadiandimension.mb.ca/frame.htm, accessed September 13, 2003. The author explains that Soros nurtured left anti-socialism movements across the former Communist countries including socialist Yugoslavia. Soros was founder of the 'Open Society Fund' soon renamed 'Open Society Institute', which was instrumental in funding various social nongovernmental movements throughout the former Yugoslavia. Soros also financed Belgrade based radio station 'B-92' and subsequent movement "Otpor" ('The Resistance') giving them "suitcases of money" to topple Milosevic's government of Yugoslavia in the coup of October 5, 2000. In sharing the spoils of the NATO's war against Yugoslavia, Soros used his connections with "Bernard Kouchner, chief of the UN Interim Administration in Kosovo (UNMIK)...to acquire the most profitable mining complex in the Balkans...the Trepca mines...[which] Kouchner closed for 'health reasons' [and] Soros invested $150 million in an effort to gain control of Trepca's gold, silver, lead, zinc and cadmium, which make the property worth $5 billion." Ironically, as Cottin notes, while Kouchner justified the closure of Trepca by stating that pollution from this Kosovo's mining complex "was raising lead levels in the environment...he cheered when the 1999 NATO bombing of Yugoslavia rained depleted uranium on the country and released more than 100,000 tons of carcinogens into the air, water and soil."

55. Rifati, op. cit.

56. Parenti, op. cit.

57. Ibid.

58. Like Baudson (1996), Chossudovsky (1996, 1997), Parenti (2000), Samary (1995), et al.

59. Samuel Huntington. "The Clash of Civilizations" in Foreign Affairs. New York: Council on Foreign Relations. Volume 72, Number 3, Summer 1993, pp. 37, 38.

60. Smilja Avramov. Postherojski Rat Zapada Protiv Yugoslavije (my translation: Postheroic War of the West Against Yugoslavia). Belgrade: Idi, Veternik, 1997, p. 100, my translation. Retired Professor Dr. Smilja Avramov taught International Relations and International Law at the University of Law in Belgrade.

61. Ronald Hatchett. "Foreword" in America's Intervention in the Balkans: A Collection of Papers Presented at the Lord Byron Foundation's Third Annual Conference Devoted to U. S. Policy in Southeast Europe. London: The Lord Byron Foundation for Balkan Studies in cooperation with Chronicles: A Magazine of American Culture, 1998, p. 5.

62. Ibid. p. 6.

63. While Franjo Tudman, Croatian President at the time, wrote a similar book entitled Bespuca in which among other things he diminishes the impact and numbers of victims of

genocide in World War II, his Serbian counterpart Slobodan Milosevic did not write anything resembling such historic manipulation and chauvinism. Yet Milosevic was definitely
a leader in Communist demagogy, which was obvious in all of his speeches.

64. Sir Alfred Sherman. "Introduction: What is Good for America..." in America's Interven-
    tion in the Balkans: A Collection of Papers Presented at the Lord Byron Foundation's
    Third Annual Conference Devoted to U. S. Policy in Southeast Europe. London: The
    Lord Byron Foundation for Balkan Studies in cooperation with Chronicles: A Magazine
    of American Culture, 1998, p. 10.

65. Hatchett, op. cit., p. 6.

66. Ibid., pp. 6,7.

67. Ibid., pp. 7, 8.

68. Avramov, op. cit., p. 46, my translation. She is referring to George Bush's Speech "To-
    ward a New World Order: Address before a joint session of Congress," Washington, DC,
    September 11, 1990. U.S. Department of State Dispatch, September 17, 1990, pp. 91-92.

69. "Toward a New World Order." A transcript of former President George Herbert Walker
    Bush's address to a joint session of Congress and the nation. From the National Archives,
    September 11, 1990. http://www.sweetliberty.org/issues/war/bushsr.htm, accessed July
    30, 2003.

70. Avramov, op. cit., p. 82.

71. Ibid., p. 96.

72. Ibid., p. 95.

73. Ibid., p. 96.

74. Ibid., p. 97.

75. Ibid., p. 448.

76. Karl Polanyi. The Great Transformation: The Political and Economic Origins of Our
    Time. Boston: Beacon Press, 2001 (1944). Polanyi's contribution to modern thought and
    the revived actuality of his work is primary based upon his argument that the liberal idea
    of self-regulating market was a pure utopia from the start. The intimate relationship be-
    tween the politics and economics is central to his historic analysis, particularly of the nine-
    teenth century Europe that was marked by four institutions: the balance-of-power system,
    the international gold standard, the self-regulating market and the liberal state. As well,
    he emphasized the new role of emerged haute finance that stood behind the international
    banking system and functioned "as the main link between the political and the economic
    organization of the world," p. 10.

77. National Post, Montreal, January 29, 2003, p. A 13.

78. Michel Chossudovsky. "Euro versus Dollar: Rivalry Between America and 'Old Europe' "
    in Global Outlook, Number 5, Summer/Fall 2003, p. 30.

79. Ibid.

80. See Paul Taylor "Ethnic crisis revives Balkan map debate" in The Globe and Mail, March
    17, 2001, p. A 20.

# Chapter Four
# Ethnic Cleansing in Multinational Yugoslavia

We have seen that the peoples of Yugoslavia have been ruled by various imperialistic powers across history. For this reason, their history embraces a legacy of continuous resistance and struggle against foreign occupation. As such, the civil wars in the twentieth century are primary due to external Balkanization and its division of the South Slavs. This chapter illustrates that while Yugoslavia, in particular Bosnia, was a 'mixture' of various nations and cultures, their inhabitants additionally 'mixed' among themselves. Not surprisingly, they were particularly intermingling during the twentieth century in spite of the ethnic nationalism and civil wars. This fact is also obvious in the findings of my preliminary survey, which shows that the vast majority of the respondents, regardless of whether their immediate family is 'mixed or pure,' have a 'mixed' national family background for the past several generations, spanning throughout the twentieth century. In fact, while only one nuclear family is nationally 'pure' and has 'pure' family origins, another family stated that while their nuclear family is 'pure' in a national sense, their relatives are 'mixed,' thus having a multinational background.

My goal in this chapter is to demonstrate that the former Yugoslavia was indeed 'Europe in miniature' in terms of its richness of nationalities, religions and customs. It was probably the most heterogeneous European country with well-pronounced and protected rights of numerous national minorities. As various Yugoslav nations and national minorities were 'mixing' among themselves, particularly in Bosnia, it is practically impossible to 'ethnically purify' such historically mixed regions. To draw ethnic border-divisions, particularly in Yugoslavia's mixed regions, meant to divide families and to commit crimes. In addition to an analysis of the geographies of ethnic cleansing and the national identities of refugees from Bosnia and Yugoslavia, with particular attention to

the respondents, I also examine the multinational popular and political resistance to the absurdity of ethnic divisions and civil-fraternal war. In this chapter, therefore, I provide empirical support for my claim that Yugoslavia was not an artificially imagined community, but rather a viable multinational state whose citizens, on the eve of the war, protested and demonstrated their disagreement and fear of the future. This popular and political resistance is also examined in my analysis of two episodes of the popular television comedy show, 'Top List of Surrealists,' performed by Bosnian artists from Sarajevo. We will finally see who 'these Yugoslavs, Bosnians and 'Eskimos' are and what happened to them in terms of their civil, social and human rights, detailed in the last chapter. While this chapter elaborates my claim that the ethnic division of the country and consequent civil war were imposed on its citizens by internal and external forces, the final chapter deals with the subsequent massive displacement of the Yugoslav population from a historical perspective on the phenomenon of statelessness.

## The 'Purification' of Heterogeneous Territories

To further illustrate the absurdity of the war and the geography of the crimes, the following fable provides the best portrayal of the former Yugoslavia, which was, as Crnobrnja reminds us, "a country of diversity" that had "seven neighbours, six republics, five nations, four languages, three religions, two scripts, and one goal: to live in brotherhood and unity."[1] The following short description of the seven neighbours of Yugoslavia (from the North to the South) and their historic relations offers a valuable background to better understand the broader international setting, the national minority question, the complexity of the Yugoslav state and its cultural diversity.

According to Crnobrnja, *Italy*, historically acted as an invading power in Yugoslavia, from the times of Venice to fascist Italy, thereby leaving a strong cultural impact, especially along the coast of the Adriatic Sea. To protect its interests, Italy was largely against the idea of the very existence of Yugoslavia as a unified state. The most Northern neighbours, *Austria and Hungary*, both separately and together as the Dual Monarchy ruled over Slovenia, Croatia, Vojvodina, and for a very short time Bosnia. They also left powerful cultural traces in these regions, which are notably the most economically developed parts of the former Yugoslavia. Like Italy, they both disliked and resisted the creation of Yugoslavia. Not to mention that the confrontation between the Austro-Hungarian Empire and Serbia over Bosnia led to World War I. On the other hand, there emerged no historic disputes with Romania up to this day.

*Bulgaria* shares borders with both Serbia and Macedonia. As previously explained, Macedonia was the central reason for the confrontation between Serbia and Bulgaria resulting in the second Balkan War. Aside from this conflict, relations with this Eastern neighbour were and still are peaceful and respectful, without any major issues. The Southern neighbour, Greece, is a traditional ally of Serbia, historically fighting side by side against Bulgarians, Turks, and Albanians. I agree with Crnobrnja that "the question of Macedonia" could again, like in the past, "be[come] a reason for new alliances and confrontations among the neighbouring countries."[2] Crnobrnja also states that the relation with the seventh neighbour, *Albania*, except for a short period after World War II, was "very tense," partially because of "the penetration of Albanian population into traditionally South Slav territories, partly because of claims for a Greater Albania reminiscent of the one that was formed as a puppet state during the latter years of the Ottoman Empire."[3]

A further brief overview of relevant socio-economic data from the six republics of Yugoslavia based on a controversial Census held on the eve of the war in April of 1991 will provide valuable insights into the national and ethnocultural heterogeneity of the republics. *Bosnia and Herzegovina* "had around 4,365,000 inhabitants" of whom almost "44 percent declared themselves Muslims, 31.5 percent Serbs, and just over 17 percent Croats. The rest belonged to other nationalities, including 5.5 percent declared Yugoslavs."[4] Not only was Bosnia called "little Yugoslavia" because of its pronounced ethnocultural diversity, but it was also the republic with the highest rate of mixed marriages, with 16 percent of children from mixed marriages.[5] For this very reason, Crnobrnja rightly asserts that the new divisions, or current Balkanization, of Bosnia "cut not only through territories but also through families."[6] In economic terms, Bosnia belonged to the group of less developed republics, with a GNP per capita between 70 to 80 percent of the Yugoslav average. *Croatia* had 4,760,000 inhabitants, of whom 78 percent were Croats, around 12 percent were Serbs, 2.2 were Yugoslavs and about 1 percent were Muslims. Additionally, there were about 110,000 Croats living in Serbia, mainly in the autonomous province of Vojvodina, and 756,000 living in Bosnia, concentrated mostly in the southern region of Herzegovina, or mixed with other Bosnians. Croatia's GNP per capita was about 25 to 35 percent greater than the Yugoslav average.[7] *Macedonia* had just over 2 million inhabitants: 65 percent of Macedonians, 21 percent (over 400,000) of ethnic Albanians, 4.8 percent of Turks, 2.7 percent of Roma people and 2.2 percent of Serbs. Macedonia was the poorest republic and, like Bosnia and

Montenegro, received financial aid for development from the richest republics, that is, from Slovenia, Croatia and Serbia.[8]

Furthermore, according to Crnobrnja, *Montenegro* had "just over 600,000 people," of which "62 percent declared themselves Montenegrins, 15 percent Muslims, 9.5 percent Serbs, 6.6 percent ethnic Albanians, and 4.5 percent Yugoslavs."[9] It was also one of the under-developed republics with a GNP per capita around 80 percent of the Yugoslav average. Crnobrnja notes that Slovenia was the so-called "Alpine state," with a population of approximately 2 million. It was the most ethnically homogeneous republic with more than 90 percent Slovenes.[10] Slovenia was the most developed and rich republic, with a GNP per capita about 60 percent higher than the Yugoslav average. Crnobrnja asserts that Slovenia was divided for centuries mostly between "German and Austrian rulers," and that socialist Yugoslavia was often "involved in disputes about the ethnic rights of Slovenes in both Italy and Austria."[11] Finally, the sixth republic, Serbia was the largest republic with regard to its size and population. Serbia had about 9,800,000 people, of which there were "65.8 percent Serbs, 17.2 percent Albanians, 3.5 percent Hungarians, 3.2 percent Yugoslavs, 2.4 percent Muslims, 1.4 percent Montenegrins, and 1.1 percent Croats."[12] Although Serbia's GNP per capita "was somewhat below the Yugoslav average (93-95 percent)," it was nevertheless "among the better-developed republics," and therefore, it contributed aid to the less developed republics.[13] Like Baudson, Hayden and Samary, Crnobrnja also emphasizes that:

> A crucial issue in both the construction and the destruction of Yugoslavia has been the fact that many Serbs live outside Serbia. The total number of people declaring themselves Serbs in 1991 was just under 8.5 million. Of that number 6.4 million live in Serbia, 1.4 million in Bosnia and Herzegovina, 580,000 in Croatia, 57,000 in Montenegro, and 44,000 in Macedonia.[14]

As I have already discussed, along with the Croats, Macedonians, Montenegrins, Slovenes and Serbs, the sixth nation of Yugoslavia were the Muslims that together with the popular Communist slogan of 'brotherhood and unity' were both Tito's inventions for the purpose of the preservation of national tranquillity. The seventh nation consisted of the 'Yugoslavs' who were, in fact, both a nation and a national minority in their own country. Also, Crnobrnja rightly points out that instead of four languages as the above fable states, there were in fact three since Serbo-Croatian and Croatian or Serbian language are almost identical. The other two are Macedonian and Slovenian, which are clearly distinct languages. As we have also seen, the three major religions are Roman Catholic, Greek Orthodox and Islam. The two scripts are Cyrillic and Latin, both in official use. In terms of their usage, the Yugoslav population was split in half with regard to both scripts. However, gradually, the Latin script prevailed as the former Yugoslavia was more oriented towards the West than the East.[15]

Similarly to this description, the aforementioned French economist, Catherine Samary, emphasizes that Yugoslavia was a multinational and multicultural country with a pronounced religious and linguistic diversity that she calls "The Mosaic of People."[16] In addition to Map 2, which shows the multi-ethnic and multicultural composition of the former Yugoslavia, we can further visualize this national and cultural diversity in Table 1, which juxtaposes the Census data from 1981 and 1991.

**Table 1:    Ethnic Composition of Yugoslavia according to the 1981 and 1991 Census**

|  | 1981 Census in % | 1991 Census in % |
|---|---|---|
| "Peoples" or Nations |  |  |
| Serbs | 36.3 | 36.2 |
| Croats | 19.7 | 19.6 |
| Muslims | 8.9 | 9.8 |
| Slovenes | 7.8 | 7.3 |
| Macedonians | 5.9 | 5.6 |
| Montenegrins | 2.5 | 2.2 |
| "Minorities" |  |  |
| Albanians | 7.7 | 9.1 |
| Hungarians | 1.8 | 1.4 |
| Roma (Gypsies) | 0.7 | N/A less than 1 |
| "Undetermineds" |  |  |
| 'Yugoslavs' | 5.7 | 2.9 |
| "Others" | 3.0 | 5.9 |
| TOTAL POPULATION IN NUMBERS | 100% 22,424,000 | 100% 23,529,000 |

Source: Catherine Samary, 1995, pp. 15, 19. See also Crnobrnja (1994) and Hayden.

To begin with, I need to point out that Samary's data from 1981 in her table misses the last category of 'Others.'[17] As her sum total for 1981 is only 97%, I assumed that the missing 3% belongs to the category of 'others,' and therefore, I added it to my Table 1. Moreover, while Samary's data for 1991 includes 5.9% of 'Others,' it excludes national minorities with less than 1% of the population, which means that Roma people are excluded.[18] As Samary did not specify who belongs to the category 'Others,' I assume that it includes other minorities, undetermined and unspecified others, for example 'Eskimos.' In the dedication page of her book, Samary remarkably describes the popular and political resistance in Yugoslavia, and she also conceptualizes the term 'Eskimo' by devoting the book to,

> All the men and women who resist, to my friends—Serbs, Croats, Slovenes, Gypsies, Montenegrins, Macedonians, Muslims, Albanians, Jews—Bosnians, Yugoslavs, 'Eskimos'...[that is] many former Yugoslavs who reject national divisions have taken to calling themselves 'Eskimos,' even on census forms [in 1991], instead of Serb, Croat, Muslim, etc. The term is meant in an entirely positive sense.

Although Table 1 shows that the highest increase of a single nationality occurred among Albanians, from 7.7% in 1981 to 9.1% in 1991 (due to the highest birth rate in Yugoslavia), there is another significant change that is even more important for the purposes of this book. Indeed, we can see that while the percentage of the 'Others' *increased*, from 3.0% in 1981 to 5.9% in 1991, in contrast, the percentage of people who declared themselves 'Yugoslavs' *decreased*, from 5.7% in 1981 to 2.9% in 1991. This phenomenon is well explained by Crnobrnja, Hayden and Samary. While I have already discussed the issue of the national identity of the 'Yugoslavs' in previous chapters, I want to return to the rather bizarre dispute that occurred—whether 'Yugoslavs' are, or could be, a nation. As Crnobrnja points out, the number of declared Yugoslavs ranged in various post World War II Censuses from 3% to 6.2% of the total population of Yugoslavia, indicating that they were at least "a well-established 'national minority' in their own state."[19] According to the last Census in 1991, Crnobrnja states that more than half a million people, or 2.9% in the above Table 1, were nationally "undecided," that is, they were 'Yugoslavs'. As Samary points out, in the Census of 1981 there were 1.2 million of Yugoslavs, or 5.7 as shown in Table 1.[20] According to Samary, this statistical confusion or discrepancy between the categories of 'Yugoslavs,' 'others' and 'undetermineds' is due to the fact that,

For many years, people could not call themselves 'Yugoslav' in the census. This word referred to the citizenship (affiliation with the Yugoslav state) that everyone shared, but not to a 'nationality' (in the ethnic-cultural sense) that any one person could choose. Rejection of the 'unitary' character of the first (pre-World War II) Yugoslavia, which attempted to impose a Yugoslav nationality on everyone, contributed to a suspicion of any cultural or 'ethnic' 'Yugoslavism,' which was seen as a threat to particular identities. But people could tell the census-taker that they were 'undetermined,' which is what more than 1.2 million 'Yugoslavs' did in 1981: 7.9 percent in Bosnia, 8.2 percent in Croatia, 0.7 percent in Macedonia, 5.3 percent in Montenegro, 4.7 percent in Serbia—but 8.2 percent in Vojvodina and 0 percent in Kosovo—and 1.3 percent in Slovenia.[21]

Indeed, as we saw in the second chapter, centrifugal and centripetal forces have historically interacted in Yugoslavia. As both Djilas and Crnobrnja maintain, while the former centrifugal tendencies were rooted in its many nations, different languages and religions, the latter centripetal forces emphasized the common South Slav ethnic origin of the majority of the population as the basis for pronounced cultural and linguistic similarities. Also, we have seen that the development of the Yugoslav idea and the emergence of 'Yugoslavism' has a very long history. In order to properly understand Samary's statement about 'Yugoslavism,' we should also recall that the Yugoslav idea and the national question embraced different types of 'Yugoslavism,' including the 'new' one that emerged in the 1950s. I argue that the relatively small percentage of declared Yugoslavs in the Census of 1981 is, above all, due to the development of the 'supranationality' of the 'new Yugoslavism,' as well as the fact that multinational Yugoslavia was a republic, thus, a political community of the working people, or citizens, and of the nations. Therefore, people were simultaneously both Yugoslavs and Croats, Serbs and so on, whereby the former referred to citizenship and the latter to ethnicity or nationality. As mentioned, people who officially declared themselves 'Yugoslavs' might well be considered the seventh Yugoslav nation, even though they were only partially recognized. While they existed as a statistical category, they were not recognized as a nation. However, we will see further on that mixed marriages and the number of declared Yugoslavs were very likely to increase had the collapse of Yugoslavia not happened.

The decrease of Yugoslavs from 5.7% in 1981 to 2.9% in 1991 was, according to Hayden, due to the fact that many people were scared to lose their jobs or even property if they declared themselves as Yugoslavs "in the chauvinist political climate then dominant."[22] Similar to Samary, Hayden maintains that many people who declared themselves Yugoslavs in the 1981 Census had to declare themselves Serbs, Croats, Muslims, etc., in 1991 due to a chauvinist atmosphere and, as mentioned, a politics of fear. This significant change between the categories 'undetermineds-Yugoslavs' and 'others,' from 1981 to 1991, which demonstrates a decrease of 'Yugoslavs' by almost half, can be also explained by the increase in the category 'others'. Indeed, many people, particularly in the ethnically heterogeneous regions like 'mixed' Bosnia, preferred to declare themselves 'others' rather than Serbs, Croats or Muslims. In this regard, Hayden, like Samary, states that "some respondents to the census [of 1991] registered a protest against the whole process by listing themselves as *Eskimos, Bantus, American Indians, Citroens, light bulbs, and refrigerators—among other fanciful categories.*"[23]

This important variation between the categories 'Yugoslavs' and 'Others' from 1981 to 1991 exemplifies both the nonsense of ethnic nationalism and the absurdity of the civil war in such a multinational and multicultural country as was Yugoslavia. More importantly, if we sum up both categories, there is approximately 9% (8.7% in 1981 and 8.8% in 1991) of the total population of Yugoslavia that accounts for *more than 2 million* people who were nationally 'undecided/Yugoslavs' or 'Others/Eskimos'! These people, combined with 'mixed' families and their children, if not already included in these categories, in addition to the 'old' national minorities, such as the Jewish and Roma peoples, and the newly created minorities, such as Serbs, Croats and Muslims in Bosnia, constituted the vast majority, if not all, of the civilian victims of all forms of ethnic cleansing. In my account, ethnic cleansing encompasses not only *all* the committed atrocities, but also the massive displacement of people or refugees, whose forced migration was enhanced by the bureaucratic ethnic cleansing or constitutional nationalism, and the new phenomenon of 'humanitarian ethnic cleansing,' as is the case in Kosovo regarding Roma people (known also as Gypsies or Cincars in Yugoslavia) and other national minorities who still live there, aside from the massive expulsion of Serbs.

As Bosnia is the focus of this book, it is important to note again that it was the only republic without a majority ethnic group, while all of the other republics had one majority nation. In the 1991 Census, Bosnia had over four million people, of whom 44% declared themselves Muslims, 31.5% Serbs, 17% Croats, 5.5% Yugoslavs, while the rest belonged to other national minorities. Bosnia also had the highest rate of mixed marriages, notably, 16% of children were from mixed marriages. The current division of Bosnia that emerged due to both external and internal Balkanization, cut not only through territories but also families, since ethnic borders often went through bedrooms. As Bosnia was such an ethnically diversified region, it does not come as a big surprise that ethnic cleansing was so systematic and brutal. There is also no mystery as to why the refugee figures were particularly large in this republic. The demographic structure of Bosnia (and of other mixed regions) has since completely changed: more than half of Bosnia's prewar population is displaced internally or abroad. Although refugee figures are discussed in the next chapter, it is noteworthy to mention that the highest concentration of Bosnian refugees in a single state are to be found, according to UNHCR statistics, in both Germany and Milosevic's Yugoslavia, as each of them received an equal number of 330.000 persons.[24]

For all of these reasons, I argue that the former Yugoslavia was not 'an artificial' country, which, as such, was bound to be dismembered sooner or later. The geographies of violence in the region demonstrated the 'purification of the Balkans,' that is, the underlying agenda of building ethnically 'pure' Nation-States in heterogeneous territories. Hayden and Samary, among others, offer a more complex and critical point of view than the 'good and bad guys' version usually presented by Western media and politicians. This contrary picture is well depicted by Samary in her introductory statement about ethnic cleansing in the former Yugoslavia: "First minority communities are expelled. Then children of mixed marriages are attacked, and all the 'bad Serbs,' 'bad Croats,' and 'bad Muslims': i.e., everyone who tries to elude the tightening net that hinders any expression of diversity of thought, interest, identity, or political choice."[25] Similar to Samary and Baudson, Hayden emphasizes in his analysis of the destruction of Yugoslavia that:

> The logic of 'national self-determination' in Yugoslavia not only legitimates homogenization of the population but has also made that process so logical as to be irresistible. The course of the war has followed this logic of establishing the nation-state by eliminating minorities. What can be done bureaucratically by a majoritarian regime in a state with a numerically overwhelming majority, however, must be accomplished in other ways if the majority is not secure in its rule—specifically, military conquest and subsequent expulsion of the unwanted population.[26]

Hayden rightly argues that the geography of violence in the former Yugoslavia is a crucial issue, because the wars occurred almost entirely within 'mixed' regions where various peoples of Yugoslavia were also most intermingled. Indeed,
the victims of ethnic cleansing were mostly from the mixed territories of Yugoslavia, such as Krajina in Croatia, all of Bosnia, and more recently, Kosovo and
Macedonia, both having mixed populations and regions. Like many authors
who argue against the primordialist explanation and media representation of ancient ethnic hatreds as the deep-seated cause of violent ethnic nationalism and
civil wars, Hayden claims that:

> The extraordinary violence that has shattered these places was not the fury
> of nationalist passions long repressed by communism, as many journalists
> and politicians would have it. I argue instead that the wars have been about
> the forced unmixing of peoples whose continuing coexistence was counter to
> the political ideologies that won the free elections of 1990. Thus extreme na-
> tionalism in the former Yugoslavia has not been only a matter of imagining
> allegedly 'primordial' communities, but rather of making existing heteroge-
> neous ones unimaginable.[27]

Hayden's analysis of the various constitutions of the successor states of the former Yugoslavia shows that they 'legitimized' ethnic cleansing, which thus includes constitutional or 'bureaucratic ethnic cleansing.' In other words, these
new constitutions aimed to construct homogeneous nation-states in heterogeneous territories. For Hayden, such a policy may be achieved through forced assimilation or expulsion, as well as through border revision. In his words: "I
consider 'bureaucratic ethnic cleansing' as well as direct violence, recognizing
both as consequences of the same logic in different social settings."[28] Hayden
maintains that the constitutions of the successor states are a combination of
"easy naturalization of nonresidents," for example of emigrants, with the
"denaturalization" of residents or 'new' national minority groups, such as Serbs
in Croatia.[29] It is clear then why the conflicting Yugoslav nations sought to
avoid the national minority status. As previously discussed, the disintegration of
Yugoslavia and the outbreak of the war were avoidable and, as such, were not a
consequence of religious, ethnic, cultural or economic differences. Crnobrnja
emphasizes that ethnic cleansing was not caused by "'age-old animosities' between ethnic groups," but rather "the break-up of Yugoslavia, the wars, and ethnic cleansing were a consequence of deliberate nationalist policies, seen as
measures of 'statecraft' " and therefore "the war was about state borders, and was

a direct consequence of the politics of intransigence."[30] Like Crnobrnja and Baudson, who argue that the main cause of war was the incompatibility between the administrative borders of Yugoslav republics with 'invisible' ethnic borders, Hayden rightly states that,

> The separate nationalist political movements were justified on the grounds of 'self-determination'...A statement in the first line of the 1974 Yugoslav Constitution about 'the right of every nation to self-determination, including the right to secession' referred, not to populations or citizens of republics, but to the nations, *narodi* (singular: narod), of Yugoslavia, ethnically defined. While these 'nations' were recognized as having their several republics, it was the 'nations,' not the republics, that were described as having united to form the Yugoslav state; the Yugoslav republics, unlike those of the Soviet Union, did not have a right to secede.[31]

Hayden maintains that after the elections of 1990, by definition, people who did not belong to the majority nation could only be second class citizens. He asserts that the separatist republics rewrote "their respective republican constitutions to justify the state on the sovereignty of the ethnically defined nation (narod) in which others might be citizens but could not expect an equal right to participate in control of the state."[32] For this reason, among the majority of the victims of ethnic cleansing were 'mixed' people and 'Yugoslavs' from the most intermingled and heterogeneous regions of the territory of the former Yugoslavia. He claims that,

> ...in some regions the various Yugoslav peoples were not only coexisting but also becoming increasingly intermingled...they served as living disproof of the nationalist ideologies. For this reason, the mixed regions could not be permitted to survive as such, and their populations, which were mixing voluntarily, had to be separated militarily.[33]

Hayden accurately maintains that the territories of socialist Yugoslavia were increasingly heterogeneous, or populated by peoples of different national origins. As well, there was a clear trend toward the increase of ethnic intermarriages, and a growing number of people who declared or considered themselves to be 'Yugoslavs.' His findings demonstrate that this increasing heterogeneity across Yugoslavia was actually parallel with the increase in the intermarriage rates between various nationalities. While the ethnic heterogeneity of the regions between the Censuses of 1981 and 1991 augmented in Montenegro, Macedonia,

Slovenia, and Serbia, it decreased only in Croatia and Bosnia. From the 1950s to the 1980s, the growth of 'mixed marriages' occurred almost everywhere in Yugoslavia. It was especially widespread in Bosnia between Serbs and Croats as well as between Serbs and Muslims. This viability of the Yugoslav political community is also apparent in Hayden's observation that:

> Not surprisingly, the highest rates of intermarriage occurred in the places in which the populations were the most intermingled: the large cities, the province of Vojvodina, Bosnia-Hercegovina, and the parts of Croatia [Krajina] that had large numbers of Serbs and Croats...

> ...Yugoslavia was developing an increasing sense of community and that support for the multinational community was likely to increase, as would self-identification as Yugoslavs.[34]

## Multiethnic Resistance and Disappearance of Yugoslavs

Following this brief overview of the complexity of the internal and external Balkanization that brought about wars and ethnic cleansing, we are now able to better understand the findings of my survey, particularly regarding the crucial research question: Who are the refugees from Bosnia? My findings strongly support Hayden's and Samary's argument about an anti-nationalist atmosphere in the former Yugoslavia, with an ever-increasing sense of a multinational community and self-identification as Yugoslavs. My argument is that Yugoslavia was not an artificial country, but rather a successful experiment of both multinational federation and socialist self-management (*samoupravni socializam* in Serbo-Croatian) based on a non-profit economy and social ownership. Due to external Balkanization, or lasting colonization, Bosnia was the most 'mixed' republic of the former Yugoslavia that, as such, developed and maintained a strong sentiment for a multinational and multicultural peaceful and interactive co-existence. Bosnian peoples, in particular, strongly intermingled, which resulted in a high rate of mixed marriages and in ever-increasing self-identification of its peoples as Yugoslavs. Although their differences, especially religious, were a source of conflict, nevertheless, before the latest civil war, differences were above all regarded as unique cultural treasures worth of respect and careful maintenance. In spite of their contested national histories, especially with regard to territorial rights, and despite sometimes conflicting religious differences, cultural and linguistic similarities prevailed among various peoples of Bosnia, and Yugoslavia at large. Their differences were viewed, in principal, as a source of mutual enrichment and not, as such, an issue. It was exactly this cultural diversity that facilitated a distinct Bosnian and Yugoslav identity, both renowned for openness, kindness and hospitality.

It is not surprising then, that my findings show the vast majority of my respondents to have ethnically 'mixed' families, or close relatives, for the past several generations, thus within the twentieth century. In terms of the ethnic composition of the respondents, I succeeded in interviewing two 'pure' Serbian and two 'pure' Muslim families and three mixed families, of which two are mixed between Serbs and Croats and one between Serb and Muslim. I was not able to find a 'pure' Croatian family from Bosnia or one 'mixed' between a Croat and a Muslim. This failure to include all three major national combinations is partially due to the inaccessibility of data about refugees, and partially due to the rare 'mixture' between Croats and Muslims in Bosnia, as we saw in Hayden's portrait of mixed marriages, i.e., mixed marriages in Bosnia were particularly common between Serbs and Muslims, and between Serbs and Croats, but more rare between Croats and Muslims. Table 2 illustrates the ethnic composition of the respondents and their responses regarding national identity over a period of time.

In order to understand this "Bosnian Blend," as Samary calls it, of various national identities before and after the civil war, we need to keep in mind the specificity of Bosnia as the most mixed republic. As Samary suggests, the essence of this blend is best expressed by Xavier Bougarel: "If Bosnia-Herzegovina has one distinctive and enduring feature, it consists in belonging to no one people, in being a permanent site of intermingling and assimilation, a crossroads of civilizations and a periphery of empires."[35] As Table 2 illustrates, this mosaic of ethnic or national identities varies through different periods of time. Before 1990, thus prior to the outbreak of the war, the majority of the respondents declared their nationality as Yugoslavs. For the purpose of my analysis, it is important to note that those declaring themselves 'Yugoslavs' gradually disappear from column to column. That is, while there were 5 of them before 1990, in the last Census of 1991 there were only 3 Yugoslavs, in official Canadian immigration documents there were just 2 of them, and at this moment there is only one Yugoslav left. It is important to note that the term 'Yugoslav' here refer exclusively to the former Yugoslavia (SFRY: 1945-1991); none of the respondents refers to the last Yugoslavia under Milosevic (FRY: 1992-2003).

Table 2:    Ethnic Composition of the Respondents and their National Identity

| Ethnic composition of respondents | Nationality declared prior to 1990 | Nationality declared in Census 1991 | Nationality declared in Canadian papers | Current national declaration |
|---|---|---|---|---|
| 'Mixed' family: Serb and Croat | Serb and Yugoslav | Serb and Yugoslav | Serb and Yugoslav | Serb and Yugoslav |
| 'Pure' Muslim family | Yugoslavs-Bosnians of Muslim creed | Bosniak of Muslim creed | Bosniak | Bosnian of Muslim creed |
| 'Mixed' family: Serb and Muslim | Yugoslavs | Eskimos, but we were not allowed to do so, thus, we remained Yugoslavs | Mixed marriage of Serb and Muslim, thus Yugoslavs | Canadians |
| 'Pure' Serbian family | As Yugoslav is too broad a term, we are Serbs; in Bosnia one had to specify one's nationality | Same response: Bosnian Serbs, or Serbs from Bosnia | Same response: Bosnian Serbs | Same response: Bosnian Serbs |
| 'Mixed' family: Serb and Croat | Yugoslavs | Croat and Serb | Croat and Serb | Croat and Serb |
| 'Pure' Muslim family | Yugoslavs | Yugoslavs | Muslim from Bosnia, I had to specify my nationality | Bosnian, and no more Yugoslav |
| 'Pure' Serbian family | Serbs from Bosnia | Serbs from Bosnia | Serbs from Bosnia | Canadians |

Source: Conducted Interviews in Montreal, 2001

I argue that this disappearance of Yugoslavs is due to the disintegration of the former Yugoslavia and the consequent 'ethnic purification' of Bosnia, and Yugoslavia at large. As we can see in Table 2, one of the respondents who used to identify as Yugoslav in the first two columns before 1990 and in the 1991 Census, explicitly states that after 1991 he/she could not remain Yugoslav because he/she had to specify nationality, and therefore, he/she declared to be a Muslim from Bosnia. On the other hand, another respondent emphasizes that in Bosnia even before the 1990s, one could not be nationally undetermined, that is, "since Yugoslav is too broad a term we are rather Serbs, because in Bosnia one had to declare nationality whether as a Serb, Croat or Muslim." In other words, although people identified themselves as Yugoslavs or Bosnians, they were primarily Serbs, Croats or Muslims, or belonging to other national minorities living in Bosnia. This is to say that, as previously discussed, peoples were simultaneously both Yugoslavs, or Bosnians, but above all they were Serbs, Croats, etc. While the supranational Bosnian and, especially, Yugoslav identity existed in reality, it was never as apparent in statistical figures. As the respondent suggests, Yugoslav was too broad a term, which ultimately meant that it referred to citizenship and not to one's ethnicity.

Table 2 shows that while the majority of respondents in my survey declared their nationality prior to 1990 to be Yugoslav, there were also some Serbs from Bosnia (Bosnian Serbs), Bosnians of Muslim creed (Bosnian Muslims) and one Bosnian Croat. With respect to the national identities of 'Bosanac' (or Bosnian in English) and 'Bosnjak' (or Bosniak in English), the essential difference is that 'Bosanac' is an 'old' Yugoslav term referring to citizens of all nations and national minorities living in Bosnia, while Bosnjak is a neologism that emerged in the current ethnic partition of Bosnia, referring exclusively to Bosnian Muslims. In Samary's words:

> The official terminology has changed in Bosnia, and been codified in the constitution of the new Croat-Muslim federation. The term Muslim now refers only to religion. A member of the Muslim ethnic-national community is now called a Bosnjak—as distinct from Bosanac, which refers to a citizen of Bosnia in general.[36]

As can be seen in Table 2, only one respondent mentioned the new term 'Bosnjak/Bosniak,' while the others rather still use the old one: 'Bosanac/Bosnian.' The essence of the term 'Bosanac' is rooted in Bosnian multinational and multicultural identity, embracing all peoples living in Bosnia, namely, Serbs, Croats, Muslims and other national minorities. This fact demonstrates that the interviewed refugees, in particular Bosnian Muslims, do not necessarily support the recent nationalist ideology and its new terminology. Since a majority of respondents, regardless of their nationality, declared themselves 'Yugoslavs' prior to the war, they obviously shared the destiny of this seventh South Slav nation: the uprootedness, homelessness and statelessness. Ultimately, ethnic nationalism destroyed the extraordinary Bosnian example of a multiethnic peaceful coexistence that was, and still is, inherent in the term and concept 'Bosanac/Bosnian.' Therefore, a logical question arises: Why should refugees, regardless of their nationality, be in favour of an ethnic nationalism that dismantled their country and homes?

As I have already mentioned, the multiethnic makeup of Bosnia represented and reflected the former Yugoslavia as a whole. In other words, it was 'Yugoslavia in miniature.' This attachment to multicultural and multinational Bosnia, and Yugoslavia at large, is the common ground of all the respondents. It is well summarized by one of them who points out that *Bosnian people* (Bosanci), regardless if they are Serbs, Croats, Muslims or others,

> ...were tied to the Bosnian soil, territory, country. Bosnia was a heart of Yugoslavia, a tie that kept Yugoslavia together and united. This is well expressed in the popular saying 'jebes zemlju koja Bosne nema' (to hell with the country which does not have Bosnia)'. We are all 'uprooted' people that are eradicated from our root—multicultural Bosnia. As multicultural Montreal reminds and resembles Sarajevo, we, people from Sarajevo feel very good in Montreal which additionally has a cosmopolitan spirit lacking in Sarajevo.

As we saw earlier, the peoples of Yugoslavia resisted ethnic division of the country and their families, as exemplified in the Census of 1991 when some of them sarcastically declared their nationality as Eskimos, Bantus, American Indians, Citroens, lightbulbs, refrigerators, etc. In this regard, we can see in Table 2 that there is one family whose members wanted to declare their nationality as 'Eskimos' in the Census of 1991. As officials did not allow them to declare themselves 'Eskimos,' they remained 'Yugoslavs' as they were prior to 1990. This family represents *a typically 'mixed' Yugoslav family*, whose members mostly declared themselves 'Yugoslavs' prior to the civil war. On the eve of the war, in the last national Census held in April of 1991, this family, similar to other mixed Yugoslav—especially Bosnian—families, viewed and considered themselves to become 'Eskimos,' being the only appropriately sarcastic answer to the nonsense of the whole process of ethnic differentiation, the growing revival of aggressive-chauvinist nationalism and the consequent danger of the civil war. To understand properly why people were against the war, one should keep in mind that memories of the past civil war and mutual atrocities committed during World War II are still very vivid in peoples' mind. Especially alive are memories of numerous civilian survivors and soldiers (Tito's partisans) who fought against both internal and external Nazi forces. Also, as explained previously, this switch in national identities from the category of Yugoslavs to Eskimos, or to the category of 'Others,' was due to the emergent chauvinist political climate and politics of fear of the 1990s. Finally, as Table 2 illustrates, this typical Yugoslav 'mixed' family declares their current nationality to be Canadian and no longer Yugoslav. Thus, they were Yugoslavs until they became Canadians.

Obviously, the disintegration of the former Yugoslavia also meant the disappearance of the 'Yugoslav' national identity, because the very existence Yugoslavs and of 'mixed' families was denied. The new projects of building homogenous nation-states, or of ethnic 'purification' of heterogeneous territories, entailed that the populations themselves had to be 'homogenized' along with the territories they inhabited. It seems to me that 'Yugoslavs' and 'Eskimos' were among the first to chose to become Canadians, or any other nationality depending of the country of their immigration. Although the next chapter elaborates these issues pertaining to the phenomena of statelessness, homelessness and rightlessness, as well as the respondents' life experiences of resettlement and rebuilding a lost home in Montreal, it is important to note that Bosnian refugees who loved their multiethnic and multicultural Bosnia (and Yugoslavia) highly appreciate the similar atmosphere of multicultural Montreal.

To sum up, Table 2 shows that the majority of interviewed Bosnian refugees, regardless of whether they have 'pure' or 'mixed' families, declared their national identity as Yugoslavs before the war. Symbolically speaking, they became 'Yugoslav Eskimos' in 1991. With the dismemberment of Yugoslavia, these people, particularly mixed families, by definition, lost not only their state but also their native homeland, that is, they became *apatrides*, or *'heimatlosen'* (the oldest group of stateless people or persons who lost their native land). Table 2 also illustrates that Yugoslavs are gradually disappearing from column to column across time, adapting themselves to less problematic national identities, including Canadian as a most recent one. In terms of their current declaration, we can see that while there is only one Yugoslav left (out of 9 respondents), the remaining respondents demonstrate a 'traditional' variety in declaring their national identities. There are two Canadians, two Serbs, one Croat, one Bosnian/Bosanac, one Bosnian Serb and one Bosnian/Bosanac of Muslim creed. Therefore, the destiny of all of these nationalities, particularly the 'Yugoslavs,' should be seen as the destiny of the victims of ethnic cleansing in Bosnia as well as across Yugoslavia.

In this regard, much of the Western media has shown a great deal of bias in interpreting the various national identities of Yugoslav and Bosnian refugees. To date, media reports have not included nor ever mentioned the peoples of Yugoslavia who considered or declared themselves to be Yugoslavs, Bosnians/Bosanci or Eskimos. Together with the 'newly' created national minority groups, these peoples were the majority of the war victims and targets of ethnic cleansing. Yet these Yugoslavs, Bosnians and Eskimos are 'invisible' victims who are non-existent in the mainstream official 'truth' maintained by media and politicians inside and especially outside the former Yugoslavia. One might assume that ethnic cleansing of Yugoslavs has been completed as officially there are fewer and fewer people declaring themselves 'Yugoslavs' within and outside the former Yugoslavia. In reality, there are today still many people who consider themselves to be 'Yugoslavs,' particularly in the present day union between Serbia and Montenegro, the successor state of the third Yugoslavia (FRY). These last official 'Yugoslavs' will soon join the destiny of the very name and the state of Yugoslavia, that is, they will also become only a part of history, which, arguably, is not too bad since it implies immortality. However, this disappearance of the former Yugoslavia as a name, a state and a national identity does not mean that its existence will automatically or rapidly be erased from peoples' memory, which is much harder, if not impossible, to 'abolish.' Ultimately, bad memories tend to vanish faster and hopefully forever, while good memories and beautiful souvenirs tend to follow us for the rest of our life.[37]

I hope that it is clear by now that the Yugoslav nations, particularly in multinational Bosnia, did not historically hate each other. In contrast to Western media and politicians' portrayal of deep-rooted ethnic nationalism and ancient hatreds, as well as the supposed 'artificiality' of the former Yugoslavia, I argue that various peoples of Yugoslavia, particularly of Bosnia, developed a multicultural and multinational society that they loved. For this reason, the majority of Bosnian peoples ('Bosanci'), including all nations and nationalities of Bosnia, resisted ethnic nationalism and the consequent civil war. On the one hand, the overwhelming presence of the 'Yugoslavs' in my findings supports my argument that the majority of victims of the ethnic cleansing were Yugoslavs and mixed families, along with 'the new' minorities whose status all conflicting parties tried to avoid. On the other hand, the symbolic presence of one Yugoslav or Bosnian 'Eskimo' additionally supports my argument about the anti-nationalist orientation and sentiments of peoples, being particularly true for mixed Bosnia, who also, in this way, demonstrated their multiethnic resistance to ethnic separation and the war.

In this regard, it is important to note that throughout 1991 and 1992, the majority of people across Yugoslavia protested against the emerging danger of civil war. As Smilja Avramov points out, while the federal government of Yugoslavia and the governments of the Republics held a series of unsuccessful meetings in 1991 throughout Yugoslavia to discuss its future and searching for a peaceful agreement, the Yugoslav peoples jokingly called these actions and actors "The Traveling Theatre (*Putujuce Pozoriste* in Serbo-Croatian)."[38] At the same time, a majority of Yugoslav peoples massively demonstrated against nationalist disputes and the civil war in many major cities across Yugoslavia. In Belgrade, the Army was sent into the streets with tanks to end a massive anti-war protest in 1991. Multiethnic resistance in Bosnia was particularly pronounced, since it was the most heterogeneous republic.[39] A massive multiethnic anti-war demonstration in front of the Parliament Building in Sarajevo on the eve of war at the beginning of April 1992 resulted in six people being killed by unidentified snipers. Moreover, there were strong multiethnic anti-war women's and feminist protests across Yugoslavia that were also unsuccessful. As renowned intellectual and feminist Dubravka Ugresic notes, "In the autumn of 1991, women in Sarajevo protested against the war...A few days later hundreds of women from Croatia and Bosnia set off for Belgrade, where they were to be met by women from Serbia."[40]

These are only a few examples of how people from all across the former Yugoslavia protested against the war and the break up of Yugoslavia. However, republican nationalist governments and foreign 'engineers,' or free market 'planners,' thought and acted differently. As we have seen, there is strong evidence that the war in Yugoslavia could have been avoided if the International Community, led by the U.S. and EU influenced by Germany, had not lit the fuse that inflamed both multiethnic Bosnia and Yugoslavia as a whole. The television documentary entitled "Yugoslavia: The Avoidable War" presents an almost identical argument, along with evidence of International involvement in the dismantling of Yugoslavia. Even Lord Carrington, who was the first appointed peace negotiator of the European Community for the former Yugoslavia, emphasizes the crucial role of the West, particularly that of Germany and the U.S., in disabling any kind of peaceful solution in the Balkans. With respect to Bosnia, Lord Carrington, and many other political analysts, claim that the war could have been avoided if the U.S. Ambassador for Yugoslavia, Warren Zimmerman, would not have encouraged Bosnian President Alija Izerbegovic to withdraw his signature from the Lisbon Plan in 1992 which would have prevented the eruption of the war.[41]

Two episodes of a very popular political comedy television show entitled "Top List of Surrealists"[42] prophetically depicted and satirized the nonsense of ethnic nationalism and the division of Yugoslavia, Bosnia and Sarajevo. It also bitingly depicts the crucial role of foreign intervention of the International Community, led by the European Community and United Nations, both acting as central players in the search for a 'solution' to Yugoslavia's crisis. These two episodes explicitly demonstrate and best summarize my argument that internal Balkanization is a consequence of external Balkanization, and that ethnic nationalism and the consequent division of Bosnia was, above all, a product of the interference of the International Community. The whole TV serial 'Top List of Surrealists' was written and performed by an alternative theatre group from Sarajevo (the capital of Bosnia) composed mostly of artists from the popular punk-rock band "No Smoking," whose most prominent member since 1986 is internationally renowned film director Emir Kusturica.[43] The "No Smoking" band was formed in 1980 and it soon gained popularity across Yugoslavia as the main promoter of a (multinational) cultural resistance movement named "New Primitivism," whose sharp critique of a rigid and monolithic one-Party system matured in their political satire "Surrealist Top List."[44] However, very similar progressive alternative youth or sub-cultural movements emerged throughout Yugoslavia in the 1980s, and *all* of them criticized the Communist nomenclature (apparatchiki) by implicitly or explicitly demanding democratic changes. *None* of them ever demanded or promoted the destruction of Yugoslavia as a common state of South Slavs, and even less, a civil war. Yugoslav youth were united in the struggle for democratization and for the creation of a better future, but never did they aspire to destroy their country or to engage in civil war.

According to the respondents that I called back (I was able to reach 5) these two 'surrealist' episodes were made and broadcast in the late 1980s (in 1989), prior to the outbreak of the war. All of the respondents that I reached had seen both episodes that were in their view "visionary," or prophetic, projections of reality. To sum up, all of them stated that "nobody in Bosnia or Sarajevo believed that something like this could happen. It is a comedy with Nostradamus-like force. As if the war was made according to the scenario of the 'Surrealists,' because these episodes predicted everything that happened, as if the 'Surrealists' knew everything in advance."

According to one of the respondents, the first episode was ironically entitled "United or Harmonious Brothers" (*Slozna Braca* in Serbo-Croatian). This episode shows Sarajevo before the war. There are two old friends (as close as 'brothers'), a Muslim and a Serb, playing pool, drinking beer and having fun in a bar. On the street, there are two already drunken foreign observers in white uniforms, complaining about the peaceful atmosphere and their consequent inability to write up any report about national hostility and conflict, as demanded by their supervisors. As their deadline for the report approaches, they decide to try to create a conflict between the Muslim and the Serb whom they already knew. They buy a case of beer and go to the bar. The Muslim and the Serb laugh at the attempt of the observers to induce a seed of national mistrust and conflict, because they have been friends since childhood, 'brothers' who know each other well. After drinking a case of beer however, the observers finally succeed in provoking a fight between the now drunken Muslim and Serb. While these two fight in the bar, the observers laugh and run off to write their reports.

While the first episode satirizes the crucial role of the International Community, or in my terms, external Balkanization, the second episode illustrates the nonsense of internal Balkanization and the civil war in multinational Bosnia, and especially, in the entirely 'mixed' city of Sarajevo. This episode shows a typical Bosnian family from Sarajevo in their apartment, divided according to each family member's nationality, shooting at each other with the Russian machine-gun 'Kalashnikov.' Since their extended family was a 'multinational mixture,' composed of Bosnian Muslims, Croats and Serbs, they end up warring against each other, fighting for every inch of what was previously the common bathroom, kitchen, living room, corridor, cold room/canteen, etc. This episode was, unfortunately, an all too accurate prediction of what would happen in the 'real' war in Bosnia and Sarajevo, the native city of the 'Surrealists.' One of the respondents said that there are additional similar episodes (which I have not had access to). Another episode depicts a prototypical skyscraper in Sarajevo inhab-

bian, Croatian, other nationalities and mixed families) end up fighting against each other for domination of the floors in the building, for example, the Muslims control the first floor, the second floor is Serbian, there is an ongoing battle for the third floor, and so on.

This is largely what the war in Sarajevo, Bosnia and Yugoslavia looked like. Not only did yesterday's friends and good neighbours became enemies shooting at each other, but families were divided, and sometimes, even brothers shot at each other. These 'surrealist' biting, yet poignant, episodes are the best depiction of both the absurdity and the criminality of the division of Yugoslavia, and particularly of Bosnia, along ethnic lines, given that the ethnic division of the territories of Yugoslavia and Bosnia also separated families. Finally, the episodes brilliantly illustrate the intimate relationship between external and internal Balkanization, whose forces were both at work in dismantling the former Yugoslavia, especially multinational Bosnia.

Similar to this 'surrealist' prophetic vision of the civil war, another Yugoslav artist, the famous pop-rock singer Dorde Balasevic, wrote a meaningful song entitled "Requiem," in the late 1980s. The following selected verses best describe the socio-economic impact of the IMF's macro-economic reforms (stabilization) that triggered the political crisis in the 1980s and the emergence of ethnic nationalism, or 'neotribalism' in Balasevic's terms (or 'new primitivism' as 'No Smoking' and the 'Surrealists' called it). The 'Requiem' consequently sounds a death knell for the naive and deceived 'Yugoslavs,' the first victims of the ethnic division of the former Yugoslavia, since they had 'only Yugoslavia.' With the disintegration of their homeland, Yugoslavia symbolically became 'Eskimos' or refugees in foreign lands, because they could not be "wind up dolls" and change sides or nationalities:

*The story about us will remain in the books: 'The Balkans at the end of an era.'*
*Every tribe draws a borderline; all of them want their page...[in history books]*
*Dreams are melting like icebergs, hey Commandant...[Marshall Tito]*
*Flags are on the barricades again; people are turning out as if it were a holiday*
*They are pulling their children out of morning classes:*
*To see the hungry workers...*
*And where are we, the naive ones...[Yugoslavs]*
*Who used to stand and sing for "Hey Slaveni" [National anthem of Yugoslavia]*
*As if, alongside that story, we were made up...*
*And deceived...*
*I am not a doll they can wind up; I only have Yugoslavia...*[45]

## Summary

This examination of the historical and socio-political background of the disintegration of the former Yugoslavia offers a different perspective and critical insights into the complexity of both external and internal Balkanization. I have sought to illustrate how external Balkanization historically produced, and still produces today, internal Balkanization. Historically speaking, national disputes and conflicts over borders and territories in what was known as Yugoslavia are the outcome of external Balkanization, or the 'Divide and Rule' politics of both old and new world orders. We have seen that this external Balkanization did historically contribute, by and large, to the ethnic and cultural diversity of the Balkans of which Yugoslav peoples were so proud. At the same time, this legacy was also a germ for potentially violent national and religious conflict emerging from 'latent or dormant hatreds,' as the most recent ethnic cleansing demonstrated. However, the work of Samary and Hayden, among other scholars, reveals that the war was not about ancient ethnic or religious hatreds, but rather it was about ambitious projects to build 'pure' or homogeneous Nation-States in the heterogeneous regions of the former Yugoslavia. This could only happen by the expulsion of old and new minorities, mixed people and Yugoslavs—by simply expelling and eliminating the 'undesirable' populations. As Bosnia was the most 'mixed' republic of Yugoslavia and the only one without a single majority national group, it is not a surprise that ethnic cleansing resulted in 2.5 million displaced people or refugees out of a little less than 4.5 million of prewar Bosnia's total population. There is a clear silence in the Western media about the anti-nationalistic orientation of various peoples of the former Yugoslavia, and the consequent multiethnic resistance to the civil war. Such people as the Yugoslavs and so-called Eskimos are completely excluded from biased media reporting as if they had never existed. These people are therefore made to disappear in silence without leaving any traces behind them. Yet as we know, popular and political resistance will always be the subject of 'heroic' stories, songs and other forms of artistic expressions, reflecting peoples' history and destiny, as exemplified by "Top List of Surrealists."

## NOTES

1. Mihailo Crnobrnja. The Yugoslav Drama. Montreal: McGill-Queen's University Press. 1994, p. 15.

2. Ibid., p. 33.

3. Ibid., p. 34.

4. Ibid., p. 22.

5. See Crnobrnja, 1994, p. 23 and Hayden 1996, p. 789. See also Samary, 1995.

6. Crnobrnja, 1994, op. cit., p. 23.

7. Ibid., pp. 24-26.

8. Ibid., pp. 27, 28.

9. Ibid., p. 28. As mentioned, the Census of 1991 is very controversial since many people boycotted it, like the Albanians in Kosovo. However, it also seems to me that the data varies from source to source, for example, in Samary's book there were 68% of declared Montenegrins in Census of 1991. See Catherine Samary Yugoslavia Dismembered. Translated from French by Peter Drucker. New York: Monthly Review Press, 1995, p. 19.

10. Again, according to Samary, there were 87.6 % of Slovenes, op. cit.

11. Crnobrnja, 1994, op. cit., pp. 29, 30.

12. Ibid., p. 30.

13. Ibid., p. 32.

14. Ibid., p. 30.

15. Ibid., pp. 15-19.

16. Samary, op. cit., p. 17.

17. See ibid., p. 15.

18. See ibid., p. 19.

19. Crnobrnja, 1994, op. cit., p. 22.

20. See Samary, op. cit., 1995, pp. 28, 160.

21. Ibid., note 10, pp. 159, 160.

22. Robert Hayden. "Imagined Communities and Real Victims: Self-determination and Ethnic Cleansing in Yugoslavia" in American Ethnologist. Vol. 23 (4), 1996, p. 789.

23. Ibid., p.797, note 9, my emphasis.

24. See Mihailo Crnobrnja. "Migration, Displacement, and the Legacy of 'Ethnic Cleansing' in the Countries of Former Yugoslavia" in Refugees and Migrations in Central and Eastern Europe, From Principles to Implementation: the Role of NGOs. Montreal: Canadian Human Rights Foundation, 1997, Tables 3 and 4, p. 69. At the time, Crnobrnja was Vice-President of the Canadian Human Rights Foundation.

25. Samary, op. cit., p. 9.

26. Hayden, op. cit., p. 795.

27. Ibid, p. 783.

28. Ibid, p. 785.

29. Ibid, p. 793.

30. Crnobrnja, 1997, op. cit., pp. 65, 66.

31. Hayden, op. cit., p. 787.

32. Ibid, p. 788.

33. Ibid.

34. Ibid, pp. 788, 789.

35. Samary, op. cit., p. 87, my emphasis.

36. Ibid., p. 162, note 22.

37. I am convinced that I will not be the only one who will die as a Yugoslav by conviction, regardless of where I will leave my bones.

38. Smilja Avramov. Postherojski Rat Zapada Protiv Jugoslavije (my translation from Serbo-Croatian: Postheroic War of the West Against Yugoslavia). Novi Sad: Idi. 1997, p. 140.

39. See more details in Samary, op. cit., particularly pp. 103, 104

40. Dubravka Ugresic. "Because We're Lads" in What Can We Do for Ourselves: East European Feminist Conference, Belgrade 1994. Belgrade: Center for Women's Studies, Research and Communication, 1995, p. 135.

41. In the television documentary "Yugoslavia: The Avoidable War," broadcast on the History channel (No. 47), April 2, 9 and 16 at 10 p.m. in 2001, produced by Frontier Theatre and Film Inc. For the same argument see also Avramov, 1997 and Baudson, 1996.

42. In Serbo-Croatian "Top Lista Nadrealista," translated in English: "Top List of Surrealists" or "Surrealist Top List." I saw these two episodes with one of the respondents who had videotape recorded them from the television, and therefore, I do not have a precise reference.

43. Some of the respondents (as well as myself) enjoyed their concerts in Montreal in the new millennium (in summer of 2000, 2001) when they officially closed 'The Montreal International Film Festival'.

44. See the biography of the "No Smoking" band at http://www.emirkusturica- nosmoking.com/eng/BrdBiog.html, accessed on February 24, 2003.

45. Translated by Tamara Vukov, my explanations in brackets.

# Chapter Five
## Stateless Peoples

Central to this chapter is a historic examination, including current implications, of what a politics of sorrow is really about. My analysis of the greatest sorrow in the world, that of losing one's homeland, also includes an attempt to understand and explain how one goes on living after a murder, especially in the context of a country (like Yugoslavia) where it has occurred too often in the past century. Indeed, the political fragmentation, or reconfiguration, of the Balkans in the twentieth century represents for some peoples of Yugoslavia a hundred years of homelessness, statelessness and rightlessness. Hannah Arendt's diagnosis that these phenomena will symbolize the twentieth century has proven accurate, notably with respect to Yugoslavia. Her examination of the new modern phenomenon of statelessness is an in-depth account of the roots of the contemporary ever-growing refugee numbers, including those from the former Yugoslavia. Drawing on Arendt, I argue that there is an intimate relationship between the phenomena of statelessness, homelessness and rightlessness and present day refugees from Bosnia, or Yugoslavia at large. This linking element puts all the parts of this book into a comprehensive whole by looking at current refugee conditions from a historical perspective. It further contributes to my analysis of the legacy of Yugoslavia's apatrides or refugees resulting from external, and consequently internal, Balkanization. As we witness today and as Arendt predicted, totalitarian solutions, or tendencies, have indeed survived both known regimes, Nazism and Stalinism, as is exemplified by ethnic cleansing in Yugoslavia or by the genocide in Rwanda which both produced floods of refugees.

Before turning to these issues I will briefly discuss some of the main relevant points of Arendt's extraordinary historical and political analysis of the origins of totalitarianism and statelessness, a condition *sine qua non* for understanding both the disintegration of the former Yugoslavia and the refugee crisis that followed. This concise historical background on Europe in the last century, from its beginning marked by the end of World War I which paved the way for World War II, is more than necessary since it explains why the twentieth century can be accurately called 'the stateless century.' To understand the core of the present day refugee problematic we need now to stop for a moment and look at the very origins of statelessness, which goes hand in hand with the legacy of modern totalitarian tendencies and solutions.

## Totalitarian Solutions

According to Arendt, the origins of totalitarianism and statelessness are traceable to the political climate of the post World War I world order that produced the very momentum of the emergence of the police state and its management of 'undesirables' as a prelude to forthcoming totalitarian regimes.[1] Arendt argues that the failure of the European Nation-State system to provide legal protection for stateless people after the Great War resulted in the transfer of state authority over the refugee problematic to the police. This meant that for the first time in Western Europe, the police was allowed "to act on its own, to rule directly over people...[to] become a ruling authority independent of government and ministries."[2] Such a political atmosphere had accommodated the emergence of the police state, which consequently, enabled the police to rise "to the peak of power" in totalitarian regimes.[3] This atmosphere also facilitated the shameful collaboration of local police with the Nazis in conquered countries. As Arendt points out, the fact that,

> ...the Nazis eventually met with so disgracefully little resistance from the police in the countries they occupied, and that they were able to organize terror as much as they did with the assistance of these local police forces, was due at least in part to the powerful position which the police had achieved over the years in their unrestricted and arbitrary domination of stateless and refugees.[4]

According to Arendt, the legacy of the dormant but permanent danger of the reappearance of radical evil, or the totalitarian solutions, is anchored in modern societies that are based on the Nation-State principle and the Rule of Law. She argues that there is a constant danger that the nation might conquer the state, as occurred before the Second World War when "the transformation of the state from an instrument of the law into an instrument of the nation had been completed" and, for this reason, there is no doubt that "the danger of this development had been inherent in the structure of the nation-state since the beginning."[5] Indeed, the unprecedented rise of stateless peoples that began with the failure of the international legal system to protect national minorities and refugees in the European nation-states after World War I largely contributed to the ensuing process: mass denationalization of citizens who belonged to 'undesirable' national minority groups. Some of them disappeared in subsequent Nazi extermination camps in World War II. For Arendt, the danger that the state can become an instrument of the nation is embedded in the precarious relationship between nation and state in modern societies. As she explains:

> But insofar as the establishment of nation-states coincided with the establishment of constitutional government, they always had represented and been based upon the rule of law as against the rule of arbitrary administration and despotism. So that when the precarious balance between nation and state, between national interest and legal institutions broke down, the disintegration of this form of government and of organization of peoples came about with terrifying swiftness.[6]

While the specificity of totalitarianism is that the "demand" for "unlimited power" resides in its very "nature," the uniqueness of totalitarianism lies in its striving, not "toward despotic rule over men, but toward a system in which men are superfluous" and reduced to "Pavlov's dogs;" that is, obedient and uncomplaining people who are reduced to "conditioned reflexes."[7] In Arendt's words, "the ideal subject of totalitarian rule is not the convinced Nazi or the convinced Communist, but people for whom the distinction between fact and fiction (i.e., the reality of experience) and the distinction between true and false (i.e., the standards of thought) no longer exist."[8] I find Arendt's following comment still relevant and an incredibly accurate description of current worldwide totalitarian inclinations and solutions, notably with regard to the violent disintegration of the former Yugoslavia and ethnic cleansing: "the totalitarian belief that everything is possible seems to have proved only that everything can be destroyed," and that "there are...absolute evil...crimes which men can neither punish nor forgive."[9] In this sense, she warns us against the constant danger of the recurrence of the 'radical evil of totalitarianism' where all human beings are ultimately superfluous, regardless of whether they are perpetrators or victims. Since totalitarian tendencies and solutions are inherent to modern Nation-States, they might reappear whenever there is a problem of over-population, of economic redundancy or of socially rootless peoples. In Arendt's words:

The Nazis and the Bolsheviks can be sure that their factories of annihilation which demonstrate the swiftest solution to the problem of over-population, of economically superfluous and socially rootless human masses, are as much of an attraction as a warning. Totalitarian solutions may well survive the fall of totalitarian regimes in the form of strong temptations which will come up whenever it seems impossible to alleviate political, social, or economic misery in a manner worthy of man.[10]

The rising phenomena of loneliness and isolation are companions to this modern condition. Entrenched in the everyday life of our times, loneliness is ever accelerating due, notably, to rapid social changes brought about by today's informational technology revolution. Since the legacy of radical evil is also grounded in these growing sentiments of isolation and loneliness, which are preconditions for total domination, there is both a constant attraction and a warning against totalitarian solutions in our times. Arendt rightly claims that in our current condition "what prepares men for totalitarian domination in the non-totalitarian world is the fact that loneliness, once a borderline experience usually suffered in certain marginal social conditions like old age, has become an everyday experience of the evergrowing masses of our century."[11]

The following pages reveal, in retrospect, that the twentieth century illustrates indeed a history of statelessness for the diverse national groups of Yugoslavia, which in turn runs parallel to the occurrence of totalitarian regimes, solutions and tendencies. It is a century long story of mass migrations in the Balkans in the process of 'ethnic unmixing' of peoples. Although there is no doubt that the history of the Balkans and especially of Yugoslavia is the history of migration of both peoples and their land, I focus on the past century because it implies the emergence of a new phenomenon of statelessness, notably for some national minorities. As Arendt explains, regardless of the preceding existence of minorities, what was really new after the Great War was the fact that the subsequent Minority Treaties were guaranteed by the League of Nations; an international legal body which recognized officially the existence of the minority as a stable formation acknowledging that "millions of people lived outside normal legal protection and needed an additional guarantee of their elementary rights from an outside body, and the assumption that this state of affairs was not temporary but that the Treaties were needed in order to established a lasting *modus vivendi*—all this was something new, certainly on such a scale, in European history."[12]

As already mentioned, the creation of the first Yugoslavia in 1918, named the 'Kingdom of Serbs, Croats and Slovenes,' marginalized Montenegrins, Bosnian Muslims and Macedonian peoples, the future nations of socialist Yugoslavia, since their territories became a part of Serbia and these peoples were considered to be Serbs. As well, at that time, national minority rights were directly jeopardized and many people left the country. For this reason, some of Yugoslavia's minority groups were among the first modern European *apatrides* (in French), or *Heimatlosen* (in German), or stateless people, who emerged due to the post World War I world order enhanced by Peace and Minority Treaties. These first apatrides were later to be joined by a new major wave of political emigration after World War II, which was further followed, in our time, by the floods of refugees and displaced persons due to the violent disintegration of Yugoslavia. All such various peoples, for different reasons and in different periods, have in common their lost homeland.

Since the twentieth century is indeed the century of stateless people and since the phenomenon of statelessness is inherent to the history of the Balkans, it is necessary to analyze the present day refugee crisis caused by the civil war in the former Yugoslavia through this prism of historical continuity of statelessness and totalitarian solutions or tendencies; because, without an understanding of the origins of statelessness, it is hard to understand its current implications. My survey findings support this claim, as the vast majority of the respondents considered themselves to be apatrides and refugees, or more specifically, to be homeless, rightless and stateless. They are 'uprooted' people who, as such, did not have 'freedom of choice' in planning their emigration. It is this 'unchosen' or forced emigration that brought them to Canada and Montreal in their desire and hope to build a new life in a peaceful and prosperous country. Besides sharing the common trauma of a lost home and a 'good or normal life' in Bosnia, the respondents also share an exceptionally advanced professional and educational background (a legacy of socialist Yugoslavia) that are supposed to be an advantage towards their integration in Canada. These advantages however are diminished by their age, their 'insufficient' knowledge of both official Canadian languages as well as the absence of a multiethnic Yugoslav community. Bosnian refugees are apparently disadvantaged because they lack both the support of Montreal's community agencies and, in particular, the support of their non-existing multiethnic Yugoslav organization. The fact that Bosnian and Yugoslav refugees (like Yugoslavs and 'Eskimos'), who are anti-nationalists and, as such, do not fit into divisive ethnic categories, were and still are excluded from both Western media reports that omit these 'other' ethnic identities and from the multicultural agenda of Canada, ultimately constitutes one of the main obstacles to a better and faster integration in Canadian society, or more specifically, in Quebec society and the city of Montreal, as we will see further on.

## A Hundred Years of Homelessness and Statelessness

With regard to the national identities of refugees from Bosnia, Catherine Samary rightly states that "many individuals and families are of mixed origin, which ethnic maps do not reflect."[13] For this reason, 'mixed' families and/or people who declared themselves as 'Yugoslavs,' Bosnians or more recently as 'Eskimos' are non existent refugees, since, as such, they are not included in the official statistics whose data is either ethnically categorized or based on the republic of last permanent residence. At best, these people are reduced to the vague category of 'mixed family,' which again is excluded from both media reports and ethnically defined refugees' categories, such as Croats, Muslims, Serbs, etc. As well, the official data about internally displaced people and refugees from the former Yugoslavia is confusing and usually vary from source to source, since reports rarely specify whether victims or, more accurately, survivors are internally displaced persons or refugees. Even if specified, it is hard to distinguish between internally displaced persons and refugees, since people often belong to both categories either at the same time or in a sequence. For these reasons, the statistical accuracy as well as the validity of the data about the number of refugees and their ethnic identities should be questioned. In a broader sense, one should question the national identities of the victims of all forms of ethnic cleansing, including both casualties and survivors. One example of blurry statistics with respect to the differences between displaced people, refugees and asylum seekers is Samary's data (otherwise quite similar to the official statements inside and outside Yugoslavia from 1994-1995) which shows that there are "2.5 million people displaced in Bosnia—3.5 million refugees from the entire Yugoslav area, on top of 750,000 people who have applied for asylum abroad."[14]

Although the question of statistical (in)accuracy is beyond the scope of this book, it is nevertheless important to note that survivors of the civil war and ethnic cleansing in Yugoslavia often belong to both categories: they were either first internally displaced persons (IDPs) and then they became refugees, or vice versa. There is ultimately no difference between these two categories, especially in Yugoslavia's context, because both concepts include forced migration or displacement. Refugee status is, however, an older and much broader term that to some extent includes internally displaced people who have fled their homes for the same reasons as refugees, that is, a fear for one's life, but who have remained within the internationally recognized borders of their native homeland. In other words, refugees are defined as persons who are *outside* of the country of their nationality and who are unwilling or unable to return due to a well-founded fear of persecution because of their race, religion, nationality, political opinion or membership in a particular social group. Like refugees, internally displaced persons are defined as people who have been forced to flee their homes as a result of armed conflict, internal strife, systematic violations of human rights or natural or man-made disasters, but who, in contrast to refugees, *have not crossed* an internationally recognized State border.[15]

This basic difference between remaining within the State borders or leaving the country is at the heart of the statistical confusion regarding refugees from the former Yugoslavia since people were commonly both IDPs and refugees. At the very least, if they were strictly IDPs, they often attempted to become refugees and leave their country. As we have seen in the previous chapters, the question of the republican borders that became the new inter-State borders was the key issue within the Yugoslav federation and within the International Community. Indeed, which borders were then accounted to be the State borders for the purpose of obtaining refugee status: the international borders of the former Yugoslavia or the borders of the new successor states? And which criterion, if any, was established for people that had double or multiple nationalities and were, therefore, able to move legally across former republics, or new states, and could change status from IDPs to refugees either in another republic or abroad. Generally speaking, people, if they could, moved back and forth in order to survive and obtain necessary documents, of which, providing they could, chose several, or the one that offered the most opportunities for a better life. However, the vast majority of people were not able to move freely and legally: they were usually trapped in the war zones or in designated accommodations for displaced persons or refugees. The most recent example of this phenomenon is exemplified by the Roma people in Kosovo, a Serbian troublesome province whose status is still unsolved and which is far from being internationally recognized as a state. As we have seen, the essential difference between IDPs and refugees is that the former implies an inferior status without the possibility to leave the region and, moreover, of being restricted to live in camps with poor facilities and, generally speaking, very bad life conditions. According to Sani Rifati, out of the numerous national minorities living in Kosovo, only Roma people live in its IDP camps! Some logical questions then arise: Why can't Roma people become refugees and leave Kosovo? What criterion is used to define IDPs and refugees? And which borders are considered to be the state borders of Kosovo?

Since the civil war moved from republic to republic, traveling across borders like a virus of fragmentation, internally displaced persons would be, according to the above definition, those people who were displaced within their own republic or elsewhere within the borders of the former Yugoslavia, since all of its territories were encircled by armed conflicts. In reality, as people of various nationalities were forced to flee their homes due to the war, they usually moved to another 'safer' republic where they were only able to obtain internal refugee status, and then had to face the war again. These unfortunate peoples, regardless of whether they were labelled as IDPs or refugees, became, above all, denationalized citizens of the former Yugoslavia, *les misérables* of an avoidable civil war and *les indésirables* of Europe, who, once banished from their native land, were also banished from the family of all nations and, therefore, were welcomed nowhere. If and when their internal refugee status, granted within the former Yugoslavia, was formally recognized by the United Nations High Commissioner for Refugees (UNHCR), this meant international recognition as official refugees as well. This (Geneva) Convention refugee status opened the door to their successful emigration process.

It is a matter of fact that survivors of war, of physical and bureaucratic ethnic cleansing (denaturalization of citizens or constitutional nationalism), could fit simultaneously in both official definitions: that of the internally displaced persons and of (internal) refugees, since both groups had to flee their homes and were displaced either within their own republic or elsewhere in the former Yugoslavia. Some of them, the 'lucky' ones, succeeded in leaving the country either to become refugees abroad or to leave as tourists, economic or independent immigrants, 'illegal' immigrants, etc. However, the official terminology of the new successor states, as well as their media, classified these incoming floods of displaced people as refugees (or *izbjeglice* in Serbo-Croatian and *begunci* in Slovenian language) rather than IDPs. According to the previous definitions, for example, Bosnians who remained in Bosnia were IDPs, but they became refugees when, or if, they moved to another former Yugoslav republic. This was largely the case given the fact that people were trying to escape the war, which was virtually impossible since the war followed them. Once refugees in their own state and former homeland, some of them applied for political asylum abroad, or for the UNHCR's official refugee status, a complicated and highly selective procedure that opened the door to leaving Yugoslavia. Others, however, remained within former Yugoslavia as refugees or IDPs who, it is hoped by now, have become citizens of one of the new successor states of Yugoslavia.

This typical trajectory of refugees is particularly true in the case of my respondents. Once they fled their homes in Bosnia, all of them sought shelter in the neighbouring Yugoslav republics. Although I did not ask my respondents to identify the republics in which they sought shelter, it is well known that Serbian (and mixed) families usually, but not exclusively, fled to Yugoslavia (FRY), while Muslims and Croats fled to Croatia or Slovenia. Despite not explicitly asking if they were also counted as internally displaced persons within Bosnia, all of the respondents stated to only have had official refugee status once forced to flee their homes, that is, to leave Bosnia. In accordance with the UNHCR definition, all of them were refugees since all had moved to another new successor state of the former Yugoslavia (SFRY), being, thus, outside of Bosnia. Prior to their arrival to Canada, not one of the respondents had their last permanent residency in Bosnia, since all of them fled Bosnia, but remained within the borders of the former Yugoslavia. In each case, they were only granted internal refugee status and not citizenship, regardless of which neighbouring republic they fled to. Therefore, none of the respondents belongs to the official Canadian data of 4,963 received Bosnian refugees who prior to their resettlement in Canada had their last permanent residency in Bosnia, even though the vast majority landed between 1994-1996.[16] It seems to me then that these respondents (like other displaced Bosnians) could accurately be defined as both internally displaced persons and refugees, since they moved from Bosnia to another Yugoslav republic until the final destination of their 'chosen' country of immigration. If not IDPs, who, then, are these refugees from Bosnia who had their last permanent residency in Bosnia before coming to Canada? According to the previous definitions, only IDPs could have their last permanent residency in Bosnia! Since, in order to be recognized officially by the UNHCR as a refugee, that person had to be outside of Bosnia.

Clearly, these definitions and statistical categories are very vague and seem to vary from country to country. However, what is really important here is the fact that if we take into account that prewar Bosnia had almost 4.5 million inhabitants, of which approximately 2.5 million were forcibly displaced or 'uprooted' in three years of war, then we can better understand the impact of ethnic cleansing: the complete transformation of the demographic structure of what had been before the war the most heterogeneous republic of the former Yugoslavia.

Besides questioning the accuracy and reliability of statistics, I have so far offered a different historical perspective and theoretical background, including empirical data, which give a more realistic picture about national identities and ethnic cleansing in Bosnia and Yugoslavia at large. Ultimately, this enriches our understanding of the circumstances and reasons that made Bosnian refugees decide to resettle in Canada. As my findings show, all of the respondents lost "everything they had," including their property and personal belongings. Not surprisingly, this total loss occurred regardless of whether they belonged to the 'new' national minority or the majority that, in both cases, included Serbs, Croats or Muslims/Bosniaks. Ironically, in terms of mixed families this meant both cases, that is, while one spouse belonged to the minority, the other belonged to the majority. In any case, all of the respondents were forced to leave their homes and were displaced due to the ongoing war and consequent violence. All of them thus left Bosnia in search of a safer place within Yugoslavia, where they then became refugees, that is, as one respondent pointed out "without any status," a status in Arendt's analogy not worthy of any man. As the refugee status was precarious and the dangers of war combined with the economic disaster were spreading across the former Yugoslavia, none of the respondents could envision any prospect for their future, particularly for their children. Also, none of them felt welcomed or safe anywhere in the former Yugoslavia. Not surprisingly then that when asked, all of them agreed with Euripides, the last representative of Greek classic tragedy, who stated in 431 BC that "*there is no greater sorrow on earth than the loss of one's native land*" (appropriated by UNHCR as logo on their web site at www.unhcr.ch). For the respondents, the disintegration of Yugoslavia, therefore, meant the loss of their homeland, and the consequent end of their human, social and civil rights.

The moral dilemma of both refugees and internally displaced persons is still present and actual even among citizens not only of Bosnia but also of peoples across the former Yugoslavia. This real dilemma of whether to remain in the Balkans or go abroad, emigrating to an unknown place but where there is hope for a decent and 'normal' life, both during the war and in times of peace was omnipresent, particularly in parts of the former Yugoslavia that were directly touched by the war. Since the outbreak of civil war in 1991, all peoples across the country shared a common loss of 'normal' life conditions, and consequently, many faced this essential refugee dilemma of either remaining or leaving their homeland. This loss of normality and the subsequent imposition of the 'refugee' dilemma is the central theme of the excellent Bosnian film entitled "The Milky Way,"[17] which shows the 'abnormality' of life conditions in Sarajevo in 2000 due to the catastrophic economic situation, rampant unemployment and high cost of living which cause people otherwise very tied to Bosnian soil to want to emigrate. As the following selected verses from the eponymous song,[18] the musical theme of the film, reveal:

> Oh, if it was only possible to awaken,
> somewhere far away from everything, to kiss a foreign soil
> there where pride exists, so I could remind myself what it is like to have some ...
> there where hope exists, so I could hug and hold onto it.
> If I go, I will wither; if I stay, I will go mad
> Not even I have hundred lives
> And if I did, it would be shameful how I live.[19]

This song poignantly captures the impact of 'uprootedness' for both people and plants: they may wither if transplanted! The refugee moral dilemma thus implies going mad if one remains in an unbearable situation, like war, or withering if one leaves one's native land. I also agree with one protagonist of "The Milky Way" who comments that something is wrong if people are leaving Bosnia in peacetime: "I understand that people were running away in war, but now in peace, I do not understand it." On the one hand, the reason why people still today try to emigrate from Bosnia (and other former Yugoslav republics) is the 'abnormal' life situation that has been imposed on the region, where people are reduced to the struggle for survival in an economically destroyed country. On the other hand, the reason why they can no longer obtain immigration papers is that in the current peacetime 'mixed families' have priority in immigration selection according to "The Milky Way," which is based on a true story.[20] The main protagonists, one Croatian and one Muslim family who are barely surviving in peacetime Sarajevo with their 'temporary' jobs, cannot obtain immigration visas for New Zealand because they are 'pure' and not 'mixed' families. Soon, the local Mafioso, acting as the employer and friend of both husbands, succeeds in convincing them to undertake a process of 'hybridization,' that is, to 'cross' or exchange wives in order to become 'mixed' families that have priority in the immigration process. While both families initially resist this 'crossing' option, the Mafioso (starring Dragan Bjelogrlic) best summarizes the 'abnormality' of their current lives in Bosnia, underlying the fact that they have no other choice but to 'mix' if they want to leave the country: "In normal circumstances you would live a normal life in a normal country with normal people, but, normally, this is not the case."

One might then conclude that it is better to lose one's homeland, even though, according to Euripides, this is the greatest sorrow on earth, than to live in a native country which has become 'abnormal,' or anomalous. Who can ultimately resolve this moral dilemma? We have seen that the paradox or absurdity of the civil war in Yugoslavia centred on the reality that people who 'mixed' voluntarily had to be separated by military force, or by legal divorce as was the case with some 'mixed' marriages which, in turn, had, and probably still have, priority in the immigration procedures of many countries. While during the war there were cases of 'mixed' families divorcing in order to survive the process of 'purification' of Yugoslavia's mixed territories and peoples, now, in peacetime, some are probably divorcing if they are 'pure' families in order to engage in mixed marriages and be able to embark on 'the milky way,' regardless of the danger that they might wither if they emigrate.

Arendt remarkably analyzes these modern phenomena of rightlessness, statelessness and homelessness in her excellent book *The Origins of Totalitarianism*.[21] Her examination of these phenomena is, more then ever, applicable to present day refugees in general, and in particular for Bosnian and Yugoslav uprooted peoples. The actuality of Arendt's argument regarding the ever-increasing figures of refugees worldwide is particularly true in terms of the mass migration of Eastern and Southern Europeans into Western Europe after the fall of the Berlin Wall. This wave included a large portion of refugees from the former Yugoslavia, among whom there was also one of my respondents. In the beginning of the 1990s, Jürgen Habermas, an internationally renowned German social philosopher, pointed out that:

> *Hannah Arendt's diagnosis—that stateless persons, refugees, and those deprived of rights would come to symbolize this century—has proved frighteningly accurate.* The 'displaced persons' that the Second World War left in a devastated Europe have long since been replaced by asylum seekers and immigrants flooding into a peaceful and prosperous Europe from the South and the East. The old refugee camps can no longer accommodate the flood of new immigrants. Statisticians anticipate that in coming years twenty to thirty million immigrants will come from eastern Europe alone.[22]

As mentioned, the origins of statelessness are traceable to the post-World War I world order, which caused some national minorities from Yugoslavia to join other European minorities in becoming, in Arendt's terms, "The Nation of Minorities and the Stateless People." In this sense, the history of Yugoslavia reflects, for some peoples, a century long destiny of being apatrides and refugees, or simply of being stateless people. This legacy of Yugoslav apatrides is anchored in the external Balkanization of the old and new world orders, which influenced both the formation and the destruction of Yugoslavia(s) and failed to resolve the question of national minorities and human rights. In this regard, Arendt argues that World War I, and the consequent Peace Treaty, entailed both the appearance of national minorities in post-war Europe and a growing number of refugees produced by revolutions and civil wars. She maintains that the post-war Peace and Minority Treaties were futile in resolving the problem of minorities in multinational states, particularly in Yugoslavia and Czechoslovakia where the Western principle of the Nation-State was questioned by the existence of more than one nation, large national minorities and numerous nationalities.[23]

Along with the wish among the South Slavs for the unification in a common state, the first Yugoslavia (1918-1941) was also a product of the post-World War I world order enhanced by the Peace and Minority Treaties. These Treaties failed to protect national minorities discriminated against in this first Yugoslav state, for example, the Bosnian Muslims, Albanians, Hungarians, Germans, but also Jews and Roma people and other nationalities.[24] We should recall Gerard Baudson's argument that the first Yugoslavia was created on a French initiative to surround Germany with 'a security belt.' Also, as Baudson notes, "one of the Yugoslav paradoxes is the fact that in the war from which Yugoslavia was born, the future co-citizens were fighting on opposite sides."[25] The Serbs, on the side of the victors, had a choice of either creating Serbia within borders recognized by the allies in 1915 or to form Yugoslavia. Baudson explains that in contrast to the losing side, the Slovenes and Croats, the victorious Serbs were able to choose "between the creation of 'the Greater Serbia' and creation of one common state on 'the Yugoslav territory'...they [Serbs] chose the latter possibility, induced by France to which they could not refuse anything, because Serbian *narod* [people, nation] considered France to be their second homeland [motherland]."[26]

To revisit this history further, the 'Kingdom of Serbs, Croats and Slovenes' was created in December of 1918 and renamed 'The Kingdom of Yugoslavia' in 1929. According to the first Census held in 1921, it had a total population of approximately 12 million inhabitants. Table 3 shows the rich national structure of the first Yugoslavia.

**Table 3:     The National or Ethnic Composition of the first Yugoslavia in 1921 Census**

| Nationality | No. | % |
|---|---|---|
| Serbs | 4,665,851 | 38.83 |
| Croats | 2,856,551 | 23.77 |
| Slovenes | 1,024,761 | 8.53 |
| Bosnian Muslims | 727,650 | 6.05 |
| Macedonians | 585,558 | 4.87 |
| Other Slavs | 176,466 | 1.45 |
| Germans | 513,472 | 4.27 |
| Hungarians | 472,409 | 3.93 |
| Albanians | 441,740 | 3.68 |
| Rumanians, Vlachs, Cincars | 229,398 | 1.91 |
| Turks | 168,404 | 1.40 |
| Jews | 64,159 | 0.53 |
| Italians | 12,825 | 0.11 |
| Other | 80,079 | 0.67 |
| TOTAL | 12,017,323 | 100.00 |

Source: Ivo Banac. *The National Question in Yugoslavia: Origin, History, Politics.* Itaha: Cornell University Press. 1984, p. 58. Cited in Mihailo Crnobrnja *The Yugoslav Drama.* 1994, p. 52, Table 1.

In addition to the French initiative to create the first Yugoslavia discussed by Baudson, and Djilas' account of the origins of the Yugoslav idea, Crnobrnja rightly points out that "the peoples that came together knew very little about each other."[27] Supplementing Djilas' general analysis of the national question in Yugoslavia(s) and, in particular, his argument about the central role of the Serbs and Croats in the formation (and destruction) of Yugoslavia(s), Crnobrnja describes this first common state in an interesting manner. He maintains that while "it is true that Serbia did not want Yugoslavia as strongly as Croatia did," it is also "true that the Yugoslavia that Croatia obtained was not exactly the Yugoslavia it was looking for. The other nations, Montenegrins, Slovenes, and Macedonians, played a secondary role, if at all, at this stage...[thus] the newly created country, though not artificial, did not have a very sound structure."[28] With regard to the political system and the question of national minorities in this first South Slav state, Crnobrnja explains that:

> The Serbs brought a tradition of a centralist and unitarian state. Until the Balkan Wars this state [Serbia] had been nationally homogeneous with no minorities. The sensitivity of the Serbian polity to questions of national minorities was therefore understandably, if regrettably, small. But the Serbs also brought a tradition of a functioning parliamentary democracy with limited sovereign powers, and the sense of a free political spirit, gained through long struggle against an oppressive foreign power. They had attained their freedom on their own and were proud of it. The way in which they attained that freedom had a direct impact on the political structure, favouring strong, central decision-making.[29]

In terms of the unresolved question of national minorities, we should recall Djilas' remark that in 1919, the Yugoslav Communist Party was strongly opposed to any form of national oppression, protesting against the central government's discriminatory policies toward non-Slav minorities, particularly Albanians, Hungarians, but also Germans. The second Congress of the Communist Party in 1920 again demanded that persecuted national minorities be accorded the same civil and political rights as those enjoyed by the South Slav citizens of Yugoslavia.[30] As we can see in Table 3, "The Kingdom of Serbs, Croats and Slovenes" was indeed a multinational state, composed of more than three recognized nations and a variety of national minorities, mainly consisting of peoples from neighbouring countries. Many authors[31] who provide a historical background on Yugoslavia emphasize the existence and central role of the massive migrations of peoples in the Balkans. Indeed, the history of Yugoslavia reflects these large-scale migrations, or in Serbo-Croatian *velike seobe naroda*. The large and small-scale migrations of peoples involved both nations and national minorities, and were particularly common during the centuries long Ottoman rule when people were massively fleeing from invading Turks, who were, in addition, moving peoples around and rearranging the demographic structure in the territories they occupied. The history of the Balkans, especially of Yugoslavia, is a history of mostly forced migrations of both peoples and their land, which often, perhaps too often, changed landlords and state rulers.

In this regard, Rogers Brubaker claims that "migration has always been central to the making, unmaking, and remaking of states."[32] With respect to the relationship between the creation of the first Yugoslav state and the migration of its 'newly created' national minorities, Brubaker maintains that "a ruling ethnic or national group in a multinational empire was abruptly transformed, by the shrinkage of political space and the reconfiguration of political authority along national lines, into a national minority in a set of new nation-states."[33] These new states, like Yugoslavia, emerged after the dissolution of multinational Ottoman and Habsburg Empires, which resulted in 'the large-scale migrations' and massive 'ethnic unmixing' of the Balkan peoples in Brubaker's terms. The collapse of the Ottoman Empire hit particularly hard the Muslim Turks and non-Turkish Muslims, or respectively Balkan Turks and Balkan Muslims, who emigrated from the new successor states. Similarly, ethnic Hungarians and Germans left newly created states in the Balkans after the demise of the Habsburg, or Austro-Hungarian, Empire.[34]

Some national minority groups of the first Yugoslavia subsequently joined the so-called European 'Nation of Minorities' that was composed of various European minorities with similar problems, all victims of the post-World War I Peace and Minority Treaties. As Arendt explains, since these European national minority groups were perceived in their new states as being "not-nationals" and since they lacked the International protection of both the League of Nations and the Minority Treaties from their forceful assimilation, they soon gathered together "in a minority congress which...contradicted the very idea behind the League treaties by calling itself officially the 'Congress of Organized National Groups in European States'."[35] This 'Congress of National Groups' was dominated by Jews and Germans who showed interregional connectedness and solidarity since they lived in almost all new successors states across Eastern and Southern Europe, including Yugoslavia, which in turn enabled them to 'press' governments throughout Europe. As discussed, the post-World War I world order had created three new states, Poland, Czechoslovakia and Yugoslavia in order to surround Germany with a 'security zone.' In this regard, Arendt notes that these states were also "the belt of mixed population" as none of them was "uni-national."[36] The fact that some Yugoslav national minorities were among the first European apatrides due to the post-World War I Peace and Minority Treaties supports my argument of a century-long Yugoslav history of apatridism and homelessness. This history of statelessness is also reflected in the aforementioned short story of Ivo Andric, The letter from 1920,[37] in which a Bosnian Jew, a medical doctor from Sarajevo, leaves Bosnia forever and emigrates to the Western Europe, to Paris, joining thus, in Arendt's analogy, 'the European Nation of Minorities' and stateless peoples. The irony of the doctor's destiny, however, is that he left Bosnia because he could not hate people of other nationalities and religions. He also could not stand that others hated him. He firmly believed that escape was the only rescue, that is, the best way to deal with hatred is to leave such a place. Ironically, he died in the Spanish civil war (as did many other Yugoslavs) where he was a volunteer in the Republican Army, because he was driven by his professional and personal ethics to help people in need and to share their suffering. The doctor died together with his patients in the hospital that was destroyed in the 1938 by the Air Strikes and, therefore, Andric concludes the story by noting that "and thus ended the life of the one who escaped from hatred."[38]

Arendt further argues that these historic events (the Peace Treaties, revolutions and civil wars) undermined the internal stability of European Nation-State system between the two World Wars. In particular, she emphasizes that civil wars at that time were followed by massive migrations of deprived peoples who, in contrast to previous migrations due to the religious wars, "were welcomed nowhere and could be assimilated nowhere. Once they had left their homeland they remained *homeless*, once they had left their state they became *stateless*; once they had been deprived of their human rights they were *rightless*, the scum of the earth."[39] In other words, once they were banished from their nation, they were banished from all the family of nations. Their destiny was sealed up and they were welcome nowhere. According to Arendt, stateless people (or modern apatrides and refugees) and national minorities were "cousins-germane" since both groups had in common that once designated as the "undesirables" in their countries they became "the *indésirables* of Europe."[40]

Arendt emphasizes that the League of Nations and the Minority Treaties have failed to protect national minorities from being assimilated or discriminated against since the Nation-State principle at that time implied that "only nationals could be citizens," and therefore, "the law of a country could not be responsible for persons insisting on a different nationality."[41] She claims that with this "rise of stateless people...the transformation of the state from an instrument of law into an instrument of the nation had been completed; the nation had conquered the state, national interest had priority over law long before Hitler could pronounce 'right is what is good for the German people'."[42] For Arendt, at the heart of the emergence of the new contemporary phenomenon of statelessness were the Peace Treaties signed after World War I that directly created stateless peoples known as 'Heimatlosen,' or people who lost their homeland. The problem of statelessness was exacerbated when this oldest group of 'apatrides' who "lived outside the pale of law" were accompanied in their "legal status by the postwar refugees," the victims of mass denationalization resulting from revolutions and civil wars.[43] Since both official European policies, namely the "repatriation and naturalization," failed due to "the very undeportability of stateless person" and due to the "cancellation of naturalization or the introduction of new laws which obviously paved the way for mass denaturalization," these "indésirables" were left completely "at the mercy of the police."[44] In fact, Arendt points out that "the only practical substitute for a nonexistent homeland was an internment camp. Indeed, as early as the thirties this was the only 'country' the world had to offer the stateless."[45]

Although I did not ask my respondents if they had lived in any kind of camps, one can easily recall images, broadcasted by the media around the globe, of displaced people or refugees squeezed in overloaded trains and buses with uncertain or unknown destinations, often ending up either in the IDPs or in refugees internment camps, which also included accommodation facilities like hotels and military barracks. As well, I still remember television images of the frightened faces behind barbed wire in the prison camps that were evidently held by all three conflicting sides in Bosnia and, in general, by all warring parties in the former Yugoslavia. With regard to the phenomena of homelessness, statelessness and rightlessness, or in terms of civil, social and human rights, my findings show that the vast majority (6 out of 7) of the respondents felt homeless and rightless due to the war. As well, they considered themselves being both apatrides and refugees. Interestingly, only four respondents said that they felt stateless, or that they feel they have lost their state. This decrease regarding 'statelessness' is due to different national perceptions and personal sentiments of belonging to the present day Bosnia. This is best explained by one Serbian, one Muslim and one Croatian respondent: "Bosnia is still the state and homeland of Croats and Muslims, but no more of Serbs who lost Bosnia. Therefore, while all Bosnian Serbs will say that they are homeless, stateless and rightless, Bosnian Muslims and Croats are only rightless and homeless because they lost Yugoslavia (SFRY) but not Bosnia which is still their state."[46] Nevertheless, *regardless of the respondents' nationality, all of them are 'Yugonostalgic,'* that is, they have nostalgia for their lost homeland, socialist Tito's Yugoslavia (SFRY), but not for the last (Milosevic's) Yugoslavia (FRY) or the nowadays mutilated Bosnia. All of the respondents point out that they miss the Adriatic Sea, friends, family and, particularly the life-style they enjoyed. Two of them, a Muslim and a Serb, emphasized nostalgia for their grandparents and the hearth as their memory of Yugoslavia and Bosnia is very vague and blurry since they were too young when the war broke out and forced them to leave their native land.

My findings demonstrate that Arendt's examination of the phenomena of homelessness, statelessness and rightlessness is not only relevant but also a necessary tool for analyzing present day refugees from Yugoslavia, and elsewhere. Arendt's accurate prediction that the stateless people will mark the twentieth century is indispensable to understanding both the origins and historical continuity of this new phenomenon, which is still reflected in growing refugee figures on a global scale. In this 'stateless' sense, the refugees from Bosnia, and Yugoslavia at large, became a part of the history of the Balkans at the end of what correctly can be called 'the stateless century.' This hundred year old story of losing one's homeland is also apparent in Brubaker's analysis of "mass ethnic unmixing" in the Balkans, which includes his vision of a recurrence of this practice since "its plausibility is enhanced by the Yugoslav refugee crisis, which resulted directly from the dissolution of a multinational state and the incipient reconfiguration of political authority along national lines."[47] It seems to me, however, that in our times the world has not advanced much with regard to civil, human and social rights. The end of the twentieth century as well as the beginning of new millennium is, in this regard, an obvious continuation of modern war, or a 'politics of sorrow,' which entails the extermination of innocent people and their massive displacement, or the 'uprootedness' of designated 'undesirables'. Nevertheless, in a consoling manner, Arendt reminds us that life itself cannot be eradicated or completely destroyed, because every birth is a new beginning and every beginning brings a new hope for humanity. She closes her extraordinary analysis of the origins of totalitarianism and statelessness, which go hand in hand with the politics of the extermination, by stating that,

> ...there remains also the truth that every end in history necessarily contains a new beginning; this beginning is the promise, the only 'message' which the end can ever produce. Beginning, before it becomes a historical event, is the supreme capacity of man; politically, it is identical with man's freedom...this beginning is guaranteed by each new birth; it is indeed every man.[48]

In accordance with Arendt's diagnosis of ever-growing statelessness, the number of worldwide refugees has indeed increased and it is rising on daily basis, while, on the other hand, the protection of human rights is apparently decreasing throughout the world.[49] Not surprisingly then that the UNHCR statistics, according to Donald Moore, puts "the figure of worldwide refugees since 1945 at 60-100 million."[50] Even more striking are the figures of Avtar Brah who stresses that since the 1980s there is an unprecedented new wave of mass migrations occurring throughout the world. Brah explains that while in 1990, according to the estimation of the International Organization for Migration, "there were over 80 million...'migrants' " on a global scale, of whom "15 million were refugees or asylum seekers," already by 1992 "some estimates put the total number of migrants at 100 million, of whom 20 million were refugees and asylum seekers."[51] Such ever-increasing refugee figures as well as usual statistical inconsistency of the exact number of refugees is remarkably analyzed by Arendt who argues that between the two world wars there was no reliable statistics about refugees and apatrides, or stateless peoples, since the politicians at the time decided to resolve the problem of statelessness by simply ignoring it in order to enhance the process of repatriation, or deportation to the country from which these people previously escaped or were banished. For this reason, Arendt rightly claims that "the postwar term 'displaced persons' was invented during the war for the express purpose of liquidating statelessness once and for all by ignoring its existence."[52] In my opinion, the following Arendt's statement still best explains the statistical discrepancy surrounding refugee numbers not only then but also now, predicting much higher figures:

> While there is one million 'recognized' stateless, there are more than ten million so-called 'de facto' stateless; and whereas the relatively innocuous problem of the 'de jure' stateless occasionally comes up at international conferences, the core of statelessness, which is identical with the refugee question, is simply not mentioned. Worse still, the number of potentially stateless people is continually on the increase.[53]

With regard to the post Cold war 'New World Order,' officially announced by George Bush Senior in 1990 as the justification for the first Gulf War, Baudson demonstrates statistical evidence about its direct responsibility for the ever-increasing number of the refugees on the world scale. As Baudson lucidly remarks:

In contrast to the Roman Empire that sustained Pax Romana during two Ages on both coasts of the Mediterranean, the new world order within six years has delivered more armed conflicts and UN interventions than 40 years of the Cold War: 22 UN operations between 1988 and 1994 in contrast to 13 between 1948 and 1988. There has never been so many displaced people and refugees as since the new world order is on stage: 17 million refugees in 1991 and 27 million in 1996.[54]

I hope that it is clear by now why the legacy of Yugoslavia's apatrides and refugees is above all due to external Balkanization, or the old and new world orders, in particular within the twentieth century. This argument is supported by both Baudson's political analysis of the current new world order and by Arendt's historical analysis of the very emergence of the new modern phenomena of statelessness and homelessness resulting from the post World War I world order, which is marked then, as now, by the failure of the International Community to establish successful protection of both human and national minority rights. As we have seen, all three Yugoslavias (1918-2003) were created and destroyed primarily, but not exclusively, by powerful Western countries and their 'Divide and Rule' politics in the Balkans. Since the beginning of the twentieth century, the International Community ignored human and national minority rights, particularly true in the current context, contributing in this way to the legacy of statelessness in Yugoslavia and the Balkans at large. It is beyond the scope of this book to analyze if refugees are now easier naturalized or repatriated than in Arendt's time, which is a hard task anyway due to the enormous increase in both *de facto* and *de jure* refugee figures. Nevertheless, for the lucky ones that succeed in the very selective and demanding immigration process, it is presumably much easier to become naturalized citizens than it was in these periods described by Arendt.

However, the findings of my survey conducted with refugees from Bosnia support the well-known fact that Canada is one of the leading world's immigration countries and the appreciated 'safe haven' for refugees. This is due to Canada's well-organized immigration process, good socio-economic conditions as well as having one of the fastest naturalization policies. This fact is made obvious from the findings of my survey research. When asked "Why did you choose to live in Canada," the vast majority of respondents point out that Canada offered the best conditions, such as, well-organized paper work,[55] the immediate permanent residence with a work permit, very good social and healthcare services as well as citizenship within approximately five years. Some respondents also emphasized that they chose Canada because it is a multicultural country as well as a more 'humane' and 'safer' state than the neighbouring U.S. For the respondents, Canada has good social security policies and programs as well as fewer crimes, or a much lower crime rate, than is the case in both U.S. or Western European countries. The latter however are geographically closer to Bosnia, but all of them have much more rigorous immigration policies (except distant Scandinavia). Since the vast majority of the respondents landed in Canada between 1994-1996, they had already become naturalized citizens of Canada. According to my findings, it was easier and faster to become a Canadian citizen than a citizen of the new successor states of the former Yugoslavia (ratio 5:4 in comparison between Canada and Yugoslavia). In addition to the findings illustrated in the Table 2 where we can see that two respondents already declare their nationality as Canadians, the majority stated that besides considering themselves as citizens of Canada, they also see themselves as cosmopolitan citizens.

In this regard, the 'Yugoslav Saga' has a 'happy ending' in a multicultural and cosmopolitan Montreal for refugees from Bosnia, and Yugoslavia at large. It is needless to say that this happy ending does not relate in any sense to the banal Hollywood happy ending involving usually an American Rambo as the winner (or saviour) in the mythic struggle between the good and evil. Rather, the happy ending for Bosnian and Yugoslav refugees, particularly for the vast majority of my respondents who are already citizens of Canada, is primarily due to several very specific reasons that favour their staying in Canada as opposed to returning to Bosnia. These reasons in my account are as follows. First of all, I argue that ethnically divided and 'purified' Bosnia is also a *pure economic catastrophe*, in particular due to the second round of the IMF's and World Bank's structural adjustment reforms of the 1990s, the material destruction of the country in the war and the neo-colonizing reconstruction program under the auspices of the U.S.-led Western powers and the International Community. As we have seen, the result of 'ethnic purification' is particularly visible in the mixed parts of Croatia (Krajina) and Bosnia, which are now more or less 'pure' territories in the national sense. It should be repeated at this point that while Slovenia was and still is the most ethnically homogenous successor state of the former Yugoslavia, the last Yugoslavia (FRY), or the present day union of Serbia and Montenegro, is now the most ethnically 'mixed' or heterogeneous state which, as such, is still the 'homeland' of various nations and national minorities. Although Macedonia is also ethnically mixed, we have seen that its mixture primarily includes Macedonians and the ethnic Albanians (who are non-Slavic people originally from the neighbouring Albania) between whom there is an ongoing conflict over the territories that both groups inhabit, which is also a key issue in the neighbouring Serbian province of Kosovo and Metohija. With regard to a 'pure' economic catastrophe, Slovenia is, up to now, the only successor state of the former Yugoslavia where this fact is not as viable and tangible as is in other former republics of Yugoslavia. Slovenia is also, for now, the first and only successor state that is scheduled to join the EU in the spring of 2004, which will ultimately and hopefully improve its living standard.

Furthermore, this ethnic purification and economic disaster in Bosnia produces the so-called *fear of the future* that is also enhanced by the history of external and consequent internal Balkanization both being the deep-rooted cause of peoples' uncertain vision of the future, since looking at the future involves necessarily looking at the past. Especially looking through the prism of unpleasant 'lessons' from history. This is nicely said by Smilja Avramov who, to paraphrase her once again, reminds us that one who did not learn from history becomes inevitably its victim. In addition, there is an emerging 'panic' regarding uncertainty of the impact of the contamination by depleted uranium due to NATO's bombing campaigns in the Balkans, affecting the territories of Krajina in Croatia, of Bosnia and the whole of the last Yugoslavia.[56] Besides all of these reasons, consummating a Canadian citizenship ultimately means the end of homelessness, rightlessness and statelessness offering thus a safer and a brighter future for children of Yugoslav refugees in general and, in particular, of my respondents. All of the above mentioned factors in combination with the familiar cultural diversity characteristic to Montreal are the main reasons for choosing Canada and naturalization, instead of choosing the repatriation or return to Bosnia, or, for that matter, to any other successor state of the former Yugoslavia. Best summarized by one respondent, all reasons for not returning to Bosnia can fit in a simple sentence: "It's not worth it! (*Nema od toga nista*)."

The following responses of my respondents provide additional insights into major reasons that refrain them from returning to Bosnia, now divided along national and religious lines. These are the answers to the questions "What are the main reasons that prevent you from returning to your 'home'?" and "Under which conditions would you return?"

1) I would not return because Yugoslavia (SFRY) is dismantled and Bosnia is nationally divided. I have a mixed marriage and I feel as a citizen of the world. I would not return even if my multicultural city (Sarajevo) belonged to my ethnic group [Serbs], because I neither like nor want national divisions. For me and my child it is unacceptable to live in Muslim culture with obligatory religious (Muslim or Catholic) programs in the schools.

2) As I did not grow up in SFRY [a Muslim, under 24 years] I do not know much about Yugoslavia, but I would never go back into such problems and troubles.

3) Where to go? In such an unstable political and economic situation and in such an unemployment crisis? I would return only to the 'old former Yugoslavia' (SFRY), not in these new states. The children could never get used to the new education system and school curriculum [mixed marriage, a Serb and Muslim].

4) I would never return, because there are no more Serbs in my city, some 'new' people live there now, there is primitivism and no conditions for return. There is no future, there is nothing there [in Bosnia]; what we [our family] need is 'return to the future' [a Serb].

5) I would return if I would find a job in my profession and if there would be resembling life conditions and economic standard as it was before the war [a Croat].

6) First of all, I don't have a house or place to return to because everything is burned to the ground. Secondly, even if I would get my apartment back, I need a job that is not easy to find, as it is also impossible to get back the former one. Finally, my children have dropped out of the Yugoslav system, they are used to a Canadian life-style and education system, they don't want to go back to Bosnia [a Muslim].

7) I would not return because there is nothing left of what used to be my everyday life, nothing familiar exists anymore: neither state nor city nor people [a Serb].

In order to better understand these statements, particularly in terms of the new obligatory religious curriculum, or 'facultative' classes, in schools, we must remember that socialist Yugoslavia (SFRY), similar to other communist countries, had separated politics/state from religion/church and promoted official atheism. In consequence, Yugoslavia was a secular and modern country with pronounced religious diversity and the protection of religious freedoms. Catherine Samary's Table entitled "Ethnic Composition and Religious Affiliation in Bosnia-Herzegovina 1990" supports the above claim. Prior to the war, 46% of the total Bosnia's population was without religious affiliation while the rest was divided as follows: 20% of Orthodox Serbs out of 31% of Serbs of the total Bosnia's population, 16.5% of Muslims out of 43.7% of the total Bosnian Muslim people and 15% of Catholics out of 17.3% of the total Croatian population in Bosnia.[57]

My findings above all demonstrate a pronounced anti-chauvinist and multicultural orientation of the respondents. This is essentially due to the fact that they had a good and 'normal' life in multinational and multicultural socialist Yugoslavia, which they loved as such. These former 'Yugoslavs' and 'Eskimos' (see the Table 2) were and still are anti-nationalists enjoying cultural and ethnic diversity. For this very reason, they appreciate Canadian multiculturalism and cultural diversity in Montreal that reminds them of Bosnia, in particular of Sarajevo, as previously stated by one respondent from Sarajevo who also emphasized the additional advantage of Montreal being a cosmopolitan city.

## Rebuilding Home in Montreal

According to my findings, this multicultural climate in Montreal, and Canada at large, is a valuable contribution to making the respondents feel more 'at home' than they would in an ethnically homogeneous country. Not surprisingly then that while only two respondents still do not consider Montreal as their new home but rather see it as a temporary solution, the majority of the respondents stated that Montreal is their new home. This 'adaptation' was quite fast: four respondents said they accepted Montreal as a new home within the first year and one said after two or three years.

Supporting the above argument about the anti-nationalist and multicultural orientation of the respondents, the vast majority (6 out of 7 families) made new friendships in Montreal mainly with the newcomers from the former Yugoslavia who also arrived in the 1990s mostly as refugees of various national origins. As well, the majority of respondents stated that they spend most of their leisure time with the Yugoslav people of diverse national backgrounds. It is apparent then that the memory and soul of multicultural and multinational Yugoslavia is still alive in Montreal, which, in turn, enhances my claim that socialist Yugoslavia was quite a viable and noble idea far from being an artificial project. It seems to me that even now, after this second bloody civil war in a row of such horrifying nature occurring within the twentieth century, the majority of diverse peoples from the former Yugoslavia, including or perhaps even led by refugees, do not hate each other. On the contrary, they are still, or like before the war, living together and supporting each other, especially if they live abroad where all Yugoslav peoples are equally 'mixed' as the immigrants sharing similar integration problems. It is a matter of fact that ethnic hatreds are vanished by now, or suppressed, and the war itself is, for the majority of people, in some way 'forgotten' within and outside the former Yugoslavia, since people meanwhile, have moved on with their lives driven either by the innate and perpetual human struggle for survival or for the improvement of life conditions. In the words of one respondent: "I am not interested in ethnic origins of the person I meet, but rather if we have a common ground, common interests and problems; for this reason I am mostly with 'our' people," that is with newcomers or refugees from the former Yugoslavia of various ethnic origins. Besides these various Yugoslav national groups, the respondents' new friends also include a 'traditional' variety of other peoples, such as: the Quebecois, English Canadians, Ethiopians, Bulgarians, Latin Americans and Inuit people.

Furthermore, the vast majority stated that Montreal is, by and large, a beautiful and multicultural city. As well, some stressed the advantages of a "bilingual, European, French and cosmopolitan city." None of my respondents ever lived in a city that is similar in size to Montreal, which is understandable given that Belgrade is the biggest city in the former Yugoslavia with approximately half the size of Montreal in both its population and territory. While there is an obvious pattern of similar opinions about the city of Montreal, there are some noteworthy differences with respect to the reasons for choosing Montreal. For three of the respondents the foremost reason was that they have relatives or friends already living in Montreal. Three other respondents stated that they chose it because of its multiculturalism and resemblance to a European city. The advice of the Canadian immigration officer who interviewed them abroad and the bilingualism of the city were mentioned by two respondents for each reason. Finally, one mentioned choosing Montreal due to job opportunities as it has a developed industry in the spouse's profession, and another respondent mentioned its cosmopolitanism. We can see that multiculturalism, or more accurately interculturalism, is a key factor for choosing and staying in Montreal. As one of the participants pointed out in terms of their first impressions of Montreal: "*It has a 'soul,' something unique.*" This uniqueness of Montreal is further explained by the same person: "It has a soul; it is a university city with the concentration of young students that give a special charm to the city. It is also a cosmopolitan and an immigrant city where English and French cultures meet and dominate the basis of [cultural] 'life' that is not 'interrupted' by the immigrants whose cultures simultaneously exist."

Cultural diversity then, besides the aforementioned easy immigration procedure and good social security system, plays a major role in accepting Montreal as a new home and Quebec as a new homeland. As one respondent, who was at first a refugee in another republic of the former Yugoslavia and then an asylum seeker in Western Europe, singled out Montreal as an unique city, because "there is a lot of ethnies and cultures, and all of them are coexisting in harmony and mutual respectfulness without provocation and intolerance." Despite these positive aspects of the multicultural and cosmopolitan attractiveness of Montreal, we will see in the next section that Bosnian and Yugoslav refugees also face some negative impacts of multiculturalism as well as other obstacles that prevent a faster and more complete integration as full-fledge citizens in such an affluent city and country.

Sociological research on (im)migration demonstrates that the immigrants' age, knowledge of language(s), educational and professional skills as well as personal characteristics and motivation are key elements in the integration process.[58] As well, the immigrants' reception by their new homeland and its people is very important, especially those first hours and days. In terms of first impressions, my findings show that the respondents appreciated the services offered at their arrival, in particular those of the 'Centre social d'aide aux immigrants' (CSAI). As explained by its director, Mme Lorette Langlois, CSAI was born in the aftermath of World War II, and since 1992 is mandated by the government of Quebec, by the Ministère des Relations avec les citoyens et de l'Immigration (MRCI), "for welcoming and establishing refugees in Montreal. Since 1994, more than 2000 persons transited through the center."[59]

According to my findings, this kind of reception and accommodation of (sponsored by the government of Canada) refugees is unique to the province of Quebec where the immigration authority provides very appreciated services at their arrival, such as: the reception at the airport, the accommodation in the downtown Montreal hotel "Maritime" and the welcoming services of the CSAI for the first week, including the necessary paper work and the assistance in finding the first apartment. Besides these positive first impressions of the reception and the immediate financial security provided by the social program, or Welfare benefits, there are some other favourable elements for their successful integration. Notably, the majority of respondents have a good educational background, professional skills and long employment history. With regard to their education, two out of ten respondents have a high school diploma, three of them have the equivalent of college, two hold a Bachelor's Degree and, finally, three of them have a Master's Degree.[60] Also, all of the respondents were permanently employed in Bosnia, ranging between ten to twenty years of work experience, and were very satisfied with their job position, salary and social status. This loss of 'normal' life conditions is at the heart of 'Yugonostalgia,' or the sorrow caused by the lost good life and the lost homeland. This is true not only for my respondents but also for other refugees (or immigrants) living now outside the territories of the former Yugoslavia. This is also true for those people who remained there, since the nostalgia for Yugoslavia (SFRY) means, above all, the nostalgic memory for the lost good or 'normal' life and, therefore, it knows no boundaries.

## Obstacles to Integration

As a comprehensive analysis of the integration process is too broad an issue and, therefore, beyond the scope of this book, my focus is rather on its preconditions with the identification of some particularities of the refugees' immigration trajectory that ultimately enables or disables their successful integration. Refugees in general, and especially my respondents from Bosnia, are a very specific social group that is, by definition, disadvantaged in 'making a new life' since usually they have lost forever, or for the moment, everything they had before their immigration, including their state and property, good jobs as well as their friends and nuclear or extended family members. To put it simply, they lost a 'good' or, at least, a 'normal' life. The circumstances under which a person leaves her or his country play a key role in the integration process, because the forced migration of refugees implies different conditions and opportunities than voluntary migration, which is usually driven by economic or business purposes. Of course, *de facto* or unregistered refugees often cross or change immigration categories in their struggle to obtain valid immigration documents. While refugees primarily seek a 'safe haven' in order to rebuild a lost life, or make a new one, the economic or independent immigrants have more clear 'prior' vision and perspective of their new or better life conditions, particularly in terms of their job opportunities in the country of immigration.

The main problems and obstacles of the newcomers, particularly refugees, that prevent better integration into Quebec's society and Montreal's community network are exposed in the above mentioned community newspaper *Le Jumelé*, in the same issue with the special report on "Régions du Québec et Nouveax Arrivants: Des Actions pour Contrer l'Exclusion Sociale (Regions of Quebec and the Newcomers: The Actions Against Social Exclusion)." In particular, there are two articles about Montreal's region that best summarize issues pertaining to the barriers of refugees' more rapid and complete integration. The first article relates to art therapy in which the author Hoori Hamboyan describes the interview with an artist from Sarajevo who claimed to feel 'uprooted' since arriving in Montreal. Besides this 'uprootedness' of refugees, Hamboyan summarizes other issues and problems pertaining to their integration process: "It seems that the difference, the isolation, the difficulties with the language, the cultural shock, the lack of self-confidence, and the feeling of guilt for abandoning their country, prevent or refrain the process of integration."[61] With regard to the community's support for refugees, Hamboyan suggests that art therapy is obviously one way of helping these people in dealing with their problems of isolation and integration, especially since 'the language' of the art is universal and, for this reason, art therapy is an attractive idea for the whole intercultural community network in Quebec. Furthermore, the second article includes the description and the recommendation of the director of the CSAI pertaining to the welcoming services for refugees:

Welcoming refugees involves the awareness and acknowledgement that these people have gone through tragic events: separation, rape, torture, stress, insecurity, exile. This is why it is necessary to have a follow-up to their settling. In their settling process, we must show respect for the client, make sure that there is a good contact with organizations and businesses, that appointments are followed up and that steps taken are efficient.

To organizations that welcome refugees we recommend to be compassionate, efficient, creative, have good management and patience, hoping everything will get better.[62]

These welcoming services for refugees are very important since they are coming as 'uprooted' people who are, more often than not, deprived of the possibility for a careful choosing and planning of the emigration, or of arranging their resettlement as a desired life project.[63] Even though this 'undesired' emigration implies both the final rescue and the realisation of the dreamed about opportunity for starting a new life, the uprootedness of refugees and their forced (or 'voluntarily forceful') migration is nevertheless undermining their successful integration. This is particularly reflected in the important difference between the age groups. In this sense, the majority of my respondents are in their late forties and this disadvantage is best explained by one respondent's concluding comments:

> We, the people who have already lived and enjoyed a full and good life and who came to Canada in our late forties, we will never be 'completely' integrated as will be the young people who previously have not created neither home nor life. We, the Bosnians, are traditional people tied to Bosnian soil and if the war would not have happened I would never leave the former Yugoslavia. For us, problem number one is that after the forties integration is harder, particularly due to different life-styles and the cultural gap between Canada and Yugoslavia. It is harder to change oneself and to adapt to a new life-style when one is in the late forties. As the Bosnian popular saying reveals: 'A plant is best transplanted while young!' [biljka se presaduje dok je mlada]

Furthermore, the Canadian government sponsored all of the respondents, which ultimately means that they came without any money, and consequently, their immediate livelihood is dependent on social security assistance, or welfare benefits. While this financial resource was very welcomed and appreciated at the time of their settling, however, as time went on, it was more damaging than beneficial because it did not help them find meaningful work and created a sense of dependence. In terms of 'cultural shock,' it is noteworthy to mention the impact of the so-called 'climate shock,' that is, all of the respondents who came during the winter were quite discouraged and disappointed by the biting cold and the snow, and therefore, were less impressed by the beauty of Montreal. Notably, one respondent was 'shocked' by the lack of washing machines in households and the existence of Laundromats where people wash their laundry 'together,' since in the former Yugoslavia almost everyone had a washing machine in their apartment and one's dirty laundry was perceived as something very private and intimate. This same respondent was further 'shocked' by the healthcare system and medical services, in particular of having to wait four or five hours in the emergency room before seeing a doctor, which was not often the case in the former Yugoslavia.

Although the majority of respondents consider themselves well integrated, nevertheless, they identify the following obstacles to their faster and more complete integration. In order of importance, the key interrelated problems are: a lack of money (5 out of 7 respondents) followed by the linguistic barriers (4) and their unemployed status. Other obstacles include a lack of social connections and interactions, the isolation, the insufficient access to information regarding employment and cultural life, a lack of leisure time, the social stigma of immigrants as poor people as well their stigmatization as welfare recipients. According to the responses pertaining to the participation in urban culture, a lack of money, particularly for the unemployed respondents, is the main reason for the overall decrease in their life standard and their participation in cultural and social life. This decrease in cultural and social life is augmented by a lack of leisure time, particularly for those working. With regard to their awareness of various cultural events, the majority of respondents are not only aware but they also go to see the multitude of free cultural events in Montreal, such as, the Montreal Jazz Festival, the Montreal Film Festival, Saint Jean Baptist and Canada Day—to list just few popular ones. As well, while they show awareness of different services offered by the urban community organizations, for example, those of the YMCA, Access Montreal and 'La Maison de la Culture,' some of the respondents besides using these services also use many others offered by the affluent socio-cultural network in Montreal. On the other side of the coin, however, is the fact that the biggest disadvantage in their new life in Montreal is the lack of a multiethnic community inclusive to all peoples (nations and national minorities) from the former Yugoslavia, where they would be able to meet and to discuss various issues, or to exchange information about events in the former Yugoslavia, as well as the employment opportunities in Montreal, or elsewhere in the North America. The findings clearly point out that the negative impact of multicultural, or intercultural, politics implies both the non-existence of a multinational Yugoslav community as well as the inadequate inclusion of the respondents in the existing network of urban community agencies established for supporting and helping newcomers and refugees in their resettlement process.

In spite of their awareness of some community agencies for newcomers, the respondents have not taken full advantage of diverse services. The government of Quebec has published in 1994 the *Directory of community agencies at the service of newcomers*, which was intended to be a reference tool for helping newcomers integrate into Quebec society. This directory includes over 30 community organizations from the City of Montreal, including other Towns and Cities of the Island of Montreal and its North and South Shores. As stated in the "Introductory Note," these organizations received the financial assistance in 1993-1994 from the Quebec's Ministre des Affaires Internationales, de l'Immigration et des Communautés Culturelles (MAIICC) "for the reception and settlement of immigrants, employment assistance and assistance for the francization of immigrants."[64] Apart from the CSAI, which was the only organization that all of the respondents were aware of and had used its services, there is an overall insufficient awareness of numerous other community agencies for newcomers, since the respondents' awareness of their existence ranged only from two to eight organizations. Even more deficient is the usage of their various services; in particular, the employment assistance, given the fact that one of the key obstacles for the respondents in their integration trajectory continues to be unemployment and unfamiliarity with the job market in Montreal.

When asked for comments or suggestions for improving the offered services of urban community organizations for newcomers, only one respondent who recently arrived, between 1999 and 2000, and who is aware of only two organizations, namely the CSAI and the Montreal Women Centre (Centre des femmes de Montreal), stated that both agencies "are excellent, they are helpful as you can address your problems there, especially in terms of the settlement and accommodation." The other respondents who landed between 1994 and 1996, emphasized that:

1) I don't know what kind of services they offer as I am not aware of these organizations, except for the CSAI which gave me what was designed for me.

2) We need faster information in our maternal language [Serbo-Croatian] provided by the agencies and people who speak our language in order to avoid 'wandering' and wasting of time upon our arrival.

3) Although all of these organizations have a humanitarian ground, it is contrary to the mentality of the former Yugoslavs [who are very proud

people] to accept help in clothing and food supplies; we need primarily moral support.

4) I would close all of these organizations because they are a waste of money, with the exception of the CSAI which services should be used in the first week of resettlement. I would abolish both welfare and these organizations as needless and useless. Instead, I am in favour of support from the Immigration authority for settlement projects and for job searches, for support in adapting of professional skills through a 'stage' [training] programs in our professions, and not through existing 'stupid' programs that are offered to us.

5) If Quebec has so many organizations, it should give money also to our community [the Serbian Church] to employ our person who could direct us in the first moments to avoid 'wandering.'

6) It is very important in the first contact with Canada to be received by someone who speaks our language and who knows our mentality and our taste in order to explain which food resembles ours, for example, to show us which products are the 'real' mayonnaise and the 'real' pickled cucumbers so that we can avoid buying, for instance, the [wrong] 'sweet' pickled cucumbers. Due to the cultural differences, this is possible only if provided by a person from our cultural milieu, and in no case by Canadians.

Thus, besides discussed positive aspects of multiculturalism, there is also the lack of a 'Yugoslav' multi-ethnic community organization in Montreal and elsewhere. As mentioned, this lack is partially due to the official non-existence of multinational Yugoslavs and Bosnians, or the resisting 'Eskimos,' and partly due to the inadequate, or exclusive, multicultural policy. Consequently, people of various national origins, like my respondents, who were 'Yugoslavs' by conviction prior to the civil war and who were, and still are, anti-nationalists by definition, especially the mixed families and officially declared Yugoslavs, lack now in their new homeland, like in multicultural Canada or in intercultural Quebec, their 'own' community organization which would be based on the only appropriate principle for membership: that of multi-nationality or, in other words, the inclusive non-ethnic principle. In addition to their unsatisfactory support by the above mentioned community organizations for newcomers, the respondents are, furthermore, excluded from the existing ethnic community network in their language(s) in Montreal due to national divisions and religious affiliation of these ethnic communities that are concentrated in and around churches, like Serbian and Croatian communities.[65] The only respondent who participates in diverse activities of his/her ethnic community emphasizes that the church, or the centre, is not helping people in need at all; on the contrary, the people help the church! The other respondents, who are not affiliated with their communities in any way, stated that they did not receive any help or support from their ethnic organizations. The majority of respondents did not even contact their ethnic communities since all are 'nationalist' in essence and, as such, inappropriate for them. For this reason, the vast majority of respondents addressed the need of having "multinational organization in order to be together; and not these existing organizations divided along national lines where we do not belong and cannot find ourselves."

Besides simplistic Hollywood-like media portrayals of 'good and bad guys' in the Balkans and subsequent biased representation of many diverse ethnic identities of refugees from the former Yugoslavia, the consequent lack of the desired and much needed multinational Yugoslav community organization in both Montreal and Canada is also due to the negative impact of multiculturalism which excludes small ethnic groups, such as refugees coming from civil or ethnic conflicts. I share the opinion of Beryl Langer who argues that the experience of Salvadoran refugees in their process of settlement demonstrates the limits of multiculturalism, which for this reason should be rethought and rewritten. I find Langer's critique of multiculturalism very appropriate for understanding obstacles to the integration of refugees from the former Yugoslavia. Even though Salvadorans and Yugoslavs have different life histories and, consequently, different needs in their new homeland(s), both groups nevertheless share a common destiny of forceful emigration of refugees escaping from civil conflicts and wars. In this sense, both groups challenge the concept of 'imagined' ethnic community in multicultural states, in the Salvadoran case that of English Canada and Australia, or in the case of my respondents that of Quebec's intercultural community. Langer accurately claims that this unrealistic concept is based on the exchange of history for ethnicity that, in turn, erases refugees' contested national histories and personal identities.

According to Langer, the Salvadoran case "presents a paradigmatic challenge to the foundational concept of 'ethnic community,' for refugees from civil conflicts construct the boundaries of 'imagined community' in terms of social and political divisions not easily papered over by 'ethnicity'."[66] The same argument holds for refugees from Bosnia and Yugoslavia who, regardless if for different reasons, like Salvadorans, do not fit into 'imagined' ethnic community designed for them by the multicultural agenda of Canada or by the intercultural vision of Quebec. Langer is right to state that "the history-ethnicity exchange implicit in multiculturalism rests on a fictive separation of culture from politics which is in practice unsustainable."[67] In other words, the multicultural concept of 'ethnic communities' constructs the 'Salvadoran ethnicity' in Diaspora regardless of the fact that "being Salvadoran is not a matter of ethnicity but of citizenship, and within Salvadoran citizenship 'difference' is marked in terms of class, politics, region, and whether or not one's forebears were Indian or Hispanic."[68] Central then to Langer's critical reflections on multiculturalism and its imposition of 'imagined ethnic community' on immigrants is the claim that "in constructing national groups as 'ethnic communities,' multiculturalism proceeds on the dubious assumption that these divisions [of class, religion, race/ethnicity and region] are rendered irrelevant by the experience of migration."[69] Similar to refugees from the former Yugoslavia, who have not only disputed national histories but who are coming from historically contested country now destroyed by civil war, of whom some are also officially non existing 'Yugoslavs' belonging apparently nowhere, Salvadorans, for different reasons and coming from a different context, are also excluded from the a-historical multicultural agenda. In Langer's words:

> Contested histories which produce different subject-positions have no place within the discourse of multiculturalism, which constructs immigrants not as bearers of history but as bearers of something called 'ethnic culture'—or culture divorced from history. For Salvadorans, the journey to 'countries of immigration' like Australia and Canada is a journey from history to ethnicity, stepping out of the continuing drama of civil war and negotiated peace in Central America into the cast of an 'ethnic group' in which divisions of class and politics are glossed by unities of culture and language.[70]

For this very reason, multiculturalism allows immigrants to retain their language and to maintain their music, food, religious and folkloric practices, which is not the case with the racial, ethnic, religious or class conflicts perceived rather as something that immigrants, especially refugees, should not bring with themselves in their new homeland. Langer lucidly concludes in this regard that "migrants are expected to leave their history at the door...and embrace the convenient fiction of 'ethnicity'."[71] At the heart of this exchange of history for ethnicity, which entails the oblivion of previous conflicts, is the fact that multiculturalism, "as ideology and state policy...was negotiated in the context of post-war migration from nations which had been on different sides, and whose internal divisions were a further source of potential conflict."[72]

Furthermore, Langer asserts that one of the foremost reasons surrounding the exclusion of Salvadoran refugees from the multicultural agenda is that they are not a large enough national group, which, in addition, is internally divided and has no stable leadership. As a small and conflictual group, Salvadorans have little or no chances for successful "alternative funding claims within the framework of multiculturalism," and therefore, their destiny is to belong to "Spanish-speaking... or Latin American community" that is, in reality, unified only by "language" regardless of "the complex histories of conquest and postcolonial struggle" in the different Spanish-speaking countries.[73] Langer argues that this transformation of the diversified political body into a 'unifying' cultural or ethnic form is at the core of the multicultural politics of "misrecognition" which opposes Salvadorans their "existential need for both 'recognition' and 'dignity'."[74] For this reason, Langer is right when emphasizing that we must defend not multiculturalism but rather cultural and political diversity, which is often recognized neither within 'imagined' ethnic communities nor between these different national groups. As both cases of El Salvador and Yugoslavia demonstrate, I agree with Langer that it is more than necessary to acknowledge the historical conditions which created this diversity since "we are dealing not just with 'cultural difference' but with the contested histories through which that difference has been inscribed."[75]

In this regard, Langer's argument about 'misrecognition' of the Salvadoran refugees and their contested histories in a similar way holds for refugees from Yugoslavia, a country with not only disputed histories but also with misinterpreted complexity of the recent civil war, whose survivors evidently include people of various national identities who are 'misrecognized' in multicultural Canada and intercultural Quebec. Even worse, some survivors are suffering from 'non-recognition' as the case of the supranational, or post-national, Yugoslavs and Bosnians (Eskimos) demonstrates. While the civil war in El Salvador was, to paraphrase Langer, a profoundly political story that has nothing to do with ethnicity in spite of the slaughtering of its indigenous population, the case of Yugoslavia, in contrast, was a profoundly national story of a series of civil wars fought along ethnic or national lines involving, in principle, ambitious and criminal projects of building homogenous nation-states. As such, these two groups of refugees, both survivors of vicious civil wars, have different needs regarding community organization in their new homeland(s). While Salvadoran refugees obviously need a more fragmented community network, thus, an organization outside the umbrella of Hispanic or Latin American cultural network that would respect their internal social, or class, differences and political divisions, the refugees from socialist Yugoslavia and Bosnia (where class struggle was irrelevant) need the very opposite. That is, an united multi-ethnic organization that would include all nations and national minorities from the former Yugoslavia and which would, as such, exist in parallel to other already in place ethnic or cultural communities divided principally along religious lines and concentrated around different churches. It is important to note that these various churches were always separated from the social and cultural life, within the former Yugoslavia and abroad, since Yugoslavia's diverse peoples for historical and political reasons practice different religions.

However, the Salvadoran and Yugoslav refugees share the common destiny of being survivors of civil wars as well as the lack of adequate understanding of their contested histories in multicultural Canada, or, for that matter, in any other country that promote multicultural co-existence, like Australia. This 'mis-recognition' consequently means that both groups also share the non-existence of cultural community organizations, which would be appropriate for both cases: for the contested political identities of Salvadorans and for the multinational and unifying orientation of Yugoslavs and Bosnians. Both groups are disadvantaged in terms of funding claims within the framework of multiculturalism or inter- culturalism as they are too small an entity and without stable leadership. This fact, to different extents, holds also for the existing ethnic communities in Montreal and Canada at large, which are now due to the civil war in Yugoslavia and their subsequent 'separation' reduced to many very small groups gathered around their churches. While various peoples of Yugoslavia have always had separate religious lives and divided churches regardless of the country in which they lived, before the outbreak of the civil war in 1991 all Yugoslav immigrants living in Montreal have attended separate religious services in separate Catholic, Orthodox or Muslim churches, but their cultural and social life at the time was common, concentrated around the Yugoslav associations and social clubs. United, however, Yugoslavs enjoyed not only more affluent social and cultural life in Canada at large (like cross-Yugoslav concerts, sport events, etc.) but they have also had more chances to be included into multicultural or intercultural programs, funded by the provincial governments. For these reasons, it is evident that both Salvadoran refugees and Yugoslav peoples illustrate and challenge the limits of multiculturalism as well as strongly support Langer's claim that:

> In the context of multicultural politics, 'ethnic community' might best be understood as a rhetorical device for legitimating claims to 'leadership' and infrastructural support, on the one hand, and as a bureaucratic fiction dictated by the need to rationalize the diminishing resources available for migrant welfare services, on the other. It is, however, a rhetorical device that recognizes neither the heterogeneity of contested history nor the complex and contradictory conditions of identity-formation within the global cultural economy. Narratives of 'ethnic community' must therefore be rewritten in terms which guarantee citizenship without suppressing difference.[76]

## Summary

We have seen in this chapter that Arendt's analysis of the origins of totalitarianism and statelessness, which are traceable to the post World War I world order, accurately predicted ever-growing refugee numbers, or rising stateless peoples, and the continuation of the extermination of 'undesirables,' or superfluous population, that she sees as a permanent danger of totalitarian solutions in modernity. This condition is enhanced in our times with growing everyday experience of loneliness and isolation that are preconditions for total domination. Besides providing a historical and political background regarding the emergence of the phenomena of statelessness, homelessness and rightlessness, I have demonstrated that this modern condition is particularly true with regard to some national groups in Yugoslavia(s), for whom the twentieth century indeed symbolizes the long 'stateless century' since they experienced, in the war intervals, the destiny of being apatrides and refugees, or stateless peoples. This is particularly true for the Jews and the Roma people who besides being the oldest groups of Yugoslavia's apatrides were also the victims and the survivors of the Nazi genocide. The hundred years of the 'politics of sorrow' in the Balkans, or of loosing one's homeland due to war, produced not only floods of stateless peoples but also imposed a moral dilemma not easily resolvable for modern refugees from Yugoslavia(s): whether one should remain or one should leave the country. This 'old' dilemma is omnipresent even now in peacetime, especially in Bosnia where people are still trying to leave in order not to go mad even though they know that they can 'wither' if they leave Bosnia to live abroad. This dilemma is inherent to the history of apatrides and refugees from the last century Yugoslavia and, certainly, there were always people who left and people who remained. Sometimes, regardless of their decision, these people ended up, once more, sharing the same destiny, like dying in the Spanish civil war or living in 'shameful' life conditions due to unemployment, as is the case for both present day Bosnian people in Bosnia and refugees living in Montreal (both being equally unemployed, or underemployed).

This chapter also provided some valuable answers to my main survey research questions, such as: What are the main problems or obstacles of Bosnian refugees in creating a new home in Montreal, or rebuilding a lost one? How are they supported by the various urban community organizations, particularly by their ethnic one(s)? What kind of help do they have and to what extent are their needs being fulfilled? As we have seen, the lack of a multiethnic Yugoslav community organization is one of the foremost disadvantages in the integration process for refugees from Bosnia and Yugoslavia at large. The existence of a multiethnic Yugoslav organization, social centre or club would mean, subsequently, that these refugees would be included in the network of cultural communities in Montreal (or elsewhere). However, since their arrival to Canada, they have been excluded from this network thereby lacking any kind of community support. If they had their Yugoslav community, they would be less isolated and ultimately would have better access to information regarding employment opportunities, since unemployment is the foremost problem for these refugees and for newcomers in general, regardless if they are refugees or any other category of immigrants. With good jobs and more money my respondents would be able to enrich their participation in diverse cultural events offered by multicultural and cosmopolitan Montreal. In addition, such a multiethnic community would help these and other refugees (perhaps joined by some 'older' immigrants who came after World War II and especially by those who came in the 1960s/70s) to preserve the 'multinational and multicultural' tradition of socialist Yugoslavia. As well, it would enable refugees from across Yugoslavia to discuss their life problems and exchange opinions and memories with people who share the same destiny. Finally, it would help them and, in particular, my respondents to feel more 'at home' in Montreal, and to appreciate much more Canadian multiculturalism and Quebec's interculturalism, especially the assistance of various community agencies for newcomers and refugees.

## NOTES

1. Hannah Arendt. *The Origins of Totalitarianism*. New York: A Harvest/HBJ Book, 1973 (1948). See particularly chapter 9 "The Decline of the Nation-State and the End of the Rights of Man," pp. 267-302.

2. *Ibid*, p. 287.

3. *Ibid.*, p. 288.

4. *Ibid.*, p. 289.

5. *Ibid.*, p. 275.

6. *Ibid.*

7. *Ibid.*, pp. 456, 457.

8. *Ibid.*, p. 474.

9. *Ibid.*, p. 459.

10. *Ibid.*

11. *Ibid.*, p. 478.

12. *Ibid.*, p. 275.

13. Catherine Samary. *Yugoslavia Dismembered*. Translated from French by Peter Drucker. New York: Monthly Review Press, 1995, p. 87.

14. *Ibid.*, p. 34. Samary refers to this data in her book to demonstrate that despite these numbers the new successors states of the former Yugoslavia are still not completely homogeneous. My intention is to bring an example for clarifying the confusion surrounding data about refugees, in particular regarding the categories of internally displaced persons and refugees as well as the criterion for distinguishing them.

15. For definitions of refugees and internally displaced persons see "Annex 2: Working Definitions" in Annex B in *Refugees and Migration in Central and Eastern Europe*. Montreal: Canadian Human Rights Foundation, 1997, pp. 39, 40. The provided definition of the term 'refugee' was established and universally accepted by the Convention of 1951 and the Protocol of 1967. For the Convention refugee status in Canada see the application form or *Immigration Act* or the *Convention Refugee Determination Division Rules*.

16. See *Citizenship and Immigration Statistics 1996*. Ottawa: Minister of Public Works and Government Services Canada, 1999, pp. 12, 13.

17. "Mlijecni Put" (The Milky Way). Film director Faruk Sokolovic, MEBIUS FILM, Sarajevo, 2000. The story is written by Edina Kamenica according to real events. All translation mine if not indicated otherwise.

18. The original film music from "Mlijecni Put" (The Milky Way). Compositor Zlatan Fazlic Fazla, Copyrights NARATON, Sarajevo, 2001.

19. Translated by Tamara Vukov.

20. The Convention refugee status, or perhaps similar status based on humanitarian grounds, is probably still granted primarily to 'mixed' families. However, since the immigration category based on humanitarian grounds is a very broad one, it is possible that there also exist special immigration programs for peoples from the former Yugoslavia in general, or at least, for some of its regions.

21. See particularly chapter 9 "The Decline of the Nation-State and the End of the Rights of Man."

22. Jürgen Habermas. "Appendix II. Citizenship and National Identity (1990)." *Between Facts and Norms: Contributions to a Discourse Theory of Law and Democracy*, translated from German by William Rehg. Cambridge Mass: The MIT Press, 1996, p. 508, my emphasis.

23. Arendt, *op.cit.*, pp. 270-272.

24. Despite the fact that Roma people, or Gypsies, and Jews were not mentioned by Aleksa Djilas (1996) nor by Rogers Brubaker (1999) in their discussion of the national minority question in the first Yugoslavia, and even though they were very small ethnic groups, particularly at that time, it is necessary to mention them due to their extermination in World War II that is further enhanced, or continued and repeated, by their recent expulsion or 'voluntary' emigration in the 1990s.

25. Gerard Baudson. *Novi Svetski Poredak i Jugoslavija*. Beograd: ING-PRO, 1996, p. 105. Translated from French by Dimitrije Radovanovic. (Original version: *Le Nouvel Ordre Mondial et la Yugoslavie*. Paris: Gill Wern Editions. 1996).

26. *Ibid.*, p.106.

27. Mihailo Crnobrnja. *The Yugoslav Drama*. Montreal: McGill-Queen's University Press, 1994, p. 51.

28. *Ibid.*, p. 50.

29. *Ibid.*, p. 52.

30. Aleksa Djilas. *The Contested Country: Yugoslav Unity and Communist Revolution 1919-1953*. Cambridge Massachusetts: Harvard University Press, 1996 (1991), pp. 62, 63.

31. For example, Baudson, Crnobrnja (1994), Djilas, Samary and Brubaker (1999).

32. Rogers Brubaker. *Nationalism Reframed: Nationhood and the National Question in the New Europe*. Cambridge: Press Syndicate of the University of Cambridge, 1999 (1996), p. 148. See particularly chapter 6 entitled "Aftermaths of Empire and the Unmixing of Peoples."

33. *Ibid.*, pp. 151, 152.

34. *Ibid.*, pp. 152-166.

35. Arendt, *op.cit.*, p. 273.

36. *Ibid.*, p. 274.

37. Ivo Andric. "Pismo iz 1920" (The letter from 1920) in his collection of *Jevrejske Price* (*The Jewish Stories*). Belgrade: Narodna Knjiga, 1991 (first published in French in 1987).

38. *Ibid.*, p. 73, ("Tako je zavrsio zivot covek koji je pobegao od mrznje"), translated by Tamara Vukov.

39. Arendt, *op.cit.*, p. 267, my emphasis.

40. *Ibid.*, pp. 268, 269.

41. *Ibid.*, p. 275.

42. *Ibid.*

43. *Ibid.*, pp. 277, 278.

44. *Ibid.*, pp. 283-285.

45. *Ibid.*, p. 284.

46. The current status of the Bosnian Serbs is problematic since they lost both Bosnia and Yugoslavia and now they are confined to their 'mini' State within Bosnia, named "*Republika Srbska*" (The Serbian Republic). Bosnian Serbs are, in fact, somewhere in between both of these new Federations, one of Serbia and Montenegro and the other of Bosnia, which includes only Croats and Muslims. Even more problematic is the precarious status of the Cro-

atian Serbs, especially of those from 'Krajina' from which all Serbs were banished in 1995. Given the scope of ethnic cleansing there, it should not be a surprise that few people live in 'Krajina.' At best, some returned, mostly elderly people driven by their wish to die in their 'home.' Their return is also due to the fact that Milosevic's Yugoslavia (FRY) was flooded with Serbian refugees from Croatia and Bosnia (and now from Kosovo), for whom it had nothing to offer since the country was completely destroyed, politically by Milosevic and economically by the International sanctions. Belgrade, the capitol of the once proud and internationally respected Tito's socialist Yugoslavia, became in Milosevic's time a city that can accurately be called 'the capitol of apatrides,' or stateless people.

47. Brubaker, *op.cit.*, p. 151.

48. Arendt, *op.cit.*, p. 479.

49. Ironically, on the one hand, the 'new style' of protecting jeopardized human or national minority rights by the 'International Community' in our times includes also (NATO's or U.S.) Air Strikes and 'humanitarian' bombing campaigns against entire countries and populations, for example, against Iraq and Milosevic's Yugoslavia, or against the Serbs in Croatia and Bosnia. On the other hand, when there is no direct or indirect threat against Western geopolitical or economic interests, as was the case in the announced genocide in the strategically not so important Rwanda or East Timor, NATO and the West favour the option of inaction, or non-interference in the internal affairs of such problematic countries. This obvious 'double standard' politics in international affairs is at the core of the loss of credibility of Western powers led by the U.S., who in turn also has a strong influence on the international institutions like the UN.

50. Donald S. Moore. "Remapping Resistance: 'Ground for Struggle' and the Politics of Place" in *Geographies of Resistance*. S. Pile and M. Keith (eds). London and N.Y.: Routledge, 1997, p. 106, note 33.

51. Avtar Brah. "Diaspora, Border and Transnational Identities" in *Cartographies of Diaspora: Contesting Identities*. New York and London: Routledge Press, 1996, p. 178.

52. Arendt, *op.cit.*, p. 279.

53. *Ibid.*

54. Baudson, *op. cit.*, p. 17, my translation.

55. Including an immigration loan with a reasonable interest rate for paying their journey to Canada, which is very attractive to refugees considering that usually they have neither financial resources nor personal savings.

56. See Canadian newspapers from January 2001, such as *National Post*, *The Gazette*, *La Presse*. Also see the extensive writing on this subject by Michel Chossudovsky et al., at http://emperors-clothes.com.

57. Samary, *op. cit.*, p. 89.

58. See more details particularly in Marina Luksic-Hacin *Ko Tujina Postane Dom: Resocializacija in Narodna Identiteta pri Slovenskih Izseljencih* (my translation from Slovenian: When a Foreign Country Became a Home: Resocialization and National Identity of Slovenian Emigrants). Ljubljana: Znanstveno in Publicisticno Sredisce, 1995 and Peter Klinar *Mednarodne Migracije v Kriznih Razmerah* (my translation from Slovenian: International Migrations). Ljubljana: Zalozba Obzorja, 1985. Along with general theories of migration, both scholars also elaborate issues pertaining to migration flows in the former Yugoslavia, with special emphasizes on Slovenes since they are from Slovenia.

59. "Pour accueillir et établir les réfugiés publics à Montréal. Depuis 1994, plus de 2000 personnes ont transité par le centre," Lorette Langlois, cited in the Montreal's community newspaper Le Jumelé (Tribune Libre du Réseau Jumelage Interculturel), Vol 2, No. 1, March 2001, p. 8, my translation. 'Le Réseau Jumelage' is financed by the governement of Quebec, by the Ministère des Relations aves les Citoyens et de l'Immigration (MRCI).

60. See more about immigrants from the former Yugoslavia in Quebec, in particular about their educational and professional background in Profils des communautés culturelles du Quebec. MAIICC: Quebec, 1995.

61. "Il apparaît que la différence, l'isolement, les difficultés avec la langue, le choc culturel, le manque de confiance en soi, et le sentiment de culpabilité d'avoir 'abandonné' son pays, empêchent ou relentissent le processus d'intégration." In Le Jumelé, op.cit., p. 8, my translation.

62. "L'Accueil des réfugiés, c'est tout d'abord, la prise de conscience que ces personnes ont vécu des situations tragiques : séparations, ruptures, viols, tortures, stress, insécurité, exil. D'où, l'exigence d'un suivi après leur installation. Pour la première installation, il faut conjuguer le respect des clients, le contacts heureux avec les institutions et les entreprises, le suivi des rendez-vous et l'efficacité des démarches...Aux organismes d'accueil nous recommandons de conjuger la compassion, l'efficacité, la créativité, une saine gestion et la patience, espérant que tout va s'améliorer." Lorette Langlois, cited in Le Jumelé, ibid. Translated by Diane Bélanger.

63. See more about issues pertaining to refugees' identities and their 'uprootedness' particularly in Liisa H. Malkki, chapter 3, "National Geographic: The Rooting of Peoples and the Territorialization of National Identity among Scholars and Refugees" in Culture, Power, Place: Explorations in Critical Anthropology. Akhil Gupta & James Ferguson eds., Durham & London: Duke University Press, 1997.

64. Directory of community agencies at the service of newcomers. Gouvernement du Québec, Ministère des Affaires Internationales, de l'Immigration et des Communautés Culturelles (MAIICC), 1994.

65. As already mentioned, the majority of people in Bosnia, and Yugoslavia, were without religious affiliation, that is, people were mostly either atheists or believers who did not practice religion. For more details about existing ethnically divided cultural communities from the former Yugoslavia in Quebec, see Profiles des communautés culturelles du Quebec, op. cit., pp. 643, 644.

66. Beryl Langer. "Globalisation and the Myth of Ethnic Community: Salvadoran Refugees in Multicultural States" in Multicultural States: Rethinking Difference and Identity. David Bennett (ed.). London and N. Y.: Routledge, 1998, p. 163.

67. Ibid., p. 166.

68. Ibid., p. 167.

69. Ibid., p. 164.

70. Ibid., p. 165.

71. Ibid.

72. Ibid.

73. Ibid., p. 169.

74. Ibid., pp. 169, 175.

75. Ibid., p. 175.

76. Ibid., 176.

# Conclusion

Throughout this book, I have examined the correlation between three broad areas related to the disintegration of the Socialist Federal Republic of Yugoslavia: the national question, geopolitics and the phenomenon of statelessness. In contrast to the simplistic representation of Balkanization as internal divisions and wars among belligerent Balkans tribes over historically disputed territories, I have argued that one must distinguish between internal and external Balkanization. Both are indispensable elements in understanding the complexity surrounding the violent collapse of Yugoslavia. It is for this reason that *A Politics of Sorrow* takes into account the internal conflicts resulting in civil war(s) and the external influences, or the foreign dimension. Both Balkanizations are responsible for the innocent civilian victims and survivors of the war, for massively displaced population and refugees. Therefore, the answer to the question "What did go wrong in Yugoslavia?" cannot be solely reduced to internal factors, or ethnic nationalism. As argued, the history of Yugoslavia does not reflect ancient hatreds among Yugoslav nations nor the artificiality of its statehood. Instead, the history of external Balkanization illustrates a centuries-long struggle of the South Slavs for liberation from various colonial powers. Key to understanding the onset of the conflict is the crisis of the socio-economic and political system brought about by the 'New World Order' and its imposition of the free-market ideology. Contrary to Samuel Huntington's claims about 'ancient hatreds' in Yugoslavia and the clash between civilizations in Bosnia, the violent conflict between the Bosnian nations, namely the Serbs, Croats and Muslims is a twentieth century phenomenon. Instead of his 'clash of civilizations' there is a long history of foreign occupation of various powers in the Balkans with their specific geopolitical, strategic and economic interests. For that matter, this external Balkanization even dates prior to the settlement of the South Slavs in the

Balkans. The political fragmentation of the Balkans is thus an ancient story of 'Divide and Rule' politics, a well-known conquering formula dating from the time of the Roman Empire.

The tragedy of Yugoslavia includes crimes committed with extraordinary boldness and a huge deception about them, propagated particularly by Western/U.S. politicians and the media. Far from the Hollywood-like portrayal of 'good and bad' guys in the Balkans, the victims and perpetrators include people of all nations involved in conflicts. Furthermore, the casualties and survivors of the war in the former Yugoslavia are primarily nationally 'mixed' people and the 'newly created' national minorities, such as the Serbs, the Croats and the Muslims in Bosnia. Both groups, the 'mixed' and the 'new' minorities, became by definition 'undesirable' populations. Consequently, all sides involved in war had the same goal: to avoid becoming a national minority, which ultimately meant their expulsion or treatment as second class citizens. I advocate, therefore, shared responsibility for the crimes since none of the warring parties was innocent. The violent collapse of the former Yugoslavia then is due to the incompatibility of the 'invisible' borders between nations and the administrative borders of the republics. It is, above all, due to the early and unreasonable international recognition of the new successor states of the former Yugoslavia in their republican, thus, not national borders, without any guarantee for the protection of national minority rights.

Accordingly, the disintegration of Yugoslavia is a complex issue that, as such, far exceeds the limited theoretical frameworks of both theories of nation and nationalism, primordialism and constructivism, which focus their analysis exclusively on ethnic nationalism, or internal Balkanization, failing to embrace and explain the broader international and geopolitical context considered to be of a distant, secondary importance. The examination of the broader international context challenges this false dichotomy and reveals a multitude of external and internal factors that brought about the break up of Yugoslavia. While extreme and strong variations of both schools are exaggerated and unsustainable in practice, the weak variants are more modest and persuasive, whose convergence provide more reasonable ground for understanding the phenomena of nation and nationalism. Both theories, however, ascribe 'divine' characteristics to the nation by claiming that its origins, regardless if they are primordial or modern, and the ideal type of a stable national identity can only be found in the West. For both schools, thus, Eastern and Southern Europeans have unstable identities based on 'collectivism,' or solidarity, in contrast to Western individualism and liberalism. For this reason, both schools inaccurately refer to the seven Yugoslav nations as 'ethnic' or 'ethnonational' groups. Although their national development was interrupted by the colonization of the Balkans, all of the Yugoslav nations are 'old' nations, which have grounded their national identities in their medieval kingdoms. In discussing the civil war of the 1990s, both extreme variants reach a dead-lock by claiming either the 'irresolvability' of nationalist conflicts in Brubaker's terms or Huntington's 'clash of civilizations' and 'kin-country syndrome' in Bosnia and the Balkans at large.

Moreover, we have seen that Yugoslav nations are of the same ethnic origin and have similar rather than different cultures. As well, Yugoslavia was created and shaped by both centripetal and centrifugal forces, involving thus common civil and separate ethnic projects. While it is true that within the twentieth century there have been three wars among Yugoslav nations, it is also true that twice, in World War I and World War II, Yugoslavs were pushed to fight on opposite sides due to previous occupation and division of their territories. Although this time there was no such direct foreign intervention, the external factors, especially the role of Germany and U.S., were crucial in dismantling Yugoslavia (the war in Croatia was called Genscher's war while in Bosnia it was Clinton's war). The origins of the idea of formation of a common, modern, nation-state involved strong centripetal tendencies, or pro-Yugoslav orientation, that resulted in the unification of the South Slavs in their first state. While this Yugoslav idea about the unity of all South Slavs into one state and the creation of one modern nation is much older, traceable to the Enlightenment, the centrifugal tendencies that involved aggressive ethnic nationalism and armed conflicts are rather recent. As well, all seven Yugoslav nations (Croats, Macedonians, Montenegrins, Muslims, Serbs, Slovenians, and Yugoslavs) never described themselves as 'ethnic groups.' Like Ukrainians, they perceived themselves as 'narod' (people/nation) rather than 'nacija,' which means exclusively 'nation' in a national(ist) sense that was in essence contrary to the very idea of socialist internationalism, and Yugoslav supranationalism. The former Yugoslavia was not only a mono-ethnic state of the South Slavic nations with a variety of ethnic or national minorities, but also the Yugoslav idea involved both civic and ethnic nationalism, including thus political and cultural projects.

The development of the postnational Yugoslavism that emerged in the 1950s was a viable and noble idea in spite of a small percentage of statistically registered 'Yugoslavs.' The small size of this paradoxical seventh nation of the former Yugoslavia does not prove the 'weakness' or 'artificiality' of the state, but rather shows the 'supranational' nature of Yugoslav community, which was built on socialist internationalism and political unity of all nations and minorities, or of all citizens and working people. As such, this new Yugoslavism was a form of civic nationalism, including 'declared' and 'undeclared' Yugoslavs. In contrast to ethnic nationalism, it referred to citizenship and not ethnicity. In fact, people were simultaneously Yugoslavs and Croats, or Serbs, or Muslims, etc. While Yugoslav national identity was based on citizenship and individualism, or simply personality, the recent ethnic projects of building 'pure' nation-states transformed 'individuals' into 'nationals.' The history of Yugoslavia illustrates then recent and not ancient national hatreds. It also demonstrates the 'viability' instead of 'artificiality' of the common state of South Slavs.

The Yugoslav nations, particularly in multinational Bosnia, did not hate each other for centuries prior to this war. On the contrary, the peoples of Yugoslavia, particularly Bosnians, developed an intercultural and multinational society based on interactive peaceful co-existence and mutual respect, which they loved as such. For this reason, the majority of Bosnian people (Bosnians) resisted ethnic nationalism and the consequent civil war. The overwhelming presence of 'Yugoslavs' in my survey findings supports the above argument. As we have also seen, the vast majority of victims of ethnic cleansing, or of national 'purification,' were Yugoslavs and 'mixed' families as well as 'new' minorities whose status all conflicting parties sought to avoid. The presence of one Yugoslav 'Eskimo' in my findings symbolically supports my argument about the anti-nationalist political climate and multiethnic resistance to the war, in particular in completely nationally mixed Bosnia. The former Yugoslavia was an advanced multinational federation with an obvious trend of ever-increasing percentage of ethnic intermarriages in addition to the heterogeneous composition of the republics. Indeed, its peoples were 'mixing' even before ethnic and cultural hybridization became increasing reality on a global scale. With the break up of their country, the Yugoslavs, once its proud citizens, became over night denationalized and deprived people. They became 'Eskimos' or 'Gypsies' since they lost their national identification in the form of citizenship and their homeland; they became apatrides and refugees in their own native land or abroad.

There is no real dilemma with regard to the question of whether Yugoslavia was destroyed from the inside or outside since, evidently, both external and internal forces were at work. It was a kind of simultaneous suicide and homicide. Socialist Federal Republic of Yugoslavia was a noble and successful experiment of non profit oriented economy based on social ownership and self-management by workers united into multinational federation of its nations and national minorities. While nations, and not republics, as was the case in the former Soviet Union, were sovereign, national minorities enjoyed the same rights and duties as national majorities. Also, the vast majority of minorities perceived themselves as Aboriginals or old settlers ('starosedeoci') of the Balkans and Yugoslavia. I have argued that the outbreak of the civil war was avoidable if the International Community would have 'frozen' the international recognition of the new successor states of Yugoslavia in their republican, thus not national, borders until the protection of the 'newly' created national minorities, the previous constitutional nations, would have been established. A closer historical analysis reveals a primacy of external Balkanization since the (re)colonization of Yugoslavia has a long history, including the current application. Ethnic divisions and struggles over borders and territories, or internal Balkanization, are rather the consequence of the previous external Balkanization. That is, the territorial division and subsequent turning of the South Slavs against each other is due to the geopolitical importance of their territory and the economic interests of diverse powers across history. Prior to the recent civil war in Yugoslavia, there were massive and multinational demonstrations across the country provoked by a deep economic and socio-political crisis induced by the second round of macro-economic structural adjustment reforms of the IMF and the World Bank, which also ignited further separatist ideas and secessionist claims.

Subsequently, the Yugoslavia's tragedy resulted in the largest refugee crisis in Europe since the end of World War II, which, if seen in a historical perspective, is a hundred year old story of statelessness, homelessness and rightlessness. This is notably due to various imperialist appetites towards the Balkans and the failure of the international institutions, like the League of Nations or its successor, the UN, to protect jeopardized rights of national minorities. External Balkanization has historically either directly produced or facilitated internal Balkanization, which included totalitarian solutions of the extermination and displacement of designated 'undesirables.' The history of 'Divide and Rule' in the Balkans demonstrates that the creation or disintegration of all three states of

Yugoslavia was strongly influenced from the outside, by various big powers. In consequence, some of Yugoslavia's national minorities were among the first European apatrides, the oldest group of *Heimatlosen*, which emerged due to and after the Great War as the failure of the post-war world order to provide an effective international protection of human and minority rights. This first major wave of Yugoslavia's apatrides, or stateless peoples, was supplemented by the second world war: first by the survivors of the Nazi occupation who succeeded to flee the country and then by the political emigration of local Nazi collaborators, who existed everywhere in Yugoslavia and were composed of both nations, like the Croatian 'Ustashi,' Serbian 'Chetniks,' Bosnian 'Young Muslims' and so on, as well as the national minorities, like German 'Folksdojcers,' Italians, Hungarians, Albanian 'Balisti,' etc. These flows of political migrations were followed in the 1990s by an estimated four million refugees, the result of the massive displacement or uprootedness of 'undesirable' populations. On different scale, for different reasons and in different times, all these people lost their homeland, some forever some for a historic moment. This continuing legacy of statelessness is primarily due to external Balkanization, or to the 'old and new' world orders, which are an integral part of the history of Yugoslavia, especially of the twentieth century.

As we have seen, the nationalist movements of the 1990s re-appropriated national symbols and flags that marked the times of Nazi occupation and the shameful collaboration of local fascist, or nationalist, forces. Since the ideology and practice of these extreme right-wing movements reflect almost identical national or ethnic intolerance as during World War II, any serious analysis of the recent eruption of aggressive and chauvinist ethnic nationalism in Yugoslavia with its destructive impact should incorporate Hannah Arendt's analysis of the origins of totalitarianism, particularly of totalitarian state terrorism. However, the genocide of the Serbs, Jews and Roma people in World War II was downplayed by Tito's communist regime in order to maintain the socialist policy of 'brotherhood and unity,' a war time slogan. Tito believed that 'the dark spirits' of not-so-ancient past would be overcome by turning toward a 'bright socialist future,' by recognizing five constitutive nations of Yugoslavia (since 1963 six including Bosnian Muslims) and by giving extensive rights to national minorities. He even granted cultural and political autonomy to two Serbian provinces, Vojvodina and Kosovo, where the two largest minorities, Hungarians and Albanians, lived. As we witnessed, ten years after Tito's death, history repeated itself in the Balkans in a very tragic way. Indeed, the civilian casualties and refugee crisis in the 1990s that emerged due to ethnic cleansing and massive displacement of the unwanted population was a 'purification' of the new successor states of the former Yugoslavia: modern states uprooting 'undesirable' populations from their increasingly 'pure' new 'lebensraum.' While present day naturalization policy is easier and more successful for refugees than it was in post-World War I and World War II Europe, there is, on the other hand, ever-growing number of refugees worldwide, as Arendt accurately predicted. The modern condition then includes a rising phenomenon of statelessness and a constant warning against totalitarian solutions, or a permanent danger of the reappearance of the 'radical evil' in modern nation-states.

Furthermore, the biased and simplistic explanation of the civil war in Yugoslavia by most of the Western media and politicians, particularly regarding the ethnic or national identities of refugees, has resulted in the fact that the Yugoslavs and Bosnians, or in a sarcastic sense 'Eskimos,' practically never existed. Such and other forms of multinational resistance to the division of Yugoslavia along ethnic or national lines and to the implied civil war are omitted in most of the Western media reports. The findings, albeit limited, of my exploratory survey show that Montreal, as a multicultural and cosmopolitan city, is highly appreciated by Bosnians since it reminds them of their multinational and multicultural country that they lost, probably forever. As such, Montreal offers Bosnians, after their experiencing the horrors and suffering of this 'best of all possible worlds' in Voltaire's sense, an appropriate and fertile soil for cultivating their new 'garden,' or rebuilding of lost home. Similar to Voltaire's *Candide*[1] who realized that the world in his time was far from being 'the best of all possible ones' and that consequently life is a permanent struggle for survival, today's refugees from Bosnia, and Yugoslavia at large, came to the same conclusion. That is, to paraphrase Candide, regardless of the existing evil in the world one must work in one's garden not only to survive but also to make life more bearable and worthy of a human being.

Besides the positive implications of multiculturalism, there are also the negative aspects of it that creates additional obstacles for Bosnian refugees in the integration process, or in re-cultivating their lost garden. One of the foremost barriers is the lack of a multinational Yugoslav community, which would ultimately enable refugees to integrate more completely into Quebec's society and feel more 'at home' in multicultural Montreal. Accordingly, multiculturalism as a state policy should be rewritten in order to become more open for cultural diversity and more inclusive of small ethnic or national groups, such as Salvadorans and Yugoslavs. As well, my findings show that a lack of money, caused by unemployment or badly paid 'immigrant' jobs, linguistic barriers and, in general, a lack of leisure time are the main reasons for the overall decrease in participation in cultural and social life, or in Montreal's rich urban culture. As one respondent stated, "every beginning is hard and time consuming," particularly true if people are 'uprooted' and displaced in their mature age after losing everything they had in their lives.

This loss primarily means 'loss of a good life' and 'freedom of choice' since multinational socialist Yugoslavia was a successful country with a publicly owned non-profit economy that offered affordable public transportation, housing, and utilities. As Michael Parenti points out, "between 1960 and 1980 it had one of the most vigorous growth rates: a decent standard of living, free medical care and education, a guaranteed right to a job, one-month vacation with pay, a literacy rate of over 90 percent, and a life expectancy of 72 years."[2] To lose such a country in such a violent way that included both the extermination of undesirable people and their massive displacement (uprootedness) is exactly what the 'politics of sorrow' is about. The former Yugoslavia was a 'promise land' for the Communist bloc, especially for nearby Eastern Europeans. It was the only socialist country that achieved a Western standard of living, which demonstrates that socialism is a viable idea that can work well in reality, in contrast to the witnessed communist dystopia. Therefore, while the disintegration of Yugoslavia is a warning to the world since it can happen anywhere at anytime, the loss of this unique country is the loss not only for its citizens but also for all humanity.

This book then has hopefully enlarged the horizon for understanding the issues pertaining to the past and present life experiences of refugees from Yugoslavia, in particular why the vast majority of my respondents are still 'Yugonostalgic.'[3] The loss of a 'normal' life and 'freedom of choice' is central to the refugee problematic and is behind the imposed moral dilemma of whether one should remain or leave one's homeland that became 'abnormal.' As we have seen, this tragedy ultimately implies choosing between going mad if one remains and withering if one leaves one's native land. While this loss of one's homeland Euripides accurately described as the greatest sorrow on earth, its moral implications are remarkably expressed by Laiwan, an artist based in Vancouver:

> Try to give reason for having left
> there is no reason in leaving
> there could have been a choice
> one leaves when home is made a foreign place

*this is never for you to choose*
*there is no good reason to choose precariousness...*[4]

Drawing upon the findings of my survey, I suggest that one should advocate cultural diversity. Accordingly, multiculturalism, and interculturalism, should be rewritten in order to include small ethnic groups, which would consequently enable the establishing of a multinational Yugoslav community in Montreal and elsewhere. Regardless if such a community will ever come into existence, one should keep in mind that some of the refugees, particularly Yugoslavs, Bosnians and 'Eskimos,' have chosen resettlement, or precariousness of their new life in Canada, because they could not or did not want to answer the question: "What is your nationality? Are you Serb, Croat or Muslim, etc.?" Some refused this nonsense of the transformation of their personality into nationality and 'chose' the sorrow of leaving. Of course, people left mostly because of the outbreak of war and disastrous life conditions. Consequently, one should not believe in the Western/U.S. media established myth of ethnic nationalism and ancient hatreds as inherent to the history of Yugoslavia, because still today peoples and especially refugees, including all Yugoslav nations and national minorities, do not all hate each other. On the contrary, when they find money and time, some of them will *together* enjoy Montreal's night life by dancing and singing 'as in the old good times' in the bars where they can listen to 'their' music performed, for example, by a Montreal-based (refugee) band with the meaningful name "Gitans de Sarajevo" ('Gypsies from Sarajevo'). Besides playing beautiful Gypsy melodic rhythm so typical to the Balkans, the name of the band also alludes to the fact that multinational people from Sarajevo and Bosnia became, or can be accurately called, 'Gypsies' since they share the destiny of real Gypsies, one of the oldest groups of stateless people. In this sense, refugees from Bosnia, and Yugoslavia at large, became for a historic moment the stateless and hungry citizens of the world, welcomed nowhere.

Since every end, as was the disintegration of the former Yugoslavia, means only a new beginning that ultimately carries hope, the future of the various peoples now living in the new successor states is in the process of historical becoming. In Arendt's analogy, the only 'message' that *A Politics of Sorrow* intended to, and can, produce is hope for a better future and that history will never repeat itself in such a tragic way. My personal hope is directed toward Western powers and international institutions, particularly toward the European Union, that could perhaps now in peacetime correct some of the past mistakes by helping

Yugoslav peoples regain a lost living standard. One possible way in the current conditions would be their indiscriminate admission as equal members in the post-national unity of European nations, since all Yugoslav nations belong to the European continent in historic, geographic and political sense. Ultimately, the division of the Balkans implies the division of Europe. The only answer in closing that this book can provide to the fundamentally moral question regarding the violent disintegration of the former Yugoslavia: "Was it worthwhile?" is a definite 'no,' because it was a bold and destructive crime. Externally, it was the murder of the Yugoslav nation and state; internally, it was the recurrence of radical evil, to use Arendt's analogy, of absolute evil crimes that cannot be forgiven nor punished.[5]

## NOTES

1. Voltaire. *Candide or Optimism*. Translated by John Butt. New York: Penguin Books. 1947.

2. Michael Parenti. "The Rational Destruction of Yugoslavia." In Michael Parenti's Political Archive at http://www.michaelparenti.org/yugoslavia.html, 2000, accessed 24 May 2001.

3. While Craig Calhoun points out that in Serbia by 1996 nationalism was replaced by 'Yugo-nostalgia' (in *Nationalism*. Buckingham: Open University Press, 1997, p. 135, note 7), I saw a meaningful graffiti "Kill all Yugonostalgics" (*Ubiti sve Yugonostalgicare*) in the summer of 1997 at the bus station in Croatia (Krajina) on the highway called 'Brotherhood and Unity." I am not suggesting and I do not believe that this graffiti represents the opinion of all, or even a majority of Croatian people.

4. Laiwan. "Is there any thing other than this moment?" Burnaby, B.C., Burnaby Art Gallery: May 2000. Postcard published in the context of Asian Heritage Month. Image: Mozambique coast, early 1960s.

5. I emphasize that the crimes of the 1990s resembled those committed during World War II in their brutality and bestiality, but their scope is not comparable. While it is true that in our time people of various Yugoslav nationalities were the victims of mass murder and torture, organized also in the 'concentration' and prison camps held by all warring parties (to different degrees), these camps of the 1990s were not the 'factories of death' of the 1940s where approximately 600,000 people disappeared. In Jasenovac alone, the notorious 'Ustashi' concentration camp, around 400,000 people perished. (Statistics according to Radovan Samardzic (ed.) *History: Encyclopedic Lexicon*, Belgrade: Interpres, 1970, p. 345). This type of extermination camp was not resurrected, even though today's mass graves and unidentifiable bodies bear witness to the repetition of bestial or absolute evil crimes that occurred on a much smaller but still significant scale. This is particularly true with regard to the mass graves in Bosnia, but also holds for Croatia (Krajina) where the war likewise lasted four years and many of the traces of such crimes are yet to be found. However, the current civil war was marked more by the massive displacement of peoples than by mass extermination as was the case during World War II.

# Research

$\mathbf{M}$y methodology[1] is a combination of historical comparative research and survey research, or a combination of qualitative and quantitative approaches and data. This combination of historical comparative and exploratory study embraces the method of interviewing, historical and comparative analyses, as well as the method of observation and participation. Having in mind the historical fact and the argument of various authors[2] that Bosnia was 'a mini Yugoslavia' in terms of its multinational and multicultural social structure, I focused my sampling frame on Bosnian refugees as the best representation of the social and cultural multi-reality of the former Yugoslavia. In order to illustrate the relationship between a historical-political background and life experience of refugees from Bosnia, I interviewed people with various national origins and identities. My sample thus includes both nationally 'mixed' families (between Serbs and Croats and between Serbs and Muslims) and the 'pure' families (Serbian and Muslim ones). I maintain that this ethnic diversity of the respondents contributes to the accuracy of my research.

I was primarily interested in exploring assumed correlation between different, or alternative, points of view of various authors presented here with the opinions and experiences of refugees from Bosnia. To do so, I conducted face-to-face interviews with seven families. Four spouses of these respondents and one adult child also participated bringing the total number of respondents to twelve. Although this small strategic sample is not a representative one, I suggest that one should take seriously into account their voices as they are an exemplary representation of the socio-political complexity of Bosnia and the former Yugoslavia at large. It is an undeniable fact that these people represent the multi-nationality and cultural diversity of Yugoslavia, especially of Bosnia that was the most heterogeneous or mixed republic. With regard to my historical comparative method, a historical retrospective of the external Balkanization, or 'Divide and Rule' politics in the Balkans, demonstrates that Yugoslavs were in the first lines of the 'new wave' of migrations of modern refugees and apatrides at the very beginning of the twentieth century.

Initially, I envisioned a much bigger sample of 15-20 respondents that would include refugees from throughout the former Yugoslavia. I realized, however, very soon that the data is quite inaccessible due to both the confidentiality of official refugee documents as well as the unwillingness of people to participate in such a study. Also, after reviewing the last report of the existing Canadian statistic[3] about immigration flows of refugees, I noticed that Bosnia was the first among the top ten countries in 1996. There were 4.963 refugees, out of 28.271, who had their last permanent residence in Bosnia, of which 1.460 had Quebec as their intended destination. This data far exceeds the second largest flow of refugees that of 1.797 people from Afghanistan.[4] This ironic 'popularity' of Bosnia in combination with the inaccessibility of personal information of refugees and the representative multi-ethnic portrait of Bosnia are the main reasons for both my focus on respondents from Bosnia and the smaller survey sample.

In regard to the inaccessibility of data, I also need to point out that the reluctance to participate in the study is due to different reasons. People have little leisure time, they are too busy and above all they do not like to participate in this kind of personal survey. In particular, people are quite unwilling to talk about themselves, their present and past lives or everyday problems. After several initial refusals for interviews, I was nevertheless successful in finding respondents because I personally know a lot of them.[5] All of the respondents were very uncomfortable with the idea of recording the interview, even though I assured them that their participation was completely confidential. As I was told, none of them likes to be 'recorded'. This is primarily so because of the presence of a tape-recorder that is too official and serious, and as such, constrains their spontaneity. I am also under the impression that both 'fear of talking' and 'desire to forget' bad things that happened are important silent reasons for the unwillingness to participate in the study. Although all respondents were happy to help me in my research, I find that refugees in general and particularly those from the former Yugoslavia are very sensitive social groups, being quite unwilling to participate in studies. This reluctance makes me wonder about the accuracy of the existing statistics and personal data about refugees, especially in journalistic writings and official reports. Keeping in mind that refugees are reluctant to give personal information, I designed the questionnaire primarily as aggregate categories for all demographic data in order to emphasize the confidentiality and impersonality of data. I also excluded as irrelevant for the research any identifying categories, such as names of places or persons.

My question order is designed in a manner that provides a chronological and a comfortable flow and atmosphere. The introductory demographic questions are followed by more personal questions about social aspects of their life in the former Yugoslavia and about reasons and circumstances of their arrival to Canada. The second set of questions relates to the urban experience in Montreal as a central part of the questionnaire. The concluding part includes more delicate questions about their national identities and the issues related to the citizenship. On the one hand, all respondents felt comfortable in answering the questions and there is statistically insignificant missing data. On the other hand, all of the interviews took more time than I had predicted due to several reasons: participation of more than one respondent, writing instead of recording, and different interruptions that enhanced the comfortable atmosphere, such as cooking lunch, drinking coffee, answering telephone calls or taking care of the children. I designed the questionnaire in a manner that would essentially explore issues relating to their experience of war and the immigration process, especially in terms of human, civil and social rights. My comparison between their current everyday life in Montreal with the previous one in Yugoslavia before the civil war, although incomparable because of completely different social systems of capitalism and socialism, illustrates very important aspects of refugees' life histories being essential for understanding who these people are and how they feel in Canada, and more specifically in Quebec.

## NOTES

1. For my methodology and research design see more details in Neuman, Lawrence W. *Social Research Methods: Qualitative and Quantitative Approaches*, 1997 (1991), in particular chapters 2, 6, 9, 10, 13 and 15.

2. Baudson, 1996; Hayden, 1996; Samary, 1995, et al.

3. See Citizenship and Immigration Canada. *Citizenship and Immigration Statistics 1996*. Ottawa: Minister of Public Works and Government Services Canada, 1999.

4. *Ibid*. See Table S6 "Refugee Categorie: Top Ten Countries of Last Permanent Residence by Province or Territory of Intended Destination, 1996" on p. 12, and the graphic illustration of Table S6 in Chart 1 on the next page: p. 13.

5. I met many newcomers/refugees from the former Yugoslavia during 1995/1996 while working in CSAI (Centre Social d'Aide aux Immigrants) as well in private circles. I only met one family interviewed through CSAI.

# Selected Bibliography

Anderson, Benedict. *Imagined Communities*. London: Verso. 1991 (1983).

Andric, Ivo. "Pismo iz 1920." *Jevrejske Price* (my translation from Serbo-Croatian: *The Jewish Stories*). Belgrade: Narodna Knjiga. 1991.

Albahari, David. *Mamac* (my translation from Serbo-Croatian: *A Bait*). Belgrade: Narodne Novine. 1997.

Arendt, Hannah. *The Origins of Totalitarianism*. New York: A Harvest/ HBJ Book. 1973 (1948).

Avramov, Smilja. *Postherojski Rat Zapada Protiv Jugoslavije* (my translation from Serbo-Croatian: *Postheroic War of the West Against Yugoslavia*). Novi Sad: Idi. 1997.

Baudson, Gérard. *Novi Svetski Poredak i Jugoslavija*. Beograd: ING-PRO. 1996. Translated from French by Dimitrije Radovanovic. (Original version: *Le Nouvel Ordre Mondial et la Yugoslavie*. Paris: Gill Wern Editions. 1996).

Brah, Avtar. "Diaspora, Border and Transnational Identities." *Cartographies of Diaspora: Contesting Identities*. New York and London: Routledge Press. 1996, pp. 178-210.

Brubaker, Rogers. *Nationalism Reframed: Nationhood and the National Question in the New Europe*. Cambridge: Press Syndicate of the University of Cambridge. 1999 (1996).

—"Myths and Misconceptions in the Study of Nationalism." *The State of the Nation: Ernest Gellner and The Theory of Nationalism*. Edited by John Hall. London: Cambridge University Press. 1998.

Calhoun, Craig. *Nationalism*. Buckingham: Open University Press. 1997.

Chomsky, Noam. *World Orders: Old and New*. New York: Columbia University Press. 1994

Chossudovsky, Michel. *The Globalization of Poverty: Impacts of IMF and World Bank Reforms.* London and New Jersey: Zed Books. 1997.

—"Dismantling Yugoslavia Colonizing Bosnia." *Covert Action Quarterly.* No. 56, Spring 1996, pp. 31-37.

—"Euro versus Dollar: Rivalry Between America and 'Old Europe'." *Global Outlook.* Number 5, Summer/Fall 2003.

Citizenship and Immigration Canada. *Citizenship and Immigration Statistics 1996.* Ottawa: Minister of Public Works and Government Services Canada. 1999.

Cottin, Heather. "George Soros: Imperial Wizard" in *Covert Action Quarterly,* Number 74, Fall 2002, see www.canadiandimension.mb.ca/frame.htm, accessed September 13, 2003.

Crnobrnja, Mihailo. *The Yugoslav Drama.* Montreal: McGill-Queen's University Press. 1994.

—"Intelligentsia and Nationalism in the Yugoslav Drama." *Europe: Central and East (Critical Perspective on Historic Issues, Volume 6).* Marguerite Mendell and Klaus Nielsen (eds.). Montreal: Black Rose Books. 1995, pp. 131-140.

—"Migration, Displacement, and the Legacy of 'Ethnic Cleansing' in the Countries of Former Yugoslavia." *Refugees and Migrations in Central and Eastern Europe, From Principles to Implementation: The Role of NGOs.* Montreal: Canadian Human Rights Foundation, 1997, pp. 65-72.

Djilas, Aleksa. *The Contested Country: Yugoslav Unity and Communist Revolution 1919-1953.* Cambridge Massachusetts: Harvard University Press. 1996 (1991).

Dostoyevsky, Fyodor. *The Brothers Karamazov: A Novel in Four Parts With Epilogue.* Translated from the Russian by Richard Pevear and Larissa Volokhonsky. New York: Vintage Books. 1991.

Gershoy, Leo (ed.). *A Survey of European Civilization: Part One and Two.* New York: Houghton Mifflin Company. 1969.

Gervasi, Sean. "Germany, U.S. and the Yugoslav Crisis." *Covert Action Quarterly.* No. 43, Winter 1992-1993.

Gouvernement du Québec. *Directory of Community Agencies at the Service of Newcomers.* Québec: Ministère des Affaires Internationales, de l'Immigration et des Communautés Culturelles. 1994.

Habermas, Jürgen. "Appendix II. Citizenship and National Identity (1990)." *Between Facts and Norms: Contributions to a Discourse Theory of Law and Democracy*, translated from German by William Rehg. Cambridge Massachusetts: The MIT Press. 1996, pp. 491-515.

Hayden, Robert M. "Imagined Communities and Real Victims: Self-determination and Ethnic Cleansing in Yugoslavia." *American Ethnologist*. Vol. 23 (4). 1996, pp. 783-801.

Hatchett, Ronald. "Foreword." *America's Intervention in the Balkans: A Collection of Papers Presented at the Lord Byron Foundation's Third Annual Conference Devoted to U. S. Policy in Southeast Europe*. London: The Lord Byron Foundation for Balkan Studies in cooperation with *Chronicles: A Magazine of American Culture*. 1998, pp. 5-8.

Huntington, Samuel P. "The Clash of Civilizations." *Foreign Affairs*. New York: Council on Foreign Relations. Volume 72, Number 3. Summer 1993, pp. 22-49.

—*The Clash of Civilizations and the Remaking of World Order*. New York: Simon& Schuster. 1996

Interview with David Owen on the Balkans, The Editors. "The Future of the Balkans: An Interview with David Owen." *Foreign Affairs*. New York: Council on Foreign Relations. Spring 1993, pp. 1-9.

Klinar, Peter. *Mednarodne Migracije v Kriznih Razmerah* (my translation from Slovenian: International Migrations). Ljubljana: Zalozba Obzorja. 1985.

Kymlicka, Will. *Finding Our Way: Rethinking Ethnocultural Relations in Canada*. Toronto: Oxford University Press. 1998.

Langer, Beryl. "Globalisation and the Myth of Ethnic Community: Salvadoran Refugees in Multicultural States." *Multicultural States: Rethinking Difference and Identity*. David Bennett (ed.). London and N. Y.: Routledge. 1998, pp. 163-177.

Luksic-Hacin, Marina. *Ko Tujina Postane Dom: Resocializacija in Narodna Identiteta pri Slovenskih Izseljencih* (my translation from Slovenian: When a Foreign Country Became a Home: Resocialization and National Identity of Slovenian Emigrants). Ljubljana: Znanstveno in Publicisticno Sredisce. 1995.

Malkki, Liisa H. "National Geographic: The Rooting of Peoples and the Territorialization of National Identity among Scholars and Refugees." *Culture, Power, Place: Explorations in Critical Anthropology*. A. Gupta and J. Ferguson (eds). London: Duke University Press. 1997, pp. 52-74.

Ministère des Affaires Internationales, de l'Immigration et des Communautés Culturelle et la Ville de Montréal. *Profils des Communautés Culturelles du Québec.* Québec: Les Publications du Québec. 1995.

Moore, Donald S. "Remapping Resistance: 'Ground for Struggle' and the Politics of Place." *Geographies of Resistance.* S. Pile and M. Keith (eds). London and N.Y.: Routledge. 1997, pp. 87-106.

Motyl, Alexander J. *Revolutions, Nations, Empires: Conceptual Limits and Theoretical Possibilities.* New York: Columbia University Press. 1999.

Neuman, Lawrence W. *Social Research Methods: Qualitative and Quantitative Approaches.* Toronto: Allyn and Bacon. 1997 (1991).

Nielsen, Greg M. *The Norms of Answerability: Social Theory Between Bakhtin and Habermas.* Albany: State University of New York Press. 2002.

Nielsen, Kai. "Cosmopolitanism, Universalism and Particularism in an Age of Nationalism and Multiculturalism." *Philosophical Exchange.* Vol. 29. 1999, pp. 3-38.

Papic, Zarana. "From State Socialism to State Nationalism: the Case of Serbia in Gender Perspective." *What Can We Do for Ourselves: East European Feminist Conference, Belgrade 1994.* Marina Blagojevic, Dasa Duhacek and Jasmina Lukic (eds.). Belgrade: Center for Women's Studies, Research and Communication. 1995, pp. 52-63.

Parenti, Michael. "The Rational Destruction of Yugoslavia." In Michael Parenti Political Archive. http://www.michaelparenti.org/yugoslavia.html, 2000, accessed 24 May 2001.

Polanyi, Karl. *The Great Transformation: The Political and Economic Origins of Our Time.* Boston: Beacon Press. 2001 (1944).

Rifati, Sani. "The Roma and 'Humanitarian' Ethnic Cleansing in Kosovo" in *Dissident Voice*, October 13, 2002, accessed on Internet October 17, 2002 at http://www.dissident voice.org/Articles/Rifati_Kosovo.htm. Link also available at www.globalresearch.ca.

Samardzic, Radovan (ed.). *Istorija: Enciklopedijski Leksikon Mozaik Znanja* (my translation from Serbo-Croatian: History: Encyclopedic Lexicon, Mosaic of Knowledge). Vol. 5. Belgrade: Interpres. 1970.

Samary, Catherine. *Yugoslavia Dismembered.* Translated from French by Peter Drucker. New York: Monthly Review Press. 1995.

Secibovic, Refik. *Uvod u Opstu Geografiju Religije* (my translation from Serbo-Croatian: Introduction to the General Geography of Religion). Novi Sad: Prometej. 1995.

Sherman, Sir Alfred. "Introduction: What is Good for America..." *America's Intervention in the Balkans: A Collection of Papers Presented at the Lord Byron Foundation's Third Annual Conference Devoted to U. S. Policy in Southeast Europe.* London: The Lord Byron Foundation for Balkan Studies in cooperation with Chronicles: A Magazine of American Culture. 1998, pp. 9-14.

Smith, Anthony D. *State and Nation in the Third World: the Western State and African Nationalism.* Brighton, Sussex: Wheatsheaf Books. 1983.

Snider, Michael. "Firefight at the Medak Pocket." *Maclean's.* Canada, September 2, 2002.

Spira, Thomas. *Nationalism and Ethnicity Terminologies: An Encyclopedic Dictionary and Research Guide. Volume 1.* Academic International Press. 1999.

Taylor, Scott and Nolan, Brian. *Tested Mettle: Canada's Peacekeepers at War.* Ottawa: Esprit de Corps Books. 1998.

Ugresic, Dubravka. "Because We're Lads." *What Can We Do for Ourselves: East European Feminist Conference, Belgrade 1994.* Marina Blagojevic, Dasa Duhacek and Jasmina Lukic (eds.). Belgrade: Center for Women's Studies, Research and Communication. 1995, pp. 128-140.

Ustava Socialisticne Republike Slovenije. (my translation from Slovenian: The Constitution of Socialist Republic of Slovenia). Ljubljana: Center za samoupravno normativno dejavnost. 1974.

Ustava Socialisticne Federativne Republike Jugoslavije Z Obrazlozitvijo. (my translation from Slovenian: The Constitution of Socialist Federal Republic of Yugoslavia with Explanation). Ljubljana: Center za samoupravno normativno dejavnost. 1974.

Ustava Republike Slovenije. (my translation from Slovenian: The Constitution of Republic of Slovenia). Ljubljana: Uradni list RS, st. 33-1409/91-I z dne 28. decembra 1991 in 42-2341/97 z dne 17. julija 1997. 1997 (1991).

Ustav Savezne Republike Jugoslavije. (my translation from Serbo-Croation: The Constitution of Federal Republic of Yugoslavia). Belgrade: Savremena Administracija. 1992.

Voltaire. *Candide or Optimism.* Translated by John Butt. New York: Penguin Books. 1947.

# Index

# BOOKS OF RELATED INTEREST

## NATIONALISM AND CULTURE
Rudolf Rocker, translated by Ray E. Chase

A detailed and scholarly study of the development of nationalism and the changes in human cultures from the dawn of history to the present day.

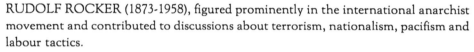

> An important contribution to political philosophy and a brilliant criticism of state-worship. —*Bertrand Russell*

> Worthy to be placed on the same shelf that holds *Candide*, *The Rights of Man* and *Mutual Aid*. —*Lewis Mumford*

> Original and illuminating. Presented in it in a novel and convincing fashion. —*Albert Einstein*

> Rocker is tolerant, modest, and aware of the essential values in culture. —*Herbert Read*

RUDOLF ROCKER (1873-1958), figured prominently in the international anarchist movement and contributed to discussions about terrorism, nationalism, pacifism and labour tactics.

592 pages, bibliography, index
Paperback ISBN: 1-55164-094-5 $28.99 ◆ Hardcover ISBN: 1-55164-095-3 $57.99


## PURE SOLDIERS or SINISTER LEGION: The Ukrainian 14th Waffen-SS Division
Sol Littman

Traces the 14th Waffen-SS Division's fortunes from its formation in April 1943, to its surrender to the British in May 1946, their subsequent stay as prisoners-of-war in Italy, and their eventual transfer as agricultural workers in Britain. In 1950 they began their immigration to Canada and the United States. Along the way they were recruited by the British as anti-Soviet spies and by the CIA as political assassins. In spelling out the Division's history, the author attempts to shed light on its true nature.

> There have been few detailed studies of Nazi war criminals who came to Canada after WWII. Littman's book...makes a welcome, if chilling, addition. —*Francis Henry, Emeritus, York University, Toronto*

> A well-researched, carefully documented forcefully presented exposé. —*Dov Bert Levy, former consultant to the U.S. Justice Department*

SOL LITTMAN is the recently retired Canadian Director of the Simon Wiesenthal Center, author of *War Criminal on Trial*, and founding editor of the *Canadian Jewish News*.

264 pages, 6x9, photographs, bibliography, index
Paperback ISBN: 1-55164-218-2 $26.99 ◆ Hardcover ISBN: 1-55164-219-0 $55.99

# BOOKS OF RELATED INTEREST

## THE PEOPLE AS ENEMY: The Leaders' Hidden Agenda in World War II
John Spritzler

Presented here is a very different, and disturbing view of WWII that argues that the aims of the national leaders were not democracy and self-determination, but were opportunities to suppress and intimidate working people from rising up against elite power. Understanding this is especially important today because the myths of WWII are the same myths being used in the "war against terrorism" by government and corporate leaders to control people and pursue ends that have nothing to do with protecting us from terrorism.

> The research is impressive...providing insights into the level of collaboration between ruling elites and their common desire to crush workers' power. The level of working class rebellion that he uncovers and recounts is amazing and often inspiring. —*Socialist Review*

> You do an excellent job unearthing the instances of class conflict...a strong argument, well-documented. —*Howard Zinn, A People's History of the United States*

> The arguments are compelling and extremely well documented. This book belongs in the libraries and classrooms of every educational institution in America. It's that important. —*Groundscore*

JOHN SPRITZLER holds a Doctor of Science degree from the Harvard School of Public Health where he is employed as a Research Scientist engaged in AIDS clinical trials.

216 pages, 6x9, WWII propaganda posters, index
Paperback ISBN: 1-55164-216-6  $24.99 ♦ Hardcover ISBN: 1-55164-217-4  $53.99

send for a free catalogue of all our titles

**BLACK ROSE BOOKS**

C.P. 1258, Succ. Place du Parc
Montréal, Québec
H2X 4A7 Canada

Or visit our website at http://www.web.net/blackrosebooks

## To order books
In Canada: (phone) 1-800-565-9523 (fax) 1-800-221-9985
email: utpbooks@utpress.utoronto.ca
In United States: (phone) 1-800-283-3572 (fax) 1-651-917-6406
In UK & Europe: (phone) London 44 (0)20 8986-4854 (fax) 44 (0)20 8533-5821
email: order@centralbooks.com

Printed by the workers of
MARC VEILLEUX IMPRIMEUR INC.
Boucherville, Québec
for Black Rose Books Ltd.